AF771495

WE WERE STILL LADIES

**IOWA AND THE**

**MIDWEST EXPERIENCE**

# WE WERE STILL LADIES

## Gender and Industrial Unionism in the Midwest after World War II

Coreen Derifield

UNIVERSITY OF IOWA PRESS, IOWA CITY

University of Iowa Press, Iowa City 52242

uipress.uiowa.edu

Printed in the United States of America
Design by April Leidig

Cover image: Women manufacturing pens at Sheaffer Pen Corporation, ca. 1955, Fort Madison, Iowa. Business and Industry, Production and Extraction, Pens, SHSI, Iowa City.



Printed on acid-free paper

Library of Congress Cataloging-in-Publication Data
Names: Derifield, Coreen, 1979- author.
Title: We Were Still Ladies: Gender and Industrial Unionism in the Midwest after World War II / Coreen Derifield.
Description: Iowa City: University of Iowa Press, [2025] | Series: Iowa and the Midwest experience | Includes bibliographical references and index.
Identifiers: LCCN 2024044625 (print) | LCCN 2024044626 (ebook) | ISBN 9781609389710 (paperback; alk. paper) | ISBN 9781609389727 (ebook)
Subjects: LCSH: Rural women—Employment—Iowa—History—20th century. | Rural women—Employment—Middle West—History—20th century. | Labor movement—Iowa—History—20th century. | Labor movement—Middle West—History—20th century. | Feminism—Iowa—History—20th century. | Feminism—Middle West—History—20th century.
Classification: LCC HD6096.I8 D47 2025 (print) | LCC HD6096.I8 (ebook) | DDC 331.40973—dc23/eng/20250117
LC record available at https://lccn.loc.gov/2024044625
LC ebook record available at https://lccn.loc.gov/2024044626

*For Tim*

# Contents

# Acknowledgments

THE IDEA FOR THIS BOOK came from my own lived experiences growing up on a farm in southeast Iowa. The struggles of my own family to keep and maintain the family farm, even after the trials of the farm crisis, left a lasting impression on me as a child. I loved hearing stories about the struggles and triumphs of everyday people and their fight to achieve the American Dream of land ownership. It was not until I left the state and began my graduate school studies that I became aware that my own lived experience was similar to that of urban workers in their struggle to achieve the elusive American Dream. Yet the reality in rural America was distinctly different from the communities in the city. Urban workers struggled to claim ownership over a small plot of land and a home, while land was abundant in the world I was familiar with and the dream was the farm. In my studies I found that many scholars have focused on the urban experience and have overlooked the experiences of rural workers. Most of the families I grew up with had parents who worked in industry, driving thirty to fifty miles to work every day. I wondered if this experience of industrial work was any less important a story in the process of class formation. I came to the conclusion that it was not, and that in rural areas land ownership was key to understanding the drive of the rural worker.

I spent many an hour discussing my ideas with Nancy Gabin, who patiently listened to me and guided my scholarship. She helped me narrow my focus to the lived experience of women, and hence the project was born. I am deeply indebted to her guidance, kindness, and humor in helping a very serious graduate student find her way. She was instrumental in the inception of this work, and I am truly grateful for the time she spent with me and the clarity of her editing in the earliest drafts.

The staff at the State Historical Society of Iowa in Iowa City were absolutely wonderful in helping my research efforts. I spent a summer poring over union records and oral histories, and Charles Scott and Mary Bennett were always close at hand to pull whatever box I needed. They made the research process so much easier and made the archive feel like home. I know they will both be happy to finally see this research in print. I am extremely grateful for their help and assistance! I am also appreciative of the Iowa Women's Archive and the assistance of Kären Mason and Janet Weaver in helping me find the voices of rural women. I am also indebted to the insightful and incisive comments and feedback from Marv Bergman. He helped me shape chapter 2 and showed interest in this work early on. I am also appreciative of the support of the *Annals of Iowa* and their scholarship fund, which gave me financial help during the beginning of this project.

I owe a heartfelt thanks to Bill Warren, who has seen this project all the way through from the beginning to end. He has also been a strong supporter of this work and has always reassured me that it was important and worthy of publication. He has read multiple drafts over the years, and I am deeply grateful for his editing and insightful comments and ideas. Doug Hurt has also been an amazing support and source of encouragement. Through his incisive comments and direct manner, he always kept me grounded in my sources. He has encouraged me to see this manuscript through to publication, giving me reassurance that this project is important. I also want to thank Darren Dochuk, who was an important part of this initial journey and also provided me with honest and kind feedback. His kindness and support were also truly meaningful to me as a young graduate student.

The late Nora Faires, who took me under her wing while I began graduate school at Western Michigan University and taught me the ropes, will always be remembered with deep respect and gratitude. She took a sheltered and rather naive young woman and taught me how to be a scholar. I learned so much those first two years I believed my brain would explode at times. Even after I pursued my studies at Purdue University, she was also such a cheerleader. I always knew she believed in me, and that has meant the world to me.

My time at Purdue University was also a truly enriching experience, and I learned so much from each of my professors as well as my fellow students. The Department of History was supportive of my research, and I am grateful for the year of additional financial support I received through a fellowship so I could finish writing my dissertation. I am very grateful for all the rich and lively conversations I had in my classes and after hours. I would like to thank Patrick Pospisek, Kate Pospisek, Timothy Lombardo, Mauricio Castro, Erica Morin, Kara Kvaran, Karen Sonnelitter, Erin Kempker, Laura Bergstrom, Sarah Morris, and Megan Birk. I am indebted to these individuals for listening to my ideas and for enriching my own personal intellectual growth. A special thanks to Carla Fisher for the endless conversations and support. Also to Elizabeth Zanoni, who provided a willing ear and thoughtful comments on my ideas. Her brilliance and capacity to understand my meandering ideas was an amazing support to me as I worked through my manuscript. Last, I owe much to Scott Randolph, my colleague and good friend. Thank you for reading drafts and providing insightful critiques. But most importantly, thank you for always supporting me even when I was not sure this manuscript would finally emerge as a published book. Thank you for the conversations, the critiques, and the bottomless resources about the business side of this project.

I am also indebted to a group of fellow graduate students studying labor history and our yearly gathering at the Midwest Labor and Working-Class History Colloquium. This yearly gathering was something I looked forward to, and I loved our discussions on labor and the working class. Our annual conversations always brought fresh ideas and new perspectives to my own studies and research interests. In particular I am thankful for Jake Altman, Matt Mettler, and the wonderful, enigmatic late Jacob Hall. I am deeply saddened that he will never see this project in print after listening to me talk about it at length for several years. Also, a huge thank you to John McKerely, who has become a friend and colleague from afar. Thank you for reading a draft of the manuscript and the crucial guidance you have given at this last stage. It is a blessing to have a friend who was there at the beginning of the project and also here at the end.

I am grateful to my colleagues at East Central College who have also expressed interest in my manuscript, even when it was outside their usual fields of study. I owe a special thanks to Bill Cunningham, Wendy Pecka, Rachel Howard, and Greg Stotler, who have made East Central College a better place to work. And a heartful thank you to the Rolla crew: Beth Rozema, Tracy Mowery, and Reginald Brigham. You have always been a delight to work with and genuinely curious about my research. I am also thankful to Robyn Walter, who has also shown support for this project and allowed me some relief from my heavy teaching load to work on the manuscript. And a note of gratitude to my numerous students (especially Ryan Lowry, Kyle Jarosik, and Levi Koch) who expressed genuine interest in my work and humored me by telling me they would like to read it.

My parents, Gary and Cathy Witte, taught me the importance of setting goals and putting in the hard work to accomplish those goals. They provided me with a supportive home and always believed in me, even when they did not always understand where my intellectual endeavors took me. I am grateful for my childhood in southeast Iowa and my grounding in a midwestern ethos of honesty, hard work, decency, and kindness. Also, thanks to my sisters—Krystal Malik and Kelly Nebel—who have provided childcare so I can find time to write and research. And a thanks to my mother-in-law, Terri Derifield, and sister-in-laws, Dana and Tina, for providing childcare so I could write.

My own little family has given me so much love and support. Even though my children are frequently unimpressed with my scholarly work, they always love and encourage me. I think someday they will see this book as a source of pride for them and for myself. I am grateful to have Sadie, Adaline, and Malcolm in my life, and their humor and curiosity enrich my life on a daily basis. And to Tim Derifield, my life partner and biggest supporter: Thank you for being my go-to editor and for reading drafts of my work over the years. This book would not have happened if it had not been for your support and belief in me. Even during the times I was willing to give up, you always reassured me this was important and that it needed to be finished. I am from the bottom of my heart truly grateful for you. Thank you.

Last, I would like to thank the dozens of women who shared their stories with the Iowa Labor History Oral Project, and it is their stories that I wish to share with my readers. Their willingness to participate in this important project has allowed historians like me to place their lived experiences into history and to make important connections and arguments about the past. Reading and listening to their interviews has been truly inspiring, and there is a certain beauty and nobility to their lives. I have been inspired by their courage to break barriers in the workplace, their loyalty to their coworkers, and their commitment to their families. I hope this book does them justice and shows how incredibly brave they were.

# Introduction

EUNICE EVANS heaved a sigh at the sight of her untidy home. "I always said that when I left for work my house looked terrible." But after a grueling eight-hour workday at the Amana Refrigeration Company, the state of her house got remarkably "better, because I was so tired, I didn't care anymore." Evans grew up on a farm near the small town of Wellman, Iowa, and as a child she "had a lot of dreams like most kids, but nothing serious. . . . It certainly didn't involve working in a factory." After a pleasant childhood, she quit high school after the tenth grade and married her high school sweetheart. Her life took a rather unexpected turn when her husband enlisted in the armed forces at the beginning of World War II. He was first stationed in Oklahoma, and Evans followed him, and they lived there for two years. She worked at the Post Exchange for a few months in order to make some extra money while her husband was busy in the army, but she soon became a mother, giving birth to two sons while living in Oklahoma. When her husband was shipped overseas, Evans moved back to Wellman to be near family. After the war, her husband joined her and their two children in their hometown. He soon began working at the Amana Refrigeration Company in the Amana Colonies, a thirty-mile drive north of Wellman. By the early 1950s, Evans began considering working herself, especially when she thought of what she could do with the extra income. "I decided I wanted an adequate diet for my children. I had one boy that had polio, and I always felt it was because he didn't have the meat and fresh fruits that he needed and with my salary we could afford to buy them." In 1951, Evans joined her husband at Amana. At first, she was uneasy about leaving her children with a babysitter while she went to work. "I think I was rather the exception of going to a factory. I probably was frowned on much more outside the home." But the extra income eased many of her concerns.

When Evans started at Amana, the factory was expanding due to Korean War contracts, and her first work assignment was pounding nails, but she quickly moved on to other jobs in the factory. During her thirty-three years at Amana, she worked as a welder, metal finisher, painter, and inspector, among other jobs. She was a dedicated worker, taking every opportunity to work overtime and never ashamed to ask for higher wages. She fought for her personal protection within the factory and kept a vigilant watch over her workplace rights to ensure the company was not taking advantage of her or her coworkers. Active in the union, she was always one of the first to file a grievance and to keep the company on its toes. She was also a pioneer, one of the first women to work in the metal finishing department, which was typically reserved for men. "When I went in that [metal finishing], it was unknown for any woman to be in there. And they tried very much to have my husband talk me out of it. He told them he couldn't tell me what to do." Evans was just too stubborn. Her industrious nature and can-do attitude were not confined to the workplace but trickled down to her home life as well. She kept a garden, canned during the summer, and stayed involved in her family's lives.[1]

The life of Eunice Evans was a microcosm of the rapidly changing socioeconomic landscape of the postwar period. Women like Evans were uprooted during the war, and as they adjusted to the uncertainties and the restrictions of the wartime period, they discovered their own resilience and the endurance of the human spirit. Once the war was over, they went home and settled into a new sense of normalcy. Even while they reestablished previous gender norms, their experiences during the war left them with a new sense of identity and purpose, one that did not fit into the model of the traditional patriarchal home. Women, for the most part, complied with these old, gendered expectations: They had children, kept a home, and supported their husbands. They also desired a chance to earn their own wages. Faced with potential economic hardships, women wanted to provide for their families and ameliorate any financial uncertainty rather than endure the deprivations they had during the Depression and the war. And like Eunice Evans, who wanted her sons to have fresh food to eat and to grow up healthy and strong, women wanted to provide.

For women, going to a job outside of the home and receiving wages for that labor was a relatively new experience in their lives. Even during the depths of the Depression, few married women worked outside of the home.[2] This quiet and subtle shift in women's lives would have a profound impact on the socioeconomic environment of the postwar period, sending ripples across American society and leaving long-lasting consequences on the cultural assumptions men and women held about gender roles and their responsibilities within a family. Before the war, married women's wage work was seen as an economic exception, done only under the most dire of circumstances, or in poor working-class communities where there was no other possibility of economic success. After the trauma and triumph of the war, women were primed for new roles in society, ones they would find satisfying while still fulfilling their duties to their families and their communities. This book is an account of that transition and how rural women processed the evolution of their identities from women caring for farm, family, and home into factory workers providing a living for their children.

The setting of this story is the towns and cities of eastern Iowa. Albeit an unlikely scene for a major socioeconomic shift in women's labor, Iowa provides a different paradigm for the transition of women from unpaid labor within the organizational structure of the family to paid labor outside of the home. Eastern Iowa is mostly rural,[3] with more people living in the country than in urban areas until the 1950s. There are many towns and small cities scattered throughout the region, and towns are typically ten to thirty miles apart from each other with populations varying from 3,000 to 20,000. When Iowa legislators began to court industrial development after World War II, the state underwent significant industrial growth. The Iowa Development Commission reported in 1955 that 1,000 of the 3,736 industrial plants in the state started in the ten-year period after World War II. In tandem with the relocation of new industries was a growth of home-based industries, such as Amana Refrigeration in the Amana Colonies, Collins Radio in Cedar Rapids, and Maytag in Newton. The amalgamation of new businesses with expanding old ones caused rapid industrial growth in the state.[4] When the thriving electronics industries sought to decentralize their production, Iowa became a prime destination. With its right-to-work laws and a labor supply of eager, hard-working women, Iowa had a lot to offer electronics producers. This movement of electronic companies into Iowa directly led to a boom in women's employment, as electronics depended on a female workforce to make their minuscule products. This tremendous industrial growth in the state led to a startling increase of job opportunities for women and provided a way to earn wages outside of the home.

The region of eastern Iowa also complicates the notion of the working class as being strictly urban. Many Iowa workers commuted to work from small towns and farms surrounding industrial centers, blurring the boundary between what was urban and what was rural. This small town/rural aspect of Iowa's female workforce offers a valuable comparison to the urban working class, especially to the often-studied midwestern cities of Detroit and Chicago. The changes to the political economy in Iowa brought on by the growth of industry in the state provide a chance to study the development of class in nonurban areas. For this reason, the study analyzes working-class women across the spectrum of a region rather than focusing on a particular plant, industry, or union.

Many of these Iowa women came from an agricultural past, where women developed their identity within a network of kin and community. The population was also very white, with only a small percentage of African Americans or other racial minorities.[5] The handful of Black women in this story have unique perspectives of being a Black woman surrounded by a sea of white faces. The meaning of race in a place that was so overwhelmingly white was challenging to untangle but necessary to understand the culture of place. Because the culture of eastern Iowa was informed by the migration and settlement of ethnically white peoples (Germans, Dutch, Swedes, Norwegians, Irish, and Yankees from the Northeast), many white women in the rural Midwest did not see race at all. While the ugly sentiment of racism lingered in the culture, and its effects were felt among the minority Black population in glaring and hurtful ways, many white women failed to recognize its existence. Because of their whiteness, they had the privilege of being of the dominant racial group in American society. Their blindness to race also gave them the advantage of seeing their culture as the only culture and forcing the assimilation of all other minority groups into the predominantly white ethnic culture. There have been some studies on working-class Black women in Iowa and the fight for equal access to jobs and work, and this study acknowledges the courage and perseverance of these women in that fight in a place so overwhelmingly white.[6]

Women were also predominantly heterosexual and sought out the conformity of a nuclear family. While there was an underground culture welcoming those who were of the LGBTQ+ community, the women of this study overtly identified as heterosexual. While some may have been closeted, the prevailing culture of the time was one of intense discrimination against sexual minorities. Gay women did not feel welcome, and therefore it is difficult to find their voices. Consequently, women in rural Iowa conformed to the concepts of the heterosexual female and the pressures to marry and have a family. The women analyzed in this study often placed themselves within the network of the nuclear family and had difficulties seeing themselves as distinct individuals. The white ethnic culture of the rural Midwest was decidedly heteronormative, which gave those women who conformed the feeling of acceptance among their peers.

To understand the lived experiences of Iowa women, this study places women within the cultural structure of the family, and by doing so argues that women's identities were formed by an understanding of themselves within that structure. By highlighting the structures of gender and family, one may glimpse the dialectical nature of the political economy of social and cultural change as it pertains to the family unit. This argument is directly informed by the work of Mary Neth and her studies on women, work, and community in the Midwest. She conducted a cultural study of midwestern families as they adjusted to rapidly changing technology in farming. She demonstrated how women negotiated their roles within the patriarchal home in ways that would provide them with significant responsibilities for the success of the family without threatening male leadership. This interpretation of family networks can be applied to the way gender roles developed within families adjusting to the socioeconomic changes of industrialization.[7]

Region as a concept is also used as a theoretical framework to analyze the formation of a gendered class consciousness. Andrew Cayton and Susan Gray present a convincing case for using region as an analytical tool. They argue regional identity, or regionality, is something cognitive and emotional that individuals cling to when affiliating with a region, stating, "regionality is about how people locate themselves intellectually and emotionally within complicated landscapes and networks of social relations."[8] A close study of the gender history of the Midwest's regionality is especially pertinent as it illustrates how kin networks formed around the primacy of men's work on the farm and were supported by the essential but secondary roles of women in the home. In analyzing the codes of behavior of midwestern women, regionality presents a way to understand how women thought of themselves within this kin network and how their codes of behavior were embedded in the long history of rural life. In Iowa, often seen as the quintessential midwestern state, these cultural norms of rural life were ubiquitous. The state originated with single families dividing the land and improving it through the collective work of the family. This rural past left deep impressions on the cultural understanding of work, family structure, and social interaction with neighbors and non-kin. In terms of gender, women learned that even though their role in the home was secondary to that of the male breadwinner, their work was still of vital importance to the success of the family farm. Women learned the value of hard work and the importance of community endeavors in support of farming, and these ideas remained embedded in women's cultural understanding of gender roles even after the dominance of agriculture declined in the region. The cultural norms of hard work, self-reliance, and neighborliness left an indelible imprint on women's learned behaviors. Midwestern women believed it was proper for women to act as ladies: to be pleasant in their interactions with others and to remain humble, polite, friendly, and acquiescent to male leadership. This type of gendered regionality directly impacted the way women acted and behaved in social spaces and provided women a mutual understanding of proper behavior and gender roles.

When Iowa women entered the industrial workplace, they found commonalities with each other over workplace experiences, backgrounds, and their cultural norms. These commonalities helped women forge a working-class identity, one that was steeped in their cultural conditioning as midwestern women. Iowa women participated in labor unions by embracing their gender roles, performing tasks that were deemed culturally acceptable for women. They held fundraisers, helped with potluck dinners, planned parties, served as local secretaries, and rarely spoke out during meetings. By performing their assumed gender roles, women were able to bridge the gender division within their local unions, and consequently the male union members embraced women as fellow workers, teaching them what it meant to show solidarity and to fight for workplace rights. As they encountered inequality in the workplace and developed a working-class consciousness based on class and gender identity, they learned how to fight for labor rights.

As women learned more about the labor movement, they grew restless with their limited roles and sought additional leadership opportunities within the union. As they struggled to overcome sexism within the union and the workplace (and even within the home), women began to embrace the ideas of labor feminism to pursue their particular goals as working-class women.[9] Meanwhile, not all women desired leadership roles or desired to challenge male sexism, and they remained content with their limited roles within the labor movement. By the 1970s, this division between women who pursued labor feminism and those women who remained loyal to traditional gender roles caused a generational split among female factory workers. It was only through a sustained effort on the part of a younger generation of female union leaders that the barriers of gender discrimination began to erode. Even these successes were limited, however. As long as women continued to view themselves as subservient to male leadership, they made limited headway fighting gender inequality.

In the light of scholarship on labor feminism and union women, this central conflict within working-class women over the issue of feminism is unsettling. While many women wholeheartedly embraced feminism as the natural outcome of their fight for their rights in the workplace, many more vehemently rejected feminism. They seemed fearful of the implications of feminism for their identity and their conceptions about their role in society. Feminism seemed to be pulling the rug right out from under their feet, disorienting and unsettling them in ways they were not willing to accept. Some of these women became vocally critical of the women who embraced feminism and sabotaged their efforts to gain gender equality in the workplace.[10]

This study is an attempt to provide an explanation for this divide and to understand why working-class women in Iowa were hesitant to embrace feminism. I conclude that Iowa women saw themselves as an integral part of a patriarchal family economy, and they viewed themselves first and foremost as members of that economic unit. Their gender identities were rooted in the cultural ideas of a rural, white heritage, and under these cultural norms, women saw their work as essential to the success of the family and not for individual gain. Because this gender identity was so engrained within rural life, it was difficult for women to separate themselves from their family and see themselves as individuals. The challenge for union organizers and feminists was to lead women to an understanding that gender inequality in the workplace was hurting their ability to support their families. The concept of individual rights for women was yet another challenge feminists faced in leading working-class women into the full embrace of gender equality. Many women did develop a feminist identity and grasped the importance of equal rights for women as individuals and for their families, but the gap between the nonfeminists and the feminists proved to be deep and wide, causing rifts between friends and coworkers.

Studies of working-class women after World War II have focused on women's participation in unions and have not focused on the ways women relied on community or family in the process of class formation. This is not to detract from the importance of these studies, which have skillfully illustrated the variety of ways women faced gender discrimination through workplace rules, union policies, and their male peers. Nancy Gabin's pioneering work on women in the United Auto Workers (UAW) was the first to argue that women's fight for both workplace rights and gender equality linked working-class women with the feminist movement in permanent and inextricable ways. This form of working-class feminism was a vital and vibrant part of the second wave of feminism in the late 1960s and early 1970s. Dorothy Sue Cobble studied how female union leaders pushed for gender equality in unions and workplaces by lobbying governmental agencies for better laws and policies. Cobble termed these women labor feminists and argued they were at the very forefront of the feminist movement advocating the rights of working-class women. And last, Dennis Deslippe demonstrated how women turned to working-class feminism during the late 1960s as they faced continual discrimination in both the workplace and the union. Denied leadership roles in unions and confronted by male union leaders and members unwilling to pursue women's workplace issues, women began using the language of unionism to pursue equal rights as women. These three authors have greatly informed this study and have skillfully shown the interconnectedness of the feminist movement of the late 1960s and early 1970s with working-class women fighting for workplace rights. The key question that these studies do not address, however, is why some women chose to reject feminism. By using an analysis of regionality, class, and gender, this study provides an explanation for the split over feminism among working-class women.[11]

This analysis begins with a description of the political economy of the region and develops the socioeconomic context of the postwar period. After the war, midwestern states began to actively seek industrial development, and Iowa was especially proactive in this search as government leaders saw the need to diversify the state's economy. The state legislature created the Iowa Industrial Commission to attract industry to the state and to diversify the predominantly agricultural economy. At the same time, large industries in the East sought to decentralize their business model and began moving factories west and south. The convergence of these push-and-pull factors led to extraordinary industrial growth in the state and consequently the increase in factory jobs open to women.

Chapter 2 discusses the social and cultural context for the change in women's attitudes toward work outside of the home. It demonstrates how industrial development in the region opened new opportunities for women by providing them with well-paying jobs that required little skill. The congruence of industrial development and women seeking paid employment led to the significant increase in women working outside of the home. Women felt a deep commitment to their families, and providing economic stability for them became more important than continued unpaid domestic housework. Within the context of farm communities, women's work was always seen as essential to the survival of the family, and with the declining opportunities in farming during the 1950s, more women sought work outside of the home to fulfill their roles and responsibilities for their families. Women did not pursue work to defy the patriarchal structures that governed their lives but to maintain economic stability of the family. This move into the workforce would, however, have tremendous consequences for the empowerment of women and the erosion of patriarchy.

Chapter 3 is an analysis of the formation of a class consciousness through the lenses of class, gender, and race. As Iowa women began working in the factory, they had several obstacles to overcome, namely a lack of industrial work experience, but they would find camaraderie and solidarity with their fellow workers. Women bonded over shared work experiences, horrible workplace conditions, and a shared regional culture. Through these bonds women formed a working-class consciousness and learned to advocate for themselves as workers. Their identities shifted as they embraced their new roles as working wives and mothers.

Chapter 4 explores the ways in which the union used a gendered class identity through the union auxiliaries, the Women's Activities Department of the Iowa Federation of Labor, and women's committees within the local unions. Women connected their regional assumptions about gender roles with their working-class identity and combined loyalty to the labor movement with the fulfillment of their gender roles. They developed a sense of working-class womanhood that blended militancy on the picket line with their work hosting card parties as fundraising events. Even though these organizations were usually on the periphery of the labor movement, it was not until women began working in the factory that they became full-fledged union members. Women began to think of themselves as union members on equal footing with their male peers.

Chapter 5 analyzes women's activities within the union itself and explores how women learned about the principles of unionism and applied them to their lives as workers and as women. Because so many female workers in Iowa came from a rural background with little knowledge or experience with unionism, unions had the extra duty of educating their female membership. Once women learned about the concepts of solidarity, many became active within their locals seeking leadership roles. Women also successfully channeled their shared grievances into strikes, which achieved safer and more equitable workplace environments. As women learned the principles of unionism and the usefulness of militancy through strikes, they began to apply these ideas and activities to their grievances as female workers. This activism within the union encouraged women to push for equal rights and opportunities with their male peers.

Chapter 6 discusses the relationship of Iowa women with the feminist movement. This last chapter shows how the rebirth of the feminist movement in the late 1960s helped working-class women fight for equal rights within the workplace. The ideas of a gendered class identity began to change from the 1950s, when women accepted their subservience to male leadership, to the late 1960s and early 1970s, when they demanded equality with their union brothers. Old notions of gender identity remained, however, and older generations of women were reluctant to embrace labor feminism. These women were introduced to unionism at a time when the fulfillment of their gender roles was their main contribution to unionism, and they clung to the traditional ideas of women's proper place. Chapter 6 argues that as a younger generation of working-class women encountered labor feminism, they embraced it as the best solution to the gender discrimination they faced in the union and in the workplace. The fight for gender equality was far from over, however, especially as labor feminists clashed with women who still clung to traditionalist ideologies. Not until working-class women could patch the divide within themselves could they move forward in accomplishing gender equality.

# Chapter One

## The Industrial Development of Iowa

Dixie Bigger, a farm wife and mother of two, began a new chapter in her life in the spring of 1968 when she started a job at the Champion Sparkplug factory in the nearby city of Burlington. The new job offered good wages, a clean environment, plenty of female coworkers, and a good union—all the things she could wish for in a job. Even though the daily commute to work would be a tedious thirty-mile drive from her farm in Illinois, she believed the job was worthwhile because of the extra benefits it offered. It was a major boon to her family as well, since the farm did not produce nearly enough income to feed her family of four.[1] Many women in Iowa, much like Dixie Bigger, began working in these small industrial factories throughout the 1950s and '60s, especially when new businesses began to trickle into the state after World War II. Champion Sparkplug was a prime example of a business on the move. Looking to escape the union territory of northeastern Ohio, Champion sought a place somewhere in the Midwest that had a dependable and nonunionized labor force.[2] Burlington, nestled along the banks of the Mississippi River in southeastern Iowa, was a desirable spot because of its transportation networks, Iowa's right-to-work laws, and a dependable, semiskilled labor supply. Champion set up shop in 1957 and joined a handful of industries relocating to Burlington. Despite the city's limited population of 30,000, sixteen plants, including Champion, Sylvania, and GE, relocated to Burlington from 1955 to 1965.[3] When Champion moved into Burlington, it provided three hundred jobs for area residents, with nearly 150 positions for women.

Burlington's story of industrial growth was typical for the state during the 1950s and '60s, as the state's manufacturing grew rapidly after World War II. Despite Iowa's renown for agricultural abundance, it did have a thriving manufacturing sector. During the nineteenth and early twentieth centuries, most of the industry in the state, such as meatpacking, grain milling, canning, and other food production, relied on its agricultural products. Coal mining was also prosperous in the southern counties, but the industry declined drastically during the 1920s. Other industries included agricultural implements, woodworking, and printing.[4] During the war, lucrative government contracts gave manufacturers a much-needed economic boost. Ordnance plants were built in both Burlington and Des Moines to supply ammunition to the armed forces, and meatpacking and farm implement firms were converted to wartime production.[5]

After participating in the war effort through food production and industrial manufacturing, the leaders of the state desired the continuation of economic growth and understood that the state needed to restructure its economy by strengthening its industrial sector and reducing its dependency upon agriculture. They did this through a dual strategy of strengthening Iowa-based industries such as farm equipment manufacturing and meatpacking, and by encouraging decentralizing industries to relocate to the state. The Iowa Legislature created the Iowa Development Commission (IDC) in 1945 to accomplish these goals. Coupled with the state's efforts to diversify the economy was a new decentralized business model of manufacturing. Scholars have referred to this as the product cycle theory—which argues that once a business has matured financially and no longer needs highly skilled labor in the production process, it searches for cheaper labor while maintaining the skilled workforce and financial center in the original location. This spatial redistribution of industry is also referred to as nonmetro industrialization. As businesses at the peak of a product cycle began looking for cheaper labor, they began to move into rural areas. Iowa, with its dependable labor supply, right-to-work laws, and central location, was an ideal spot to open peripheral branch plants. This new capital mobility, combined with the efforts of the IDC, sparked industrial growth in the state from 1945 to 1970 and, in turn, provided working women major opportunities to earn decent wages and support their families.[6]

## Growth in Manufacturing

The image of Iowa as a rural haven for the sensible farmer has been instilled in the cultural dialogue through literary and iconic images such as

Grant Wood's famous painting *American Gothic*. With the stoic farmer beside his austere daughter set against the backdrop of a pragmatic A-line home, *American Gothic* came to symbolize in many imaginations what Iowa meant: rural, sober, and practical. In many ways, Iowa fits the stereotype, as the landscape and the economy reflected the agricultural abundance of the region, with its endless rows of corn and soybeans. From the state's inception as a promising frontier in the 1830s, agriculture flourished as the settlers turned over the dark, fertile prairie soil and discovered its promise for prosperity. When the region officially became a state in 1846, pioneers streamed to the region, hoping to achieve the American Dream of the self-reliant, yeoman farmer. During the late nineteenth century, immigrant groups such as the Scandinavians, Germans, and Dutch migrated into the state, establishing ethnic enclaves where they could continue the traditions and customs of their homelands. By the turn of the twentieth century, the region was dotted with thousands of small family farms achieving the dream of independence and land ownership. These rural traditions of agriculturally based communities provided the foundation for society and culture throughout most of the state. Even as late as 1950, two-thirds of Iowans were born, raised, or lived on the farm.[7] Not until World War II did people begin to move off the land, and even then, most residents of the state retained some connection to farms, through either relatives or acquaintances who still owned land. Others earned their livelihoods outside of agriculture but chose to live in the country and commute to work to maintain the dream of country living and land ownership.

Even though many began to leave the land in the 1950s, agriculture still dominated much of the state into the late twentieth century. Iowa's urbanization was a gradual process and differed significantly from that of eastern states that had experienced the effects of urbanization and industrialization by at least the 1920s. In 1940, 57.3 percent of Iowa's population of 2.5 million still lived in rural areas, while only 42.7 percent lived in towns. By 1950, the gap between the urban and rural population had decreased, but a majority of residents still lived in rural areas, with 52.3 percent living in the country and 47.7 percent living in urban centers. By 1960, those numbers had finally crossed, with more people living in urban areas than rural, as 53 percent of the population lived in towns and cities while 47 percent still lived in the country. Table 1 illustrates the dominance of agriculture as a

TABLE 1. Occupations in Farming and Manufacturing in Iowa

| Occupations | 1940 | 1950 | 1960 |
|---|---|---|---|
| Farmers and Farm Management | 207,099<br>24% | 199,119<br>19.5% | 158,160<br>21.6% |
| Craftsmen and Foremen | 75,891<br>8.8% | 115,648<br>11.3% | 113,646<br>15.5% |
| Operatives and Manufacturers | 92,158<br>10.7% | 131,973<br>12.9% | 145,819<br>16.2% |
| Professionals | 57,145<br>6.6% | 76,658<br>7.6% | 99,335<br>7.7% |
| Total Employed | 957,869 | 1,002,180 | 1,019,002 |

Source: U.S. Census, 1940, 1950, 1960.

form of employment, and even as late as 1960, 20 percent of those employed worked in agriculture.[8]

Along with gradual urbanization, Iowa's manufacturing began to steadily increase throughout the twentieth century. There were nearly 15,000 manufacturing firms in 1900. The leading industries were in food production: meat, butter, flour, and canned fruits and vegetables. Small towns remained rooted in agriculture, while the larger urban centers became home to the growing manufacturing, especially the cities in the eastern half of the state, such as Davenport, Dubuque, Waterloo, and Cedar Rapids. Woodworking began to prosper after 1900 along with printing and the development of farm implements. As Keach Johnson noted, "The outlines of twentieth century industrialism were clearly discernible in Iowa by 1910. The manufacturing industries had broadened the scope and quickened the pace of the state's economic growth."[9]

The growth of manufacturing and urbanization was fertilized by the gradual decline of the family farm, which displaced people from the land. This happened through a collapse of the social structure, which had sustained farming communities for decades throughout the rural Midwest. Farmers who owned a large amount of land and needed hired labor to help with daily farm operations were at the pinnacle of the rural class structure. Next were the independent farmers who owned their land and operated the farm with labor from their own families, and below them were those families who rented their land. Last were those who worked as hired labor. By the 1950s there developed a significant subset of those who either owned their land or rented but could not remain self-sufficient with only the profits from the farm. This decline of profitability drove members of the family into the workforce. Typically they either worked in town or the wife volunteered to take a job off the farm to support the family. This last subset became much larger by the 1950s and 1960s as many farmers found it more difficult to stay on the land due to the instability of agricultural markets. As these part-time farmers ventured into town to find work, they often landed industrial jobs, which helped form the basis of a rural working class, and the fusion of rural and town workers created a unique working experience in small factories throughout the state.[10]

After World War II, mechanization of farm work began to dramatically change Iowa farms. Mechanization not only made farming easier, it also gave farmers the ability to cultivate and develop more land, eventually reducing the need for the hired farmhand. Soon, state leaders took note of this concerning trend and realized something needed to be done to absorb the excess labor: "As a result of modern machinery, better commercial fertilizers and improved scientific farming, agricultural production has climbed steadily upward while the number of farm workers has declined."[11] The displaced rural residents went searching for work in urban areas, which included the many young people who had grown up on farms and found it increasingly difficult to buy or support a farm of their own. Agriculture was slowly losing its dominance in the state, causing a serious threat of unemployment due to a growing pool of those displaced from farming.

Some state leaders argued for diversification of the economy in order to safeguard it from massive unemployment. Those proposing diversification reasoned that an increase in manufacturing would provide more sources of income and employment opportunities. They believed more industry would expand existing businesses, broaden the tax base, and raise the state's per capita income. As they argued, "Only when a balanced economy between farm and factory exists can there remain sufficiently sound employment opportunities to hold a population."[12] Even some farmers agreed that an increase in industrial development would be good for farm families in the state. A prominent farmer with the Farm Bureau argued, "Industry will provide additional income for farmers on the smaller farms. Many farmers who would otherwise be forced out of agriculture would have the opportunity to remain on their farms, taking off-the-farm employment. As technical development and productivity increase, there will be increasing pressure to divert human resources out of agricultural production." He also challenged the Farm Bureau to take industrial development seriously: "I have been told that because industrial development is so far removed from agriculture, we in the Farm Bureau need not be greatly concerned with the problem. To me, progress and development in our own state is just as important, perhaps even more so, than other areas of endeavor which are undertaken by the Farm Bureau."[13]

In 1945, the state legislature created the IDC to achieve the goals of diversifying the state's economy, absorbing the excess labor, and guaranteeing the protection of the economy.[14] Eleven members, all appointed by the governor, composed the new commission, including four from the legislature—two from the House and two from the Senate. The legislature gave the commission three major functions: one, to encourage new industry; two, to provide assistance to existing ones; and three, to "promote industrial development of our agricultural raw materials and products."[15] The IDC began a massive advertising campaign to entice new business into the state and started a series of publicity programs in order "to acquaint the people of Iowa with the need for an expanded industrial economy."[16] They mass produced pamphlets, brochures, and fact sheets all promoting Iowa as a state of "industrial opportunity." One of the flashier brochures was titled "Industry's Road to Opportunity Leads to Iowa," and the cover depicted a beautiful pastoral scene of Iowa's landscape behind a stolid worker in coveralls holding onto a steel rail. The brochure blended Iowa's agricultural fame with imagery of modern transportation, factories, industrial equipment, and good workers. Splashed across the tops of the pages were blurbs about how bountiful, blossoming, rich, and promising the land of Iowa was. One, for example, declared in bold letters "In Iowa—the heartland of America—bountiful nature provides advantages for industry too!"[17]

A difficult task for the commission was convincing industrialists back east that industry could indeed thrive in Iowa, despite its prominence as an agricultural state. They stressed that the state did, in fact, have urban areas, and offered the metropolitan area of Des Moines as an example.

Pamphlet published by the Iowa Industrial Development Commission, 1952.
Iowa Industries, SHSI, Iowa City.

They argued that the state had at least thirteen cities, all with a population of at least 25,000 or more, which composed nearly 28 percent of the state's total population.[18] According to them, an ideal city for a new factory would be "large enough to offer good basic services and utilities, but not so large that congestion is a problem," and also "these typical American communities, with their aggressive self-improvement programs, merit your most careful consideration."[19]

The IDC also encouraged local communities to develop their own programs and argued that "a small factory added to a community could mean an annual increase of $312,875 to retail business." The *Digest*, the commission's monthly newsletter, commented in 1961 that "almost every community in Iowa is interested to some degree in attracting some kind of industry. To date, more than 240 cities and towns have formally organized industrial development groups." One of the main ways the commission taught communities was through annual industrial clinics. The first clinic, held in February 1954, had nearly two hundred representatives from fifty-four different communities and six states. Governor William Beardsley, who was in attendance, complimented "Iowa's chamber of commerce for their efforts to fulfill the need for increased industrial development throughout the state" and asserted that "cooperation between state government and local communities was essential in realizing Iowa's great potential."[20] Local communities took the initiative and developed their own programs, and the annual clinics continued to be a huge success for several years.

The IDC was successful in its efforts to encourage industrial growth, and by 1965 there were nearly 4,000 manufacturing firms in the state, with an increase of 850 new firms from 1945 to 1965. The commission had achieved its most basic goal—increasing the industrial sector of the state and balancing the economy. The diversification of the state heralded twenty years of economic growth from 1960 to 1980.[21] The IDC broadcast this achievement in one of its many publications, proclaiming that even though Iowa was "historically regarded as an agricultural state, it is matching the income from its soil with products of industry. Nowadays there are splotches of smoke on the horizon, coming from the smokestacks rising out of the tall corn. The field and the factory, the farmer and manufacturer, are joining forces for the good of themselves, Iowa, and the nation." The commission also concluded that "the trend toward diversification of industry has found Iowa ideally situated to receive and absorb the benefits which a balanced economy between agriculture and industry can assure."[22]

While the state was actively recruiting industry to relocate, businesses themselves were in the process of decentralizing production. This began after World War II as industry, previously concentrated in the Northeast and Upper Midwest, began moving into the South. The proximity to old markets influenced business leaders' decisions to try the South, and with their success, companies began to expand westward into the Midwest as well. Companies sought small to mid-sized towns and cities as places where the community would be cooperative with their business interests and have access to a high-quality workforce at a cheaper price.[23] Many businesses found Iowa to be an ideal, though unlikely, place to set up shop. Businessmen took the process of choosing a new plant location quite seriously, and those decisions were not made at random. The commission reported that companies relocating took considerable time to investigate new places in which to invest, stating, "The era of incaution, injudicious plant location has been supplanted with scientific analyses and systematic research by most major manufacturers concerned in the trend toward industrial decentralization. Businessmen and executives . . . have as their present object the scientific determination of that one best community which offers the greatest competitive advantages."[24]

Companies that looked for new places to invest had a whole litany of things to consider, including transportation networks, tax breaks, a cheap labor supply, business climate, and community attitudes. Business climate was an especially important factor with many considerations such as employee-employer relations, employee work habits, state labor legislation, taxes, government regulations, education, character of government, and basic attitudes in the community. Manufacturers took the climate of a community quite seriously, so that even when problems were discovered, "a program of constructive action to improve the business climate is necessary because it is an integral part of the community having its 'house in order' for new industry."[25] In other words, manufacturers did not want to encounter militant unionism that could overshadow the company's agenda, and businesses wanted to guarantee that nothing would interfere with business as usual. S. B. Williams, the director of public relations for Sylvania Electric Products in Burlington, put the process of relocation this way: "Choosing a town is in some ways a lot like choosing a college for a youngster. . . . You may know half a dozen or more colleges where the book-learning would be about equally good, but where there would be a wide difference in extra-curricular activities. For instance, if the youngster were a girl, you would in all probability want a place that was fairly close to a boy's college." By using such highly gendered terminology, Williams implied that the female plant would want to be near extra perks such as the comfort of companionship in a healthy community.[26]

Companies liked Iowa's sense of community, describing Iowans as "a pretty wholesome group," and the "friendly atmosphere in Iowa" was an important qualification. Businesses also hoped they would not encounter the strong unionism they were escaping in the East. The state's right-to-work law had a significant role in this belief and helped many decide in favor of Iowa. As one businessman explained, "Iowa's laws indicate a friendly attitude on the part of government." The state's legislature passed the right-to-work law in 1947, shortly after the national Taft-Hartley Act passed in Congress. The IDC did not stress this law in its numerous publications. Rather, it was the businessmen themselves who considered this a prime motivator in moving to Iowa. Of course, the leaders of the new businesses implied that they would not exploit their rural workforce, as S. B. Williams promised when his company decided to move to Iowa. "Our program of decentralization is not based on seeking places with low labor rates. We have no intention of exploiting small town labor," Williams explained. "Exploitation, of such nature, we feel would, sooner or later, boomerang." And indeed, Iowa labor would prove to be not nearly as docile as many industrialists assumed, as the workforce would unionize in a number of the new plants.[27] Industrialists, however, were looking to escape the high wages of the East and find areas where the community wages were considerably lower. In places like Iowa, industrialists could offer good wages by the community's standards, but still lower than wages they paid back East.[28]

The state also asserted it did not give industrialists large tax breaks, claiming in their bimonthly *Bulletin*, "There would seem little for the State of Iowa to fear from those few manufacturers concerned with the employment of a cheap labor force and in search of tax favoritism. Iowa has never looked with favor upon plant and factory give-away programs and tax support, because industry seeking such subsidies would feel, in most cases, no obligation to the community in which it locates."[29] Even though the commission stressed that the state did not bend over backward in giving ridiculously low tax rates, the state did have an extremely low tax rate. The national monthly survey magazine, *Industrial Development*, claimed that the state "had the second lowest average employer tax rate in the nation during 1959, and the third lowest during 1950–1959."[30] While the exact tax rate appears to be elusive, it is safe to assume the tax rates were low to encourage the industrial development of Iowa's resources.

Improved transportation routes also provided further encouragement to industry's migration westward. With the advent of the interstate highway system, Iowa became a crossroads of the highway transportation system, and eastern Iowa was also considered part of the periphery of Chicago's greater urban network. Trucking became the major means of transporting both raw material and the finalized products, and between 1945 and 1968 intercity freight by trucks grew from 67 billion ton-miles to 415 billion ton-miles. Access to major highways was a serious consideration in a move to the Midwest.[31]

Whether industries were pulled by Iowa's natural advantages, or the labor laws, or the tax breaks, they did indeed flock to the state—not just one type or kind of industry, but a whole assortment. A brief analysis of a three-year period shows the variety of firms that were moving. Between 1953 and 1955, some of the greatest increase of business in the state occurred. In just the first half of 1953, seventeen new plants relocated or expanded, and in 1954, thirty-one new industries created approximately 1,600 jobs.[32] Some of these industries produced stock feeders, fertilizer, dairy, and electrical industrial equipment. In the first quarter of 1955 there were twelve new industries and three new expansions. Some of these included Modern Homes Incorporated and Red Dot Foods in Ottumwa, Heinz Foods in Muscatine, and W. D. Caldwell in Fort Madison. In 1955, a total of seventy-two new industries moved in, creating forty new firms and thirty-two expansions. They included nine in food processing, seven in chemicals, five in electronics, and four in machinery.[33]

The new industrial growth of Iowa built upon a solid base of existing industries, two of which provided the bulwark for the industrial sector in the state: meatpacking, food processing, and farm equipment manufacturing. These two industries had some of the largest factories in the state, and out of the twenty largest plants (all of which employed over 1,000 workers) two were farm equipment manufacturers and seven were meatpackers.[34] Both of these industries also continued to rapidly expand after the war and remained the two most important industries late into the twentieth century.[35] The IDC advertised that "since Iowa produces 10 percent of the nation's food supply, food manufacturing and processing leads all other industries in the state, accounting for more than half of the value of the state's manufactured products," and that "in manufacturing . . . 47,000 are employed in food processing (more) than in any other classification."[36] Meatpacking blossomed in the state because of the easy access to agriculturally based materials, and the industry dominated many of Iowa's cities beginning in the early twentieth century. Packing firms began as direct-buying meat centers in the rural Midwest, which allowed farmers to bring their livestock directly to these meat processing centers, and they focused mostly on pork since hogs were easier to transport than cattle.

Both Ottumwa, through John Morrell, and Cedar Rapids, through Sinclair, had the earliest direct buying centers, both of which began in the 1870s. Meatpacking continued to grow rapidly during the 1910s and 1920s, and maintained steady production long into the century until it began to decline after the 1970s.[37]

Machinery production, especially farm equipment manufacturing, provided the main bulwark to Iowa's economy. The commission noted that 40,150 people were employed in manufacturing and of those, 18,450 worked in agricultural machinery.[38] Farm equipment manufacturing grew rapidly after the invention and mass production of the tractor in the 1910s. In the 1880s, John Deere, a pioneer in the business, settled his headquarters in Moline, Illinois, just across the Mississippi River from Davenport. From there, Deere built his empire, spreading farm equipment plants across the state. Deere eventually had three major plants in Waterloo and large factories in Dubuque, Ottumwa, and Des Moines. John Deere, while perhaps the iconic figure in farm equipment, was by no means the only major manufacturer in the business, as both J. I. Case and International Harvester, among others, had major plants in the state.

The new industries that relocated between 1945 and 1965 helped to further expand the industrial sector. Many of these newer industries fell into the broad categories of chemical, electronic, fabricated metal, and machinery. Chemical manufacturing prospered in Iowa, especially DuPont, who had plants in both Clinton and Fort Madison. While the plant in Fort Madison was relatively small and only employed around three hundred to produce paint thinners, the plant in Clinton was fairly large. DuPont started production in Clinton in 1941, producing cellophane, and in 1962, built a 90,000-square-foot addition to the plant to begin producing polyolefin. DuPont employed nearly 1,300 in the Clinton area and, along with Clinton Corn Company, a grain processing plant, was a major employer of the city.[39]

Electronics boomed after World War II as well, as newer uses for electrical technology were discovered for both home and business. Electrical companies were one of the largest industrial groups and had phenomenal growth during the 1950s. In 1953 there were 9,139 electronic manufacturing plants, but by 1963 there were 19,635, a 114 percent increase (see Tables 2 and 3). Both Cedar Rapids and Burlington seemed to attract a greater

TABLE 2. Number of Manufacturing Establishments and Employees, 1939–1963

| Year | Establishments | Employees |
|---|---|---|
| 1939 | 2,541 | 88,054 |
| 1947 | 2,965 | 140,425 |
| 1954 | 3,320 | 163,669 |
| 1963 | 3,496 | 178,199 |

Source: United States Census of Manufacturers.

TABLE 3. Total Number of Employees by Product

| Product | 1953 | 1963 |
|---|---|---|
| Food | 48,374 | 50,356 |
| Apparel | 3,706 | 12,036 |
| Chemical | 5,869 | 4,946 |
| Fabricated Metal | 7,868 | 9,249 |
| Machinery | 37,237 | 35,484 |
| Electric Machinery | 9,139 | 19,635 |

Source: United States Census of Manufacturers.

amount of electronic industry, as Cedar Rapids was home to Collins Radio, Turner Microphone, and Square D, among others. Burlington experienced major growth in electronics throughout the 1950s, as Sylvania, International Resistor Company, GE, and Champion Sparkplug all moved to the city between 1953 and 1958.

The remaining industries fell into a variety of categories. These plants were usually exceedingly small, employing one hundred or fewer employees. The IDC reported that roughly 3,400 of the 3,736 plants (about 40 percent) had fewer than one hundred employees. The *Iowa Development Digest* stated, "small industry plays a significant role in the state's economy. The fact that there are many small, diversified industries rather than just a few large ones is advantageous from the standpoint of achieving a more balanced economy and is undoubtedly a major factor in the wide and even distribution of industry throughout the state."[40] A good example of a small but successful plant was Dairypak, a milk carton producer, which relocated to Clinton in 1953. The company built a 55,000-square-foot expansion to make paper milk containers and used eight hundred tons of paper each month to produce 24 million paper milk containers a year. It hired approximately 125 employees out of the four hundred who applied, and about 70 percent of those hired were women.[41]

Most of the industry was located in the five largest cities: Des Moines, Cedar Rapids, Waterloo, Sioux City, and Davenport.[42] Midsized cities and towns also experienced an increase of industry, and 2,023 manufacturing firms, or 52.4 percent, were located in towns with a population of 10,000 or less. Small towns had some industry as well, and there was a combined total of 685 manufacturing firms in towns with a population of less than a thousand.[43] Malvern, Iowa, was a good example of a small town with some industry, as the town gained Continental Frozen Foods, a St. Louis–based firm, in 1954, and planned to hire anywhere from fifty to two hundred people.[44] Despite the apparent lack of a labor supply, rural areas and small towns were able to support these manufacturing firms because businesses could pull from a labor supply in the surrounding rural area. The *Digest* reported that "the ease with which workers can commute from adjacent areas has made it possible for smaller communities to attract industries that employ larger numbers of people."[45]

Companies targeted small towns and nonurban areas as places to invest because of cheaper wages and a community willing to work with the company. From 1960 to 1970, manufacturing only grew by 4 percent in urban areas, but 22 percent in rural areas. Rural manufacturing peaked in 1974 and then began to decline during the economic stagnation of the 1970s. The new factories could provide an economic boost to an entire region, and neighboring small towns became dormitory communities as people commuted to their factory jobs, sometimes as far as fifty miles one way.[46]

Some regions had more growth than others, and the eastern sector of the state achieved the greatest industrial growth. Only two counties west of Polk County (City of Des Moines), Woodbury and Pottawattamie, had significant growth. These two counties were located along the Missouri River in western Iowa, and included the cities of Sioux City and Council Bluffs. The south central and southwest counties had the smallest amount of industry; and the southern eight counties of Adair, Warren, Mills, Adams, Clarke, Ringgold, Decatur, and Davis had the least industry in

TABLE 4. Ten Leading Industrial Counties

| County | 1953 | 1963 |
|---|---|---|
| Polk | 23,515 | 21,621 |
| Linn | 19,221 | 23,771 |
| Black Hawk | 17,582 | 18,265 |
| Scott | 14,306 | 13,535 |
| Dubuque | 11,739 | 10,911 |
| Des Moines | 11,025 | 8,314 |
| Woodbury | 10,098 | 7,300 |
| Lee | 6,651 | 6,211 |
| Clinton | n.a. | 5,732 |
| Wapello | 7,227 | 5,571 |
| Jasper | 5,860 | n.a. |

Source: United States Census of Manufacturers.

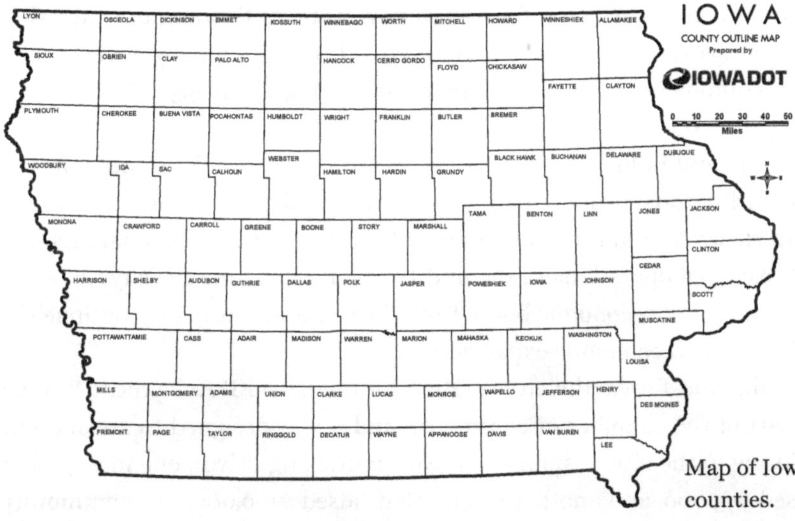


Map of Iowa's counties.

the state, with less than ten manufacturing plants. These counties also had some of the smallest populations in the state. The main concentration of industry was in eastern and southeastern Iowa, in Polk, Woodbury, Linn, Black Hawk, Scott, Dubuque, Des Moines, and Lee counties (see Table 4). Of the top twenty industrial counties, only three were west of

Polk County—Woodbury, Pottawattamie, and Webster.[47] Counties along the Mississippi River appear to be the most successful, since seven of those ten counties had at least fifty firms in 1955.[48]

## Burlington and Clinton as Case Studies

Two communities illustrate how cities in Iowa sponsored industrial development and how industrial development impacted those communities. Burlington and Clinton provide a good comparison because they were roughly the same size, with 30,000 in population, and had a significant industrial economic base. Burlington, located in the southeast part of the state along the Mississippi River in Des Moines County, expanded dramatically during World War II. In 1941, the federal government hired a private contractor, Mason and Hanger-Silas Mason, to build a new ordnance plant a few miles outside of the city. The plant needed nearly 12,000 workers to operate the new high-tech equipment that made bombs and ammunition for the war. This caused a serious housing shortage for the city as it scrambled to make room for all the new workers flooding in. The other main employer before the war was the J. I. Case Company, which made farm equipment and opened a plant in Burlington in 1937. Before these two plants opened, the city's industries consisted mostly of small manufacturers and industries such as caskets, furniture, baskets, and vinegar. The Burlington Ordnance plant, which eventually changed its name to the Iowa Army Ammunition Plant, closed for a few years in the late forties, but restarted operations in the mid-fifties. By this time the city's officials had enjoyed the economic boom from the war and wanted to continue the industrial and economic expansion.[49]

In the mid-fifties, the city created the Industrial Development Bureau as part of the chamber of commerce, and it was designed to attract new industry to the city. It sponsored two fundraising drives, one in 1957 that raised $75,000, and another in 1961 that raised $100,000. The community participated in the fundraisers and elicited contributions from all facets of the community: businesses, banks, unions, and professionals. The Burlington *Hawkeye* commented, "Burlington is quite willing to put its money where its mouth is. Most of us talk about the need for encouraging industry, both existing and new. Most of us recognize that increasing job opportunities is the key to a community's survival, not to mention its growth.

Champion Sparkplug, Burlington, Iowa.

But doing the job is something else and this campaign proves Burlington is willing to work at it."[50] The bureau had a yearly budget of $23,000 to recruit new business, and created brochures and data sheets, much like the IDC. It was able to attract new industry, and approximately sixteen new plants relocated to Burlington from 1955 to 1965. Some of these included GE, Champion Sparkplug, Advance Ross, and Sylvania. Daniel Hauser, head of the Industrial Development Bureau, gave reasons for Burlington's success: "Closeness to markets and sources of supply is the determining factor, although community attitude and other factors, some more or less intangible, play a part in the final determination." GE also listed business climate, attitude of the local public, activity of the chamber of commerce, tax rates, and public facilities as helping determine the final decision.[51] The city of Burlington actively strove to achieve industrial growth and took advantage of the state's general trend toward industrialization to benefit the community. Burlington continued to prosper, with high employment rates until the end of the 1970s.

Much like Burlington, the city of Clinton also prospered from industrial development during the 1950s. Clinton was very similar to Burlington. They both developed along the Mississippi River, had roughly the same size population, and both had a solid industrial base. Clinton was located farther north, several miles north of the Quad Cities in Clinton County. Clinton also desired to increase its industry after the war. Two major industries dominated the industrial base in the city: the Clinton Corn Company and DuPont. During the 1950s, the city's chamber of commerce began seeking ways to diversify the city's industrial economy by bringing in several smaller industries. The city organized the Clinton Development Company (CDC) in 1954, which was its own independent, nonprofit organization separate from the chamber of commerce. The goal of the CDC was to attract new industry to Clinton, increase payrolls, and broaden the economic base of the city. The CDC had 356 members from the community, including many from organized labor, and raised nearly $263,000 to help spark industrial growth. The CDC was fairly successful in its endeavors to attract new industries and expand existing ones. From 1955 to 1965, there were a thousand new jobs and ten new industries. The CDC also won several awards during the IDC's awards banquet in 1959, including first place for organization and first place in the industrial contact category. In 1965, Clinton had fifty-three manufacturing firms, with five of those firms employing over two hundred people.[52] Both Burlington and Clinton illustrate how communities in Iowa developed a diversified industry and prospered with the new industrial development.

The transformation of Iowa's economy from agricultural predominance to a mixed economy of both agriculture and manufacturing had many repercussions for the citizens of the state. It spurred Iowa's urbanization, so that by the 1970s more people lived in towns and cities than in the countryside. More people began making a living through industrial work than by agriculture, and many farmers began working in nearby factories to support their small farms. Most importantly, this industrial growth opened up opportunities for women to earn a decent income and support their families. As women began looking for work outside of the home during the 1950s, they found manufacturing companies eager and ready to provide them employment and set them to work in gender-designated jobs and tasks.

# Chapter Two

## Out of the Home and into the Workplace

As a young girl growing up on a farm, a lifetime of work in a factory seemed a far-off possibility to Pauline Fisher. She married young, shortly after high school, and followed her husband to California during World War II. They returned to Iowa when the war was over and began renting land outside Oskaloosa, a town located an hour southeast of Des Moines. They settled down to raise a family, but their dreams of thriving off the bounty of the land faded as the harsh realities of farming in the 1950s prevented them from purchasing their farm. Unable to save enough money, they continued to rent, making farming—an already challenging lifestyle—even more difficult. Fisher lamented the hardships of farming: "By the time you give the landlord half [of the income], you didn't have much left." To keep the farm, she took a job at the Ideal Manufacturing plant in Oskaloosa. She worked forty hours a week on third shift, sometimes coming home in the mornings to help on the farm. At first, Fisher hated her job and revolted at the idea of working in a factory, but she did not have much of a choice. "I had to work," Fisher recalled. "Our farm just wasn't paying at all." Despite the long, hard days, she eventually came to enjoy her job, the friendships she developed with other female workers, and the ability to make a decent income.[1] Fisher's life highlights the growing trend of Iowa women leaving the farm and heading to work in a factory. Her life was by no means indicative of all Iowa women's experiences, but it does exemplify the somewhat unusual combination of rural life with industrial work. A confluence of events in the 1950s caused many Iowa women like Fisher to leave the comfort of home and begin working in factories, workplaces many of them never intended to spend the majority of their working lives.

The presence of Iowa women within the industrial workforce presented a contrasting image of the ruddy-cheeked, corn-fed Iowa farm girl within a dark, rank factory. What could possibly pull these women into the factory, a place they never imagined they would end up? As Eunice Evans, a rural woman who worked at the Amana Refrigeration Company, recalled, "I think I probably had a lot of dreams like most kids, but nothing serious. It certainly didn't involve working in a factory." As women adjusted to the rapid social and demographic changes of the period, more women sought paid work outside of the home. In Iowa the number of women working outside of the home in paid employment increased 80 percent over a twenty-year period. These women were participants in a national economic and cultural shift during the immediate postwar period. As families began to place more emphasis on education for their children, kids spent more time in the classroom and less time working. This sparked a change in the role of women from caretakers to providers, and as Iowa women began searching for ways to provide an income, industry was moving into the Midwest. Major manufacturers began searching for a workforce that would be more pliable and less expensive, and they found midwestern women to be a perfect solution to their labor problem. The convergence of these trends propelled hundreds of Iowa women into the workforce. It also led to an indirect challenge to the patriarchal system and the division of gender roles in American households. Iowa women did not search for work to undermine the authority of their husbands over their households, but by exercising agency over their lives in their search for work, they began to redefine their gender roles. This redefinition of womanhood from a dependent housewife to a supporter of the household would begin to erode the foundation of the patriarchal household system.

## Redefining Motherhood

Nationally, the activity of women working in industry was not new, and indeed, women have been working in factories since the early days of the first industrial revolution in the 1820s. Beginning with the young New England farm girls who worked in the textile mills of Lowell, Massachusetts, manufacturers depended on women as a valuable source of labor. Continuing throughout the nineteenth century and into the twentieth, women played an important part in the industrialization of America. These women worked in the textile mills, sweatshops, and meatpacking plants, and they were usually young and single, and worked to support their families.[2] Although some married women did work outside of the home in the first half of the twentieth century, especially in the textile mills in the South, it was still unusual for married women to work. In 1920, only 23 percent of working women were married, a figure that increased slightly to 29 percent in 1930. Most of these married working women were among the poorest in the United States, often African American, and sequestered in the lowest-paying jobs. Consequently, throughout the early twentieth century it was still uncommon for married women to work, and many assumed that a young woman would quit her job once she did marry.

World War II provided a breaking point in that it challenged the cultural and social assumptions that women were incapable of performing hard physical labor. But as Alice Kessler-Harris argued, the net gains from the war were negligible. Many women who worked during the war assumed that they would return home once the war was over, even though they may have wanted to continue. The iconic figure of Rosie the Riveter spurred women to fulfill their patriotic duty, take up the rivet gun, and fight the war in the factory, but the country's leaders did not intend for Rosie to stay on the job once the war was over. Rosie went home and focused on the family, fulfilling the traditional role of homemaking. The war did not challenge the primary gender roles for women, and the home remained the principal concern of the wife and mother. What was significant about the 1950s was how these gendered assumptions began to erode as married women with children began entering and reentering the paid workforce. In 1950, 29 percent of the workforce was female; by 1975 it increased to 40 percent. This slow and steady transfer of women, especially married women with children, into the workforce provided a greater challenge to gender roles in the United States than World War II ever did.[3]

As more women began working outside of the home, public and social attitudes slowly shifted to accommodate the working wife. Although many in society believed that women with jobs would cause irreparable harm to the health and well-being of the American family, national leaders began to endorse the idea of women working. As the economy boomed after the war, public leaders realized that they needed women to spur the continued growth and stability of the economy. To support this economic stability, women needed to be not only consumers but also producers. Women provided the essential labor needed for economic growth and filled low-level positions in manufacturing. The extra wages women earned allowed families to purchase new consumer products, which in turn boosted the economy by sustaining the high rate of production. Julia Kirk Blackwelder argued that this need for working women caused a redefinition of motherhood and womanhood that allowed the public to accept the transition from homemakers to workers. "Consumer desires," she explains, "propelled mothers to supplement the family income. More and more mothers marched off to work during the 1950s, as economic forces—not for the first time—overcame the messages of popular culture, employers and bureaucrats thought they had the answer in a redefinition of maternal obligation." Blackwelder added, "a redefinition that included providing for as well as protecting children, a redefinition that ultimately prevailed." By the 1960s, Blackwelder argues, motherhood included providing for the family as well as giving nurturing care. Alice Kessler-Harris also noted this change, adding that families began turning to women's wage work as a way to handle the family economy, rather than depending on children's wages or a wife's penny- pinching, belt-tightening household budgeting. She argued that the decades after the war were "marked by the dawning recognition within families that women's functions of cushioning depression and fighting inflation . . . might be more effectively handled by wage-earning women."[4]

The redefinition of successful motherhood directly impacted Iowa women, who also began to work outside of the home in increasing numbers between 1940 and 1960. According to the U.S. Census, the number of Iowa women working overall increased 20 percent from 1950 to 1960 (see Table 5), while the participation of rural, nonfarm women increased 25 percent over the ten-year period. More urban women worked outside of the home than rural women, but the numbers for both increased from 1950 to 1960.

Many prominent leaders in the state noticed the shifting demographics and formed committees to study and analyze the changes. Governor Harold Hughes created the first Governor's Commission on the Status of Women in 1964 and tasked it with analyzing these important demographic shifts occurring within the state's female population. The governor charged the commission to realize the urgency in understanding this new movement of women working outside the home, as "the increased participation

TABLE 5. Iowa Women in the Labor Force, 1950 and 1960

| | Employed 1950 | Employed 1960 | Not Employed 1950 | Not Employed 1960 |
|---|---|---|---|---|
| Statewide | 249,524 | 318,117 | 735,645 | 680,478 |
| Urban | 165,003 | 208,842 | 339,083 | 344,244 |
| Rural Nonfarm | 51,192 | 68,327 | 177,642 | 165,029 |
| Rural Farm | 32,929 | 40,928 | 218,920 | 171,205 |

Source: U.S. Bureau of the Census, Iowa.

of women in aspects of Iowa society has changed so rapidly that our state's laws and customs have lagged in fully accepting and adjusting to the changing activities of women. A few generations ago the working woman was rare and not fully accepted. Today one-third of Iowa's women are employed."[5] The Governor's Commission noted that those working outside the home had increased by 70 percent since 1940. At the conclusion of the study, the commission filed a report on their analysis stating that the high rate of female employment was ultimately good for the state's economy and encouraged employers to continue hiring women. They distributed information to employers stressing "the positive aspects of employing women, such as, the favorable absentee rate of women who have re-entered the labor market after their child-bearing years."[6]

The governor's office was not the only state agency to take notice of this change, as the IDC also reported that approximately 190,000 women were working in the state, and of those, 23 percent were employed in manufacturing. Table 6 illustrates the increasing number of women employed from 1940 to 1960 and the economic sectors where they worked. While manufacturing claimed only 10 percent of women working, its share increased significantly during this period, as the number of female factory workers increased 140 percent in just a twenty-year period. Those women in manufacturing predominantly worked in electronics, meatpacking, machinery, and rubber. Although many mass production industries, such as the farm equipment and grain milling industries, continued to deny employment to women, there was more opportunity for women in machinery (which

TABLE 6. Women in the Labor Force, by Occupation

| Year | 1940 | 1950 | 1960 |
|---|---|---|---|
| Professional | 31,823 | 36,539 | 44,900 |
| Clerical/Sales | 51,053 | 88,453 | 114,194 |
| Domestic Service | 29,694 | 16,091 | 20,961 |
| Manufacturing | 16,530 | 30,833 | 30,636 |
| Service | 23,508 | 37,160 | 55,766 |
| Agriculture | 5,398 | 19,512 | 4,690 |
| Total Employed | 170,350 | 244,745 | 308,318 |

Source: U.S. Bureau of the Census: 1940, Table 18; 1950, Tables 28 and 31; 1960, Table 57.

TABLE 7. Women in Manufacturing

| Year | 1940 | 1950 | 1960 |
|---|---|---|---|
| Food and Kindred Products | 5,437 | 9,509 | 10,995 |
| Machinery | 1,074 | 5,447 | 10,385 |
| Durable Goods | 3,157 | 5,224 | 7,906 |
| Nondurable Goods | 3,906 | 6,952 | 7,286 |
| Apparel | 2,159 | 2,735 | 3,169 |
| Total Manufacturing | 16,564 | 30,889 | 40,304 |

Source: U.S. Bureau of the Census, Iowa: 1960, Table 62.

included electronics), durable, and nondurable goods. Table 7 illustrates the different types of manufacturing that employed women.[7]

It is important to note that these changes did not directly challenge the system of patriarchy, which privileged the importance of the male breadwinner. These women saw themselves as supporting the family, and consequently, their work served to reinforce patriarchy as the predominant structure in the division of labor. Even though they began working outside of the home, many women at this particular moment did not see themselves as challenging the traditional family structure; rather, they were supporting it through the fulfillment of their gender role. Providing for the family remained the predominant role and responsibility of the husband and father, while women's work was considered supplemental income. As discussed, the more subtle yet radical shift was the redefinition of that role from housekeeper to provider.

## The Need for Paid Labor

Iowa women pursued work outside of the home for a variety of reasons, and for the most part, women found it comforting to have their own income and felt pride in their contribution to their family's economic security. The Iowa Labor History Oral Project (ILHOP) includes numerous female voices and life stories, and by analyzing their experiences, one can see the larger economic, social, and cultural trends at play. The first of these trends was the cultural value of work and the sense of duty to family, neighborhood, and community. This culture stemmed from the long roots of an agrarian past that were still present in midwestern life, despite the slow and steady progress of urbanization across the region. Second, the shifting cultural notions of women's place in the home and in child rearing began to place a greater emphasis on provision for children rather than care within the home. As more children began attending school, mothers began to see themselves as additional providers, replacing children's potential income with their own. This shift in values and in economic reality eventually led to the birth of a new norm—the dual-income household. Last, many women went to work out of sheer economic necessity, usually because of the absence of a male breadwinner. Without a male provider, the burden of earning an income fell solely on them. Women of color also felt tremendous economic pressure, not necessarily because they lacked a male breadwinner but because the men in their lives could not make enough income to fully provide for their families. Faced with racial discrimination in the workplace, people of color had difficulty living on just one income.

Women's viewpoint on the cultural value of hard work grew from a rural agrarian culture rooted in eastern Iowa. Even though many Iowa women no longer lived on the farm, they retained an ingrained cultural understanding of the value of hard work accompanied with a deep sense of duty to the family.[8] Edith Arendt, a lifetime worker at Collins Radio in Cedar Rapids, demonstrated this point when she recalled how her father taught her the importance of work. "My father thought that hard work was good for everyone. And taught me to do it when there was any chore to be done or any repair work to go ahead and do it and try to succeed." Women like Arendt brought this understanding of work with them when they started their own families, and they in turn taught their children to value hard work. When these women found themselves in need of additional cash, they were willing and able to find a job, work hard, and provide for the family.[9]

Young women often found paid jobs outside of the home as soon as their families considered them old enough to work. Many young women began working after high school to support themselves until they got married. These young women usually worked as waitresses or clerks in department stores. Artis Hatland England, who graduated from high school in 1946 in Emmet County, Iowa, worked as a waitress to save money for her marriage. But she, like many other women, quit shortly after starting a family. Other women gained valuable work experience during the war, which helped them find employment once it was over. Mary Speer, a welder in the shipyards in Portland, Oregon, commented, "It was hard work, but I really enjoyed it. But I guess I got kind of homesick to come back home." She returned to Iowa and applied at the new Firestone Tire plant in Des Moines, remembering that she "applied for a job one morning and went to work that night on the eleven to seven shift." When it came time for women to return to the workforce, their life experiences helped ease that transition.[10]

The second major factor driving women into the workforce was the need for an additional income. This need varied according to the family, often appearing on a sliding scale from extra pocket money to cushion the family budget to dire need. At the top of this scale were women who saw paid work as a way to protect their families against economic hardship, especially after years of depression and war. Families in Iowa and across the nation desired a return to normalcy and wanted to provide their children with the extra things they went without during the Great Depression. Women wanted a better lifestyle for their children, free from the worry of economic hardships they had faced. For example, Josephine Gerard went to work at the Amana Refrigeration Company so she and her husband could afford to buy their six children the extra things she did not have when she was growing up during the Depression. She remarked, "I thought of the money that we could use. I was raised on not enough clothes, not enough food, and I swore to God that my kids were gonna have something . . . but when you got kids . . . it takes a lot." She and her husband agreed that he could "support us for basic things, but my kids would never be able to do or get anything extra, you know, if I didn't go to work and that's the reason I went to work." Some women, like Eunice Evans, who also worked at Amana, wanted to be able to afford to give their children healthier food. Fern Klopp, who did not work for several years after she was married, decided to get a job when her daughter wanted to receive nurse's training. She applied at Turner Microphone in Cedar Rapids, recalling, "I didn't work until my daughter was wanting to go to nurse's training. We only lived two blocks from the plant, so I decided that maybe I could help out until she got through nurse's training."[11]

Rural farm women also felt the economic pressures of the era, and after the war there was a movement toward dual incomes within farm families.[12] Beverly Everett, a prominent speaker in farm circles in Iowa during the 1960s, encouraged rural women to think about possible economic opportunities they could fulfill to support the farm. She testified, "Both my husband and I feel that, should weather or health fail, the other should be equipped to step in and provide an income." After her four children were in school, she decided to go back to college and gain a teaching certificate. She argued, "Whether I take a job or not, we are more ready as a family to meet a financial crisis." Everett also noted in many of her speeches that many women were increasingly working off the farm in a variety of ways to earn an income. She described the various activities of her farm neighbors: Hazel worked as a nurse, Barb owned a shop in town, Mabel taught second grade, Faye worked at a bookstore, and Lucille cooked in the school lunchroom.[13]

Rural farm women faced additional economic challenges during the 1950s, which drove them off the farm and into the workforce. Farm women were accustomed to providing for their families, as they took charge of dairy cows and chickens, selling milk, butter, and eggs to a local market. These endeavors provided women with cash to purchase food items they could not raise or grow themselves; they also used the money to purchase supplies such as shoes, clothing, and household items. This income eased the family budget and provided the overworked farm wife with some extra padding to purchase needed things. After World War II, however, these independent economic endeavors became obsolete due to the restructuring of both the dairy and poultry industries. As the poultry industry changed from decentralized backyard production to a vertically integrated farming operation, women's small flocks could not keep up. Large-scale poultry operations soon took over the industry, as farmers discovered it to be quite lucrative. Women also lost the small dairy income they had maintained through selling milk and butter. As Jane Adams comments in her study of Union County, Illinois, "The loss of markets for these agricultural products placed enormous strains on household budgets, since women's sales had virtually provisioned the family."[14]

Farm prices as a whole also failed after the war, as markets became unstable and those who operated small farms, or those who rented, found it increasingly difficult to stay afloat. As wartime price supports were removed, the market became more variable, causing general instability of prices. Either the husband or the wife needed to go in search of work to ensure economic stability of the farm. As Luella Zmolek noted, "Somebody had to work. We had to have more income, and so I decided, well, I guess I would go to work. That's just the way it was. I think, [at] first I wondered how I was going to go to work when I had six kids to take care of, but, on the other hand, I thought, well, I guess I'll try." Ilo Rhines also decided to work, and she appreciated her job at the postal service: "What saved us on the farm, what kept us so we could stay there, was an opportunity that I had to join the postal service. And you know, it was an above average wage. But that was one of the reasons that we were able to [stay]—it wasn't because farm prices got so darn great."[15]

Declining farm prices led to dual-income farm families, which reflected larger trends within the economy as more families across the nation and the state began depending on two incomes. Dual-income households affected urban women as well. As Bev Clinton, who did not work the first two or three years of her marriage, commented, "It had become part of the household to have two incomes." She went to work at Square D in Cedar Rapids, an electronics factory. Susan Rhum went to work at the ammunition plant in Burlington in 1963 because it was difficult to support her family on only one paycheck. Carol Carter worked at Champion Sparkplug in Burlington because it paid well, and she "was anxious to make a good living for [her] family." These women illustrate the growing dependence on two incomes.[16]

Even though many women worked to help support the family, others were forced into working by economic necessity. Women's economic need usually resulted from the loss of a male provider, whether through the husband's disability, divorce, or the collapse of the husband's job. For example, Joyce Burrows went to work at Flexsteel in Dubuque sewing cushions for couches and chairs because her husband lost a finger working at John Deere. Helen Erdmann went to work at Black's Department Store in Waterloo because her husband became ill. "My husband worked at John Deere's," she explained. "He'd had a serious operation. In March of 1956 he was not convalescing as fast as he could have, and at that time the insurance benefits weren't like they are now. So we thought we needed another income."[17]

Some women became the sole provider for their children because either their husbands died or, more commonly, their marriages ended. Edith Arendt farmed with her husband for a few years, until he passed away. She sold the farm and moved to Cedar Rapids to work at Collins Radio. Marlene Kruger had a clear understanding of why she had to go to work, stating, "In 1966 my first husband walked out on me and left me with three small children, and that threw me into the job market. I had to support the children, and I got a job at Waterloo Industries through a friend." Jeannette Haymond had a similar story; she married young and had two children soon after, and then her husband left her. "Well, I had been married, had two children, and got a divorce. My husband went south. And I had two children to take care of."[18]

Doris Peick, who also worked at Collins Radio, recalled how she had to go to work in a bakery when she was just fourteen years old to help her mother after her father died of lung cancer. She and her mother left the farm and moved to Cedar Rapids, where Peick got a job greasing loaf pans. She remarked, "Thank God I was a large, economical-size farm girl; you just really had to do the work of an adult, and I assumed that responsibility pretty efficiently, because I didn't get fired and I worked all the hours that I could and saved every cent I could for my school clothes."[19]

Women of color especially struggled with economic survival because they had to contend not only with gendered notions on the appropriateness of women's work, but also with extremely limited job opportunities due to racial discrimination. Even though the minority population of the state was very small, lingering around 5 percent for the twenty-year period, their experiences echoed those of white women with the additional burden of race. Black women, like white women, found it difficult to support a family on just one income. If they were married, husbands were paid on average less than white male workers. Because of this it was almost assumed that Black women would work in some capacity, but they met several challenges to finding high-paying jobs. Meatpacking plants were notorious for denying Black women jobs because of race. It was not until a handful of courageous Black women challenged the discriminatory hiring policies within the industries, by bringing it to the attention of the federal government, that hiring policies began to change. Latinas met similar difficulties. Two Latina sisters, Mercedes Aguilera and Delores Garcia, grew up very poor in a large family in Muscatine. Both of them had to search for work at a young age and migrated between Chicago and the Quad Cities searching for work. They eventually landed in Davenport working in manufacturing jobs.[20]

It was these economic forces that began pushing women out of the home and into the workplace. The trend toward a dual income household provided women with a new cultural norm that made it acceptable for them and their families to begin working outside of the home. What was distinctive about these rural, small-town women was the embedded cultural traditions surrounding work, where households understood their role in the family and that the fulfillment of their responsibilities meant the survival and success of the entire family. This cultural norm gave women further determination to pursue work outside of the home. These examples demonstrate the scaffold of patriarchy that these women operated under. Husbands supported their wives' endeavors because it eased the financial burden on them, but it did not threaten their position as head of the household. These women saw it as their place within the family to be the support rather than the main provider, and it reinforced the traditional division of labor embedded within rural cultural notions of work.

## Women's Work in the Factory

As industry moved into Iowa after World War II, it provided women with additional options for paid work, especially at a time when such options for women were few. Esther Witmer expressed this frustration, commenting,

"You know our options weren't as numerous as they are now. You could be a secretary or you could be a teacher or you could be a hired girl." Sally Putman echoed this lament: "I can remember the opportunities for young women where you could either be a beautician or a nurse or a secretary. Well, I knew that a beautician and a nurse was out for me. I just was not interested in that kind of thing. And so I took secretarial courses in high school." Young women with the foresight or the economic resources could and did receive training to become nurses, teachers, or secretaries. Industrial wage work provided a prime opportunity for women with little education and skill to earn an income. Martha Linn, a young woman in southwestern Iowa, had high hopes of attending college but was disappointed that neither she nor her family could afford for her to do so. She noted that at least "there was a Union Carbide factory in Red Oak, and they paid good wages, and so I went over there to work instead." Even though these jobs were not glamorous or easy, Iowa women like Martha Linn worked them for the simple reasons that they were there, they hired women, and they paid better than clerical or service sector jobs.[21]

In Iowa, several different industries hired women. Table 8 shows the variety of jobs held by eighty-six women who recorded oral histories with ILHOP in the 1980s and '90s. Electronics and meatpacking had the largest percentage of female workers, as these two industries had specific jobs set aside for women. Apparel was also an important industry that usually had a majority-female workforce. Apparel as an industry, however, was on the decline during the postwar years, which explained why the number of apparel jobs was lower than meatpacking or electronics. The remaining group of industries hiring women was an assortment of manufacturers who found women suited for particular jobs.[22]

Industries that hired women usually designated certain jobs within the factory as women's work, cornering women into particular spaces in the factory and keeping them there. Businesses labeled these jobs "female" jobs, and within each industry the designation differed. Ruth Milkman referred to this process as sex-typing and argued that the nature of sex-typing was highly variable. Each plant made its own rules on what was considered men's or women's work. Most jobs for women were based on women's physical characteristics: manual dexterity, attention to detail, and lack of physical strength. Over time, however, these initial explanations

TABLE 8. Distribution of Female Jobs; Sample of the Iowa Labor History Project

| Industry | Number | Percentage |
|---|---|---|
| Electronics | 25 | 30 |
| Meatpacking | 23 | 26 |
| Telephone Operator | 9 | 10 |
| Apparel | 6 | 7 |
| State Jobs | 5 | 6 |
| Miscellaneous Industries | 5 | 6 |
| Office Jobs | 5 | 6 |
| Rubber | 4 | 5 |
| Food Preparation | 2 | 2 |
| Unemployed/Auxiliary | 2 | 2 |

Source: Iowa Labor History Oral Project, Iowa Federation of Labor, AFL-CIO, State Historical Society of Iowa, Iowa City

became lost, and the jobs became known as women's work simply because women had always done them. Milkman termed this process structural inertia and explained that the early, formative period of any industry or organization is crucial "because an industry's pattern of employment by sex, once established, quickly gains all the weight of tradition and becomes extraordinarily inflexible. Employers show surprisingly little interest in tampering with it, even to enhance profitability. Workers, too—both male and female—tend to accept the sexual division of labor once established as 'natural.'" Within the factory, once certain jobs became known as women's work, it became incredibly difficult for women to move out of those jobs and into higher-paying departments that were traditionally known as men's work. In this way, the sexual division of labor worked as a double-edged sword: in one sense it guaranteed that women would always have jobs in the plant, but it also kept them in the lowest-paid positions. By creating a division of labor based on sex, manufacturers protected the supremacy of the male breadwinner and male hierarchy within the factory.[23]

Meatpacking was the first major industry in the state to employ women in special job categories. Nationally, meatpackers began hiring female laborers as early as the 1880s, putting them in canning or by-product departments to produce such things as lard, sausage, and canned meat. The greatest increase of women occurred in the 1890s, and by 1904 nearly two thousand women were working in Chicago's meatpacking industry. These women worked in the lower-paid and unskilled jobs that took very little training. As Jim Barrett noted, "The extreme division of labor and the mechanization of some operations diluted the degree of skill required for most jobs, reducing them to tasks that women were deemed capable of performing." These jobs typically included filling cans, trimming meat, making sausage casing, packing lard and butter, and canning chipped beef. The higher-paid and skilled jobs were reserved for men, since men were considered the family providers and breadwinners.[24]

In the Iowa plants, women usually worked in bacon, sausage, or canning departments. Sometimes women worked as trimmers or in cured meat departments, but they were not allowed to work on the heavy jobs such as those in the kill and cut departments. In the canning department, women cleaned, packaged, and labeled canning products. Work in the sausage department involved stuffing sausages and making lunch meat products, such as hot dogs or wieners. The bacon department contained several conveyor lines, and at each conveyor, one person, usually a male, stood at the head of the belt slicing the bacon into strips. The women lined the belt layering the bacon, and at the end, a woman weighed the layered bacon to ensure there was a pound. The women at the very end of the line were in charge of packaging and boxing. Each conveyor line involved approximately ten women, with ten to twenty lines in the bacon department, creating between one hundred and two hundred jobs for women.

These jobs in a meatpacking plant were not always easy or clean. Velma Wetzel worked on a chitterling crew unraveling large intestines from a butchered hog and flushing out the left-over manure. Wetzel would then store the intestines so the company could sell them as chitterlings. It was a very dirty job, and according to Wetzel, if you weren't careful, you could be completely covered in manure by the end of the day. Despite the dirty, smelly conditions of work in packing plants, women were proud of their work and their position in the industry. This commitment and identification with their jobs would make many women unwilling to give up their position even for higher-paying jobs.[25]

Poultry production also grew after World War II, and poultry producers

Woman slicing bacon at Rath Packing, ca. 1941, Waterloo, Iowa. Iowa Federation of Labor Collection, SHSI, Iowa City.

opened small processing plants in towns and rural areas across the country, especially in Iowa. Since women were instrumental in poultry production during the first half of the twentieth century, poultry processors continued the tradition of female employment. Deborah Fink outlined the importance of poultry processing in a rural community, discussing a small poultry plant that hired women to butcher, clean, cut, and pack chickens, turkeys, ducks, and geese. Darlene Croft worked in a poultry plant in a small town near Ottumwa, which employed approximately 350 women, where she packed and canned boneless chicken.[26]

The electronic industry, the second largest employer of women, had nearly two thousand women working in electrical manufacturing in 1950. The industry had employed men and women almost from the beginning of its history, and in the 1880s and '90s, when inventors found new uses for electricity, the industry began to grow. Men who had considerable knowledge of the science and technology of electricity were the first employees of the burgeoning industry, but as it grew and developed the basis for mass production, industrialists began to break down the modes of production into simple repetitious jobs, a process known as de-skilling. Because mass production work in electronic industries was not as physically demanding as other types of assembly work, industrial leaders viewed women as good candidates for this semiskilled type of work. Electrical production involved tedious repetition dealing with small, intricate parts, and industrialists believed that women's small, nimble fingers, accustomed to long hours of sewing, were perfect for the new work. As historian Ronald Schatz notes, "The jobs which women had traditionally held in electrical factories required speed, attention to detail, nimble fingers, and intense concentration—qualities which managers summed up in the term 'dexterity.'" And much like meatpacking, once women began working these jobs and could perform them with a high degree of proficiency, they became known as women's work.[27]

Women worked in many different aspects of electronics production, especially in inexpensive consumer products such as light bulbs or radio tubes, where they were over 60 percent of the workforce. Women were not limited to these lighter jobs, as they also worked on assembly lines in appliance production. While electronics work could be quite tedious, it also took a great deal of precision. Ronald Schatz described the process of coil winding: "These workers wrapped wire, paper, and tape tightly around metal tubes to form the coils that are used to create magnetic fields in electric motors. The size of the coils depended upon the power of thermometers in which they were placed: they ranged from an inch to several feet in length." It was also physically uncomfortable work, since "coil winders worked in a sitting position with little opportunity to move. Their fingers, wrists, arms and shoulder muscles were continuously in motion." Much of the work in the electronics industry was similar, and women usually sat at stations winding coils, assembling telephone relays, trimming small pieces of rubber, or drilling tiny pieces of metal.[28]

The appliance industry also employed a significant number of women. The best example of an appliance company in Iowa was the Amana Refrigeration Company, located in the small cluster of villages known as the Amana Colonies. The company began when George Foerstner developed a new and more efficient way to produce refrigeration and freezers. He began using the new technology in the mid-thirties to produce the freezer, and by World War II, his business boomed and expanded rapidly. Because the factory was located in a town of approximately five hundred residents, Foerstner needed to search outward for employees to produce the new, high-tech refrigeration products. He began drawing from a pool of rural and small-town residents from within a forty-mile radius surrounding Amana, and because filling the labor force would still be quite difficult, he opened employment to women as well as men. Based on grievances and union lists from 1950 to 1965, it appears that at least 146 women worked at the plant. They commuted from nearly twenty-one small towns and communities, and sixteen of those towns had a population of less than a thousand. Women at Amana usually worked as lower-class assemblers, which meant work on the line, but some also worked as welders, painters, and inspectors. Amana provided a decent income to hundreds of rural women. Leona Roberts, a lifetime worker at Amana, noted, "I know if it hadn't been [for] Amana that come into this here territory, I don't know what people would have done around here because there was no jobs."[29]

The apparel industry was the third major "female" industry in the state. Much like meatpacking, apparel had a long history in the state, especially button making. The city of Muscatine was famous nationwide for its button industry. Around the turn of the twentieth century, businessmen in Muscatine developed the industry by digging clams out of the muddy shores of the Mississippi River and processing the freshwater pearl shells into buttons. By 1910 there were forty-three button factories in Muscatine employing approximately 2,500 workers, who together comprised about two-thirds of Muscatine's workforce. The button industry was the fourth largest employer of female workers in the state, and women worked as machine operators drilling holes, pressing patterns, and polishing buttons.[30]

Besides button making, small apparel factories peppered the state in small towns and cities, employing anywhere from fifty to three hundred women. Apparel factories produced everything from overalls, to flannel shirts, to hunting garments. After World War II, apparel manufacturing continued to grow, and new factories sprang up across the state. Some manufacturers chose these new locations based on the availability of a female labor pool. In her study of rural women in Iowa, Deborah Fink noted that several farm women worked in apparel factories and argued that "these factories were specifically planted to tap the labor of rural women." As one manager confided to her, "the factory's location was chosen because the owners understood that rural women needed jobs." These factories opened mostly in the 1950s and employed around one hundred female workers. Workplaces were typically the size of a large gymnasium, with sewing stations scattered throughout the plant and cutters transporting the garment pieces to the different assembly stations. A few men worked at these factories, and they were tasked with the heavier work such as cutting and transporting the material.[31]

These factories were much like the Hinson Manufacturing Company, a family-owned business in Waterloo, which employed around three hundred women for apparel production. Hinson produced a variety of products, from automotive textile accessories, to hunting garments, to tractor accessories. Wilma Riley, who worked at Hinson after the war, ran a sewing machine while Ilene Christianson made seat covers for automobiles. Like other apparel factories, Hinson had a handful of men who worked the heavier jobs, but women filled most of the workstations.[32] Another garment factory, the Clinton Garment Company in Clinton, assembled women's dresses for Sears under the labels Tony Todd and Vicki Block. They employed approximately 250 women and about twenty men. The women did all the sewing, and many of these sewing stations took a significant amount of skill, such as collars, zigzag, and hook and eyes. Women usually worked under a piecework system that paid them for the number of garments they completed rather than an hourly rate. The women enjoyed piecework because it enabled them to make a higher rate and more money.[33]

The remaining group of industries employing women was an odd assortment of miscellaneous businesses, which found women a steady yet affordable labor supply. Much like electronics, these industries used women to do repetitious jobs that required agile hands. A good example of these industries was the W. A. Sheaffer Pen Company in Fort Madison, located in the southeast corner of the state along the Mississippi River. The company's founder, Walter Sheaffer, experimented with ways to develop fountain pens, and in the early twentieth century he perfected a new process and cultivated a thriving business in pen production. His company continued to flourish, and by 1952 the company built a new $3 million plant in Fort Madison. Sheaffer became one of the largest pen factories in the country, and produced fountain pens, mechanical pencils, ballpoint pens, and customized desk sets. The company employed nearly 1,500 workers, about 50 percent of Fort Madison's total industrial workforce of 3,000. A majority of workers at the plant were women, since the managers believed that women's small, nimble fingers were more suited to working with the small parts needed in pen manufacturing.[34]

Near Fort Madison was Sheller-Globe, a rubber manufacturer in Keokuk, which made synthetic rubber foam used in the auto industry and produced the rubber insulation for windows and doors as well as rubber foam for armrests and dashboards. Also known as Dryden manufacturing, Sheller-Globe started business in Keokuk in 1937 with only fifty employees. It grew rapidly, employing over a thousand workers (40 percent of them female), making Sheller-Globe the largest employer in Keokuk, a city with a population around 16,000, and a manufacturing workforce of nearly 4,000. Women ran presses and completed the production process by putting the finishing touches on most of the products. Betty Noe worked as a cutter at Sheller; using a pair of electric scissors, she trimmed the excess rubber from the final product. She described the process as having "so many angles in them that you must have the dexterity to be able to use a pair of sewing scissors." Women also operated on a piecework system, and it was considered women's work within the plant. Carrie Azinger, who operated a press in the factory, believed that piecework was the domain of women's work. She commented, "Most of the men would be insulted if you mentioned—would you do this or that type of piecework. No way. They would take a straight-time pay rather than that. I think they felt that that was women's work." Men handled the heavier presses and the harder work; it was not until the 1970s that women began doing those jobs.[35]

Even though an increasing number of industries were hiring women, many more remained closed to women, and some actively weeded out all

Women manufacturing sponge-rubber padded trim at Sheller-Globe Corporation, ca. 1967, Keokuk, Iowa. Iowa Industries Collection, SHSI, Iowa City.

female employees that remained after World War II. The Clinton Corn Company in Clinton was a gross offender, as the company had hired a significant number of women during the war in order to keep up production while men served overseas. After the war, several women remained working in the plant, but they were segregated in the canning and sewing departments. Between 1954 and 1960, they began to lay off most of the female employees. The few remaining women worked on the pudding line, canning and applying labels to the products. Several of the male employees began to object to women working on potentially male jobs. William Skiff, a disgruntled coworker, submitted a grievance objecting "to girls applying the label to . . . canisters for pudding powders in the package department." Skiff contended that it was a man's job even though a woman was doing it. Management agreed that it was under the umbrella of men's work and that it should be done by a man, and the company found yet another way to reduce the number of women working at the plant. By early 1961, all of the pudding packing jobs for women were discontinued. It is rather ironic to compare Clinton Corn to the meatpacking plants, where all of the canning was performed by women and it was strictly women's work. One can imagine a male meatpacker scoffing at the idea of labeling cans. Clinton Corn demonstrated the power of sex-typing jobs and how it can be used both to give women work and to deny them positions. By the mid-1950s, only a handful of women remained, and they were sequestered as janitors in sanitation or as seamstresses in the sewing room; combined, these two departments employed only a dozen women. The plant did not begin hiring women again until the 1970s when Title VII of the Civil Rights Act made it mandatory for them to do so.[36]

Alcoa, an aluminum manufacturer, provided yet another egregious example of discrimination against female workers. During the Korean War, Alcoa experienced a severe labor shortage, and, in order to maintain production, they began hiring women with the implicit understanding that they would be laid off once the Korean War was over and production was down. The women began working with the understanding that they would be the first to be laid off. The women, however, thought they could keep their jobs if there was enough work for them to complete. In effect, the company failed to inform them that their status was only temporary. The three hundred women hired by Alcoa drove fork trucks, operated cranes, and worked in the shipping department. They also received the same pay as men. In 1957, once war production was over, the company laid off all of the female employees, and not only did the union fail to protect the interests of the female workers, it cooperated with the company from the beginning. According to Everett Shadle, when all the women marched into the union meeting demanding to get their jobs back, "We was the most no-good bastards ever was born in this country!" He claimed it was the worst union meeting in his life, and said, "There was a lot of women out there that were the best friends of mine. I thought that there was nothing I could do wrong, but I'll tell you that day I was the biggest s.o.b. that ever . . . !" The women hired a lawyer and tried to sue the union and the company, but to no avail; they lost the case because they had been told when they were hired that they were subject to first layoff. Like Clinton Corn, Alcoa did not hire women again until the 1970s, after the Civil Rights Act went into effect.[37]

Even though some plants refused to hire women, many more opened their doors and created space for female employment. This provided some job security, as long as they continued to work within designated female jobs. Even though many plants remained closed to women, such as Alcoa and the Clinton Corn Company, many more found women to be excellent employees, especially in the production of small parts. The electronics industry especially found women to be ideal employees, and as electronics boomed in Iowa, hundreds of Iowa women found work there.

## Women's Agency in Finding Industrial Work

For Iowa women, the process of getting into the factory and starting a new job could be an uncertain course to navigate, especially if they were unfamiliar with industrial work. However, women did have some agency in choosing which factory suited their wants and needs. In more industrialized locations like Waterloo, Cedar Rapids, and southeast Iowa, there were more opportunities. This was not always the case in more remote areas where only one factory might hire women, but even then, women had a choice of whether to work in a factory or take a clerical job. Women also could choose not to remain at a certain factory, especially if the plant's supervisiors did not treat the workers fairly. For example, the Burlington Basket Company in Burlington had a poor reputation, as Wilma Haynes explained: "It's not the greatest place to work. They're not fair to their people, as far as I'm concerned. Women left the factory as soon as they found something better." Sometimes women left a factory because the working conditions were beyond their physical capabilities. Susan Rhum had to quit working at the Sylvania Television plant in Burlington because the work with such tiny parts became too difficult for her eyesight. She reported, "It got to be nerve wracking, hard on my eyes and hard on my nerves." She switched to the Iowa Army Ammunition Plant (IAAP) in 1963 and stayed there for nearly thirty years. Many women, like Rhum, enjoyed working at IAAP, but that plant also had a high turnover rate due to the hazardous conditions of making ammunition.[38]

Women valued workplaces that provided good wages, clean conditions, and the camaraderie of other female workers. For example, Wilma Haynes, after leaving Burlington Basket, eventually began working at the International Resistor Company (IRC), where she worked for over twenty years. Fellow worker Letha Alliman described IRC as "a nice, clean factory. It was all women. It's not like other factories I've worked in. Because it was air conditioned, it was clean, and you know, they were just kind of happy, even if they didn't make the most money on earth." Once women found a place they liked, they tended to stay for twenty-five to thirty-five years, retiring with a pension package and other benefits.[39]

Because women had choices about where to work, companies had to deal with the issue of turnover rates and had to serve workers' interests in order to keep good workers. For example, Birtman Electric Company's employee records show some of the issues in keeping employees, as they had about a 20 percent turnover rate from August 1950 to September 1952. Birtman, which produced washing machines in Davenport, hired about 138 women over a two-year period, and out of those hired, twenty-seven either quit or were fired. Six of those women quit within the first week of work (22 percent), eleven quit within the first month (40 percent), and five left within three months (19 percent). Two quit within the year (7 percent), and three quit sometime after a year and a half (11 percent). Of the twenty-seven who quit, two were rehired within the next two years. It appeared that if they made it past the first month, they usually stayed. These women gave a variety of reasons for leaving, but most often it was because they disliked factory work since it was physically demanding, hard on their health, and challenging to juggle with childcare.[40]

Once a woman decided to take a job in the factory, getting the job could be as simple as going to the plant, filling out an application, and being called within a week. Sometimes it took more effort and involved relying on personal networks. Marlene Gerst explained how she networked to get a job at Champion: "When Champion Spark Plug came to Burlington, word . . . got out that it was a real good-paying place to work. Well, I knew a lady in the personnel office. I had worked with her at the theater." It was not always easy, however, for women to go in and apply for industrial work, especially if they had very little working experience or if they had never worked in a factory before. It was especially difficult for Marlene Kruger, who was so ashamed of being divorced that she was afraid Waterloo Industries would not hire her. "I remember when I went to the personnel office, I told them very timidly that I was divorced and was that going to affect my employment there. And they said no, that just about everybody who was hired there either was single when they came or was single when they left. So they said it didn't make any difference."[41]

It was even more difficult for African American women to find employment within industry due to discriminatory hiring practices. Billye Smith Williams commented that most male and female African Americans in Burlington worked in hotels and restaurants because the industry in the city refused to hire them.[42] By the late 1950s, more opportunities began to open up, but it was still difficult to obtain employment. The IAAP hired African Americans, but only as janitors, and would not hire them for any other position in the plant. Williams worked at IAAP for a while and then tried to find work at Champion Sparkplug. There she met blatant discrimination. She commented, "You'd go over to Champion Sparkplug . . . and ask for an application, and the personnel manager or girl would tell you . . . blatantly tell you, 'It won't do you any good. You can fill it out and when you're gone I'll tear it up and throw it in a wastepaper basket.'" She eventually got a job at IRC and was the first African American to work there.[43]

There were often other limitations and requirements that women had to meet before they could get a job in industry. Betty Noe had a difficult time convincing Sheller-Globe in Keokuk to hire her because she was so short. Standing only 4 feet, 11 inches, she had to give up her original career plan of nursing because no one would hire her. She recalled that Sheller-Globe was desperate for people, so they hired her despite her height: "At that time they couldn't get enough men to do the jobs and so they hired women. Now, I'm not very big and after I was hired there was some controversy over hiring bigger women. It wasn't that the smaller women couldn't do the work, it was just that somebody thought that if you were five foot ten and weighed a hundred and fifty to two hundred pounds you could last longer." Sometimes plants used height limitations as a way to restrict Latinas from employment, since many Latinas were very short.[44] Despite these limitations, women had significant leeway in their choice of industries.

## Conclusion

It was these industries with their steady work, benefits, and high wages that pulled women into the factory, and it was the national trend of women working outside of the home that began pushing women out into the workforce. The congruence of these two factors directly led to the remarkable growth of women working in industry in the state, an important and dynamic change in the daily lives of Iowa women. While the motivations for paid labor did not directly assault the patriarchal hierarchy that dominated life in both rural and urban areas, it did shift the ground under the foundation patriarchy was built on, allowing for erosion to begin. As women exercised agency in their own lives in their search for employment, earning their own wages furthered their independence and freedom from patriarchy. This erosion continued as women connected with other female workers and formed a foundation for a collective consciousness as industrial workers. These working-class women created a distinctive workforce within Iowa factories, and as women came from urban centers, small towns, and rural areas to work together in the factory, they formed a working-class consciousness based on a shared culture and common experiences on the factory floor. Their shared identity would help them navigate their transition into the working class and their evolution as working wives and mothers.

# Chapter Three

## The Crucible of the Workplace

Alice Jackson began her first day of work at the Iowa Army Ammunition Plant unphased by the stories of dangerous explosions or the lurid tales of workers losing fingers or hands. Her father was not pleased with Jackson's new employer and, concerned for her health and well-being, warned her of the dangers of her new job. Young and fearless, she brushed aside her father's concerns and eagerly anticipated receiving a large paycheck. In 1966 she started working in the slurry room cleaning empty powder bottles. Here she scrubbed bottles to remove all gunpowder residue so they could be refilled and used on the component line. Jackson liked her work in the slurry room, but she eventually switched to the component line where she could make more money. On the component line she made detonators for ammunition, which was incredibly dangerous work, as components were terribly sensitive, and one little mishap would be enough to take off someone's finger or hand. To stay safe, Jackson learned how to work with her coworkers, noting, "It can be very dangerous if you don't have a good crew to work with." Jackson even got to the point where she could "almost tell what they're gonna do before they do it. But you've gotta have trust in each other when you work out there or you'll never make it." Working under the added pressure of a possible explosion, women at IAAP worked together and learned to have faith in each other for their mutual safety. Their experiences working with dangerous material congealed workplace relationships quickly. Those who were afraid did not last long, while those who learned to trust their coworkers did not fret over the danger. Many, like Jackson, grew to love their jobs, and she liked working at IAAP despite the danger. She commented, "I'm not scared. I know the people I'm working with. I trust 'em. And that's really what it takes is a lot of trust in your fellow man."[1]

Building trust was part of a long journey toward the creation of a class consciousness that bonded workers through a mutual understanding of their place and status. Historians of labor and the working class have long pondered over the numinous process of making a class consciousness, and beginning with the influential work of E. P. Thompson, scholars have scrutinized and theorized the process of class formation. These scholars have argued that class consciousness forms through workers' shared commitment to better themselves and to resist oppression by the industrialist class. As Thompson argued, "class happens when some men, as a result of common experiences (inherited or shared), feel and articulate the identity of their interests as between themselves, and as against other men whose interests are different from (and usually opposed to) theirs."[2] Historians have shown how class happens in a variety of contexts, illustrating the formation of class through the strength of working-class neighborhoods, shared interests in material culture, or the process of passing on skilled trades.[3] Scholarship on the working class in the later twentieth century has shown how the fight for civil rights or gender equality united workers into a common cause that helped form a class consciousness. Unions have played a central role in this process, as they have funneled people's discontent and militant energy into action and helped them achieve their goals of better working conditions and higher pay.[4] Building on these studies, this chapter explores how women formed a collective consciousness based on their shared experiences as women and as workers.

To forge a collective consciousness, women first needed to overcome the barriers to class formation. What once happened in the strong working-class neighborhoods adjacent to the factory, communities that bolstered the union in the early years of the century, had been largely scattered across a large geographical space by the postwar period.[5] These large spatial distances, coupled with ethnic and racial divisions, created stark boundaries to forming a common identity. Midwestern women needed to find commonalities to bridge these divisions; they would find them through their shared experiences in the factory. In the factory they discovered their shared cultural norms—family, work, and community. These crucial experiences in the workplace and their shared cultural norms were also shaped by their shared gender and race, which added yet another layer to their mutual understanding of being both a woman and an industrial worker. The intersection of race, gender, and class shaped and defined their workplace experiences, which included the limitations in job opportunities, the division of labor according to sex, the purposeful exclusion from higher pay, and the accompanying reinforcement and entrenchment of gender differences. All these factors worked together to force a bond of collective consciousness and shared identities as both workers and women.

Yet while these experiences created a shared female class consciousness, working-class women also divided over the issue of gender difference. As women faced the oppression of the patriarchal system within the workplace, some women chose to accept the discrimination as normal and believe that women should stay in their proper place. Meanwhile, many others began to chafe at the limitations to earning more money and desired better-paid jobs, and work that required more training and skill. This ultimately divided women between those who accepted gender differences and those who began to question the inequality in the workplace. This divide became more palpable as women learned the language of rights and began pursuing a feminist identity toward the end of the 1960s. This division was also a natural outcome of shifting gender roles in society at large. As changes to the political economy allowed women to work, women struggled with how to embrace this new identity and role within the family structure. Some women in small-town Iowa felt uncomfortable pursuing wage work as it defied the cultural standards for gender roles. They were raised to believe that women's proper place was the home. Because of this shifting identity crisis, some women clung to gender difference as normal and recoiled at the idea of challenging systemic gender division in the workplace. Understanding these subtle and nuanced divisions between women serves to explain the fights that occurred between female workers in the late 1960s as the language of feminism flowered within labor circles and the nation at large.

## Gender and Sex-Based Job Categories

As soon as a new female employee stepped into the factory, gender dictated and defined where she would work and what she would do. Employers assigned jobs according to a complex system of categories that considered the skill level, physical strength, and mechanical aptitude needed for each task. Jobs were further divided between men and women based on the gendered notions of intellectual and physiological capabilities. Work that required brute strength was automatically designated as male, while intricate work that required agile fingers was female. Within each factory, company managers applied this division differently, and there was very little consistency in job categories across an industry. Ruth Milkman argued that the categories of women's work were built into the institutional formation of each specific manufacturing plant, and once established, it was extremely difficult to break down. Consequently, within the plant, what was men's work and what was women's work became embedded into the institutional lore and culture of the factory workplace and became a naturally assumed practice. What was particularly burdensome to women was how the division systematically shut them out of the higher-paid categories. Part of the gendered assumptions regarding work was the belief that men deserved higher wages. Within the cultural norms of the day and of the region, men were the breadwinners, and women's labor was simply supplemental. Therefore, those categories that required the most skill and the highest pay were reserved for men and protected men's ability to earn more than women. No matter how the work was divided, it was ultimately divided to protect a patriarchal hierarchy that defined the nation's larger society and culture.[6]

Despite the limitations within job categories, women's work varied across industries. A comparison of job categories in three different companies in the Quad Cities demonstrates the sheer range of women's work. First, the Victor Animatograph Company, which produced record players and other similar electronic equipment, employed 58 female workers out of 204 employees. These women worked as wirers, polishers, wire cutters, and assemblers. Meanwhile, the Gellman Manufacturing Company, which made heavy-duty wrenches, employed twenty-seven women to work in milling, filing, burring, light drill press, subassembly, and hand sanding. Last, at Birtman Electronic, an appliance manufacturer, women worked in automatic turning equipment and spot welding. While these jobs required some mechanical aptitude and training, all of these jobs were listed as the most basic tasks within the factory. The sheer variety and diversity of sex-based jobs deemed "women's work" demonstrates the subjectivity of job categories and how it was at the discretion of the employer to determine what exactly was women's work.

The process of sex-typing work (and consequently excluding women from higher-skilled and higher-paying jobs) was achieved through the systematic cultural conditioning of workers (management as well) to believe that men and women were innately different and incapable of performing certain functions. The gendered concept of dexterity was designed specifically for this task, as it justified the presence of women while pacifying the male worker who may have felt threatened by the female laborer. Dexterity is the idea that women are more suitable for certain work because they have small, nimble fingers and hands. The microelectronics industry targeted women for employment for this precise reason; their small hands made it easier for them to work on incredibly small parts, objects that could be as small as a watch stem. The Sylvania plant in Burlington, which hired a majority of women, made miniscule receiving tubes for televisions, and workers needed to wear special glasses just to see the tubes. This task took steady hands and precision to perform and was most often given to women. Dexterity mattered across industries throughout the country. At the IAAP in Burlington, women worked on small component parts that were highly unstable and could easily take off a finger or an entire hand.

For dexterity to divide labor effectively along gender lines, women needed to believe that they were more capable of this kind of work and in a sense lean into the concept. Believing that they had dexterity gave them a feeling of superiority over men, a feeling that was rare in the strict hierarchical nature of gender under patriarchy. Dexterity gave them a job only they could perform, and it became an essential part of their identities as female workers. Women made comments about how skilled they were at these dexterity jobs. For example, Betty Noe described her work trimming rubber with electric scissors as "duck soup" for women, because they were already accustomed to long hours of needlework and sewing. Edith Arendt commented that she was better working on small parts because as a lady she was "used to sewing and using [her] hands for fine work. It was really easier for [her] than it might have been for a man." While it is undoubtedly true that women have smaller hands and could perform this work more efficiently than men, employers also exploited the division of labor along lines of gender in order to pay women less. Since dexterity was designated as a female trait, they felt justified in paying lower wages for those jobs. Even though women believed dexterity set them apart as unique and skilled, it only served to cement the gender hierarchy in the plant, as those jobs labeled with "dexterity" would be at the middle to bottom of any listing of job categories. Because women truly believed that their dexterity gave them something special that they could do that men could not, they became complicit in the institutionalization of job categories according to gender.[7]

While dexterity was perhaps the most prominent factor in job placement for women, a company's perception of physical capabilities also played a role. Women were viewed as physically weak and were not placed in jobs requiring physical strength. At the Amana Refrigeration Company, where women had some of the widest range of jobs, they were still shut out of particular tasks because of their perceived physical limitations. When Dorothy Garringer, a diligent worker who always jumped at every opportunity for overtime work, attempted to keep her job during a layoff and requested to work in a different section of the assembly line, the foreman denied her request. This job was to be filled only by men as "units had to be lifted from skids on to the conveyor, repaired, recrated, and again restacked on skids," tasks that required physical strength. Because men were required to do some of this heavy lifting in their job categories, men received first bid on this particular job. The company denied Garringer's request because as a woman she was not required to perform this kind of heavy lifting.[8] Collins Radio was another company that attached certain qualifications to each job description, such as a requirement that an employee be able to lift a certain weight. As Pat Marshall explained, "They used to segregate women out of a lot of jobs because they had a weight factor attached to jobs, and they would say it was beyond the physical capabilities of a woman. . . . That was what kept women out, that little footnote on the physical capability of a woman."[9]

Many of the jobs in the meatpacking industry were divided according to the perceived physical capabilities of men and women. This occurred very early in the development of the industry. During the 1890s when meatpacking jobs were plentiful in the Chicago yards, companies hired women to work in the sausage and bacon departments. These positions became fixed in the industry through structural inertia, causing workers who had spent their entire lives working in a meatpacking plant to believe that women were naturally suited to work on sausage and bacon lines. According to

Women packing meat at Rath Packing, ca. 1977, Waterloo, Iowa.
Iowa Federation of Labor Collection, SHSI, Iowa City.

these theories, women did not work on the kill floor because they could not handle the heavy lifting it required. Ralph Helstein, the longtime president of the United Packinghouse Workers (UPWA), commented that jobs in meatpacking were split by gender because of the nature of the work: "When it came to lugging part of a carcass around on your back, a woman wasn't able to do that." However, he contradicted his own argument by saying, during an oral history interview, "except one woman that I knew in Grand Forks, North Dakota, who was about five by five. Christ, she could throw those carcasses around better than most men. But for the most part that was not true." This woman in Grand Forks was such an exception to Helstein's firmly held belief that women lacked physical strength that she stuck in his memory as remarkable.[10]

In general, however, women's jobs usually involved two types of tasks: running a machine or working on an assembly line. Machine work broke

Woman milling rubber at Firestone Tire and Rubber Company, ca. 1960.
Iowa Industries Collection, SHSI, Iowa City.

production into separate tasks according to the concepts of Taylorism. Experts in efficient production patterns created a manual at each workstation giving the exact motion pattern each woman was to follow. The instructions for the machine included pictures, instructions on the motion pattern, and the precise time it would take for someone to complete the task. Machines varied widely as they were designed to perform a single operation within the larger production process. International Resistor Company, for example, relied heavily on machinery in their production process. Letha Alliman ran an auto capping machine, which cemented wires to a resistor, while Wilma Haynes worked as a hand capper, which took two small wires and put them together with a resistor. Champion Sparkplug, a plant neighboring IRC in Burlington, also used machines in their production of sparkplugs. While working at Champion, Dixie Bigger worked on an FEC machine that spun around an insulator while she put in a center wire, powder, and glue.

Operating a machine was exceedingly tedious and mind-numbing work. Women complained constantly of the monotony of their jobs as they performed the exact same task all day, every day. Carol Carter noted that machine work included "the most monotonous jobs. They were more confining and required people to work continuously for eight hours. It didn't allow for much free time."[11] To break up the pedestrian nature of machine work, women often switched to different machines in the factory every few months. In this way, female employees challenged themselves to learn a new machine and perfect their rate of production.[12]

The assembly line was not much better in terms of enjoyment, as women were tied to the line and its rigid timing. The Amana Refrigeration Company, which made freezers, refrigerators, and air conditioners, divided each product into its own separate assembly process, and women worked all along the line. Erma Mantz worked as a basic assembler cleaning tubing for the freezers. She had to clean the tubes inside and out with two different brushes, and then the tubes had to be washed with carbon tet, so they could be welded onto the finished product. For a while Eunice Evans worked on the door line, where she had to lift doors, lids, and tops off the conveyor belt and stack them to be inspected. While working on the assembly line, the conveyor would move at a set speed so that everyone had limited time to perform a certain task. Wanda Beasley had exactly 3.067 minutes to complete her job of gluing strips on refrigerator doors and then putting on coils. If a woman fell behind, a lead worker jumped in to help her keep up with the line.[13] At the IAAP, women operated an assembly line making components and detonators. Fern McCarthy, who worked on the component line, described the process of building a component: "The detonator was half the size of your little finger and . . . it had to be in . . . a thin piece of aluminum . . . and then the outer fixture that went over it was about . . . a quarter inch and it was round. There was a little hole in the middle, and so you put the powder in there, and it punched it into that little fixture."[14]

Assembly lines did not always move; sometimes women worked in the assembly process on stationary tables and layouts. Women at Collins Radio performed tasks on a long assembly table full of bins with each part labeled and numbered. Each worker would have written instructions on the sequence they were to follow in making their part. "For some operations," as Pat Marshall described, "it could be just a portion of a big unit, or for a smaller unit you [might] do the whole operation yourself." The work also took a degree of training, as she had to learn the different color codes for the wires and parts and be able to read the values of the parts she was working with.

Besides the more traditional work on an assembly line or on a machine, women also held a variety of different jobs within a plant. Some women worked with tools such as screw guns or welding torches. For example, Patricia McGuire and Barbara Sexton at Amana put in gasket screws using a special torque gun that could put in the screws with fifteen pounds of torque. The women sometimes complained about these guns because they were big and heavy and awkward to use and sometimes stripped the screws. Fern Klopp worked a rather unusual job at Turner Microphone in Cedar Rapids. She worked in the basement operating a diamond-edge saw cutting quartz for use in crystal microphones. She described her job as extremely dirty, as she had to have oil running on the blade constantly, and it was just an "oily, messy job."[15]

Even though most factories had jobs clearly defined as either male or female, the division was not always explicitly stated. At Amana, for instance, women were spread throughout the plant and were involved in multiple parts of the production process, but there were certain jobs in the plant that women just did not do. There was no clearly stated policy strictly forbidding women from working on certain jobs; rather, it was an assumed practice. The majority of women at Amana worked on the assembly line performing basic tasks in the job categories of first- or second-class assembly. Women also held some higher-skilled jobs in the plant such as inspection, leak detection, brazing, spot welding, heliarc welding, and painting. They were, however, frozen out of the higher-paid skilled jobs, not because of direct company policies, but because it was assumed that women just did not work those jobs.[16] Bud Sanders noted this tradition of male job categories and stated that women did not work in the maintenance department or the tool and die department. He did not know why women "don't bid in there because they would be given the same opportunities a man would. We've had a few women in the maintenance department and we've had a couple tool and die makers that were female too. The tool and die makers didn't last long. I don't know why, if they moved on to a better job or what." It could be that women did not stay long because they felt uncomfortable as the only female in the department, or they intuitively understood they were unwelcome in this male-dominated space.[17]

In most plants, however, the division of labor was clearly delineated with the sorting of jobs into categories. An analysis of the employment records for Birtman Electric Company, which had a 40 percent female workforce, showed how women were kept in the lowest level of job categories. Birtman had ten levels of job categories, with 10 being the lowest and 1 being the highest. Women worked predominantly in grades 10 and 9 (the lowest pay grades) and the rest were scattered through grades 8 to 5. Only 25 percent of workers in categories 8 and 7 were female, and only 5 percent in categories 6 and 5. No women worked in jobs in categories 5 through 1. Other companies used similar job categories, which kept women in the lowest pay grades. According to Fern Klopp, who worked for Turner Microphone, women worked in grades 1 to 6, where grade 1 was the lowest pay level. Men worked in grades 6 and above, which were the highest and included the skilled jobs such as tool and die making.[18]

This exclusion of women from higher-skilled, higher-paying jobs meant that men, on average, were paid significantly more than their female coworkers. Sometimes men were paid more for jobs that required the exact same work as women. According to Doris Peick, she trained men to work on her job, and once they started, they made more money than she did. "I used to train men who got paid more salary than what we women did on how to do deburring, handling air blowers, and air demurrers and whatever . . . we manufactured at that time."[19] There was a push in the 1950s by some unions to maintain "equal pay for equal work," which was, in many ways, a campaign to protect wages for men so that companies did not start hiring women to replace men as cheaper labor. The International Association of Machinists (IAM) put this in their contract with Birtman Electronic in 1955, stating that "when women perform jobs formerly filled by men and fully perform from a quality and quantity standpoint, all of the parts of the job previously performed by men, they shall be paid the same wage rate or piece work rate as men, according to the job grade." The IAM officials wanted women to know of this policy to make the union more appealing to them, stating, "As a union that has long worked for justice on the job—and that has fought for equal pay for equal work in the electronics industry—the IAM definitely has a basis for broad appeal among the hundreds of thousands of unorganized women who are employed in the electronics industry today."[20]

Even though businesses hired women to work in the lowest-paying job categories, women averaged an hourly rate anywhere between $1.40 and $1.80 an hour. For example, in 1950, the Gellman Manufacturing Company in the Quad Cities paid their female employees between $1.47 and $1.67 an hour.[21] Men, however, averaged at least a dollar an hour more. By the late 1960s, wages began to gradually increase, due to the rise in the minimum wage to $1.25 in 1963, and by the mid-1960s, many women made over $2 an hour.[22]

While many women worked for an hourly rate, women also worked for an incentive rate, and in many factories, incentive, or piece work, was designated as women's work. As Carrie Azinger commented on her jobs at Sheller-Globe in Keokuk, "I'd say most all the piecework was done by women, there were some men that asked for the piecework jobs and got them. But most of the men would be insulted if you mentioned would you do this or that type of piecework. No way. They would take a straight-time pay rather than that." At Square D in Cedar Rapids and Champion Spark-plug in Burlington, women sometimes made more money than men, since women worked on an incentive rate. Even though women were limited to which jobs they could work, the incentive system did allow them to make a decent income.[23] Most incentive systems operated under a time-motion rate and involved machine work. This involved an expert observing and documenting the average time it took for a worker to complete her task. Letha Alliman explained that when the company timed a job, the union made sure they observed an average worker who went at a reasonable rate and that all operating conditions were normal. The last thing the union wanted was to set the rate too high, which would make it difficult for women to make money. Once a job was timed by a plant engineer, he established a rate, or how fast each job should be done, and women were paid according to how many products they could complete during an hour. If a woman followed the rate exactly, she made 100 percent, which would be the quota for the hour. If a woman made over the quota, producing 150 to 200 percent, she could theoretically make more money. Sometimes companies tried to raise the rate, or the quota, so that the employees would make more products while getting paid less. At IRC, foremen would try to raise rates, but female employees would either slow down to reduce the rate or file a grievance. At one point, IRC gave Wilma Haynes two machines to run at the same time so that she could produce more, but she immediately protested to the union, and the company put her back on one machine.[24]

Because time studies varied in different plants and in different years, at times it could be quite easy for women to make money, and at other times they really had to work for it. Bev Clinton at Square D recalled, "They were pretty tough time studies. I mean we made good money over there . . . but time studies in later years have gotten real tight. They have closed 'em down so you work pretty darn hard to make your money, no doubt about it." Even though women could make "good money" on an incentive system, it was still difficult work. "Remember, piecework is horrible for a human being to do," stated Betty Noe. "You are going at a rate of speed that's not normal, and they have the rates up so high that you have got to do so many just to make . . . what they call base wage."[25]

To keep the rates under control and remain both manageable and profitable, women needed to work together to control the speed and the rate. Fellow workers would reprimand a woman who worked too fast and ruined the rate for everyone. Wilma Haynes once caught a woman running two machines after there had been a lengthy discussion within the union about members running two machines. Since Haynes was the steward, she told the woman to turn off one machine and said, "I know I'm going to make you mad, but I am telling you to turn one mach. [*sic*] off. . . . I'm not planning on getting in this rate race again for no one." But sometimes, women were comfortable letting some people work faster. Billye Smith Williams was content just letting the women make higher pay, stating, "That's their business. That's their job. We just make the company understand [that] just because they can do it doesn't mean that the next person can." But at the same time, she insisted, "We won't let the company up the rates because there's one or two that can do this. Now, those are exceptional people that can go exceptionally fast anyway. Not all people is geared like that, or they can't get that fast, no matter how they try."[26]

The gendered division of labor also impacted the issue of seniority within the plant. While some factories listed all workers on a single seniority list, most industries put men and women on separate seniority lists, so that male and female employees would be laid off at different rates. This was usually the case in factories that had only a small percentage of women, like the Firestone Tire factory in Des Moines, which kept women on a separate list in order to protect the priority of the male jobs. Some places even had triple seniority lists, like Champion Sparkplug, which kept a different list for men, women, and skilled workers.

Female workers were often ambivalent about the gendered division of labor and the practice of keeping separate seniority lists. Some women accepted it as the status quo, while others felt limited and desired the option to make more money in higher pay grades. At Champion Sparkplug, women were often unwilling to work what they referred to as the "men's jobs." Marlene Gerst was quite vocal about her opposition to working a "man's" job:

> I say . . . women really don't want to do the jobs that have been historically men's jobs, because they're the heavy jobs, dirty jobs. They take skill that most women don't have, like on the automatic machines, that all releases some heat, you know, and it's hot and it's dirty and it's oily, and they just don't really want to go back into those jobs. And I really think, unless a woman is very, very mechanically inclined, those jobs that historically were men's jobs aren't desirable jobs for women. I don't think—and maybe I could get crucified by some of my fellow women workers—I just don't think the women have the ability mechanically. Now, there's exceptions to every one of those rules, but . . . some, I'm sure, don't know the difference between an Allen wrench and a screwdriver. You know, we're just not mechanically equipped to do it.[27]

Gerst was insistent in her belief that men and women belonged in their "proper place." As a full-time industrial worker and a mother, she had left the sphere of the home to pursue paid work. Gerst's sentiments echoed the feelings of other women of her generation who tried to balance full-time work with the domestic sphere. One way women could reconcile their conflicting actions and beliefs was to import the domestic sphere into a physical space that was clearly male. Gerst's words portray her desire to maintain a sense of gentility and femininity in the workplace by performing jobs that were clean and not laborious. She could not understand why women would work in jobs that were clearly "male"—dirty and physically demanding. Gerst reconciled her inner conflict by insisting that she maintained her proper place within the workplace, even when she was clearly violating gender norms by working outside of the home.

Gerst was not alone in these contradictory ideas of femininity and the proper place for women, nor was Champion Sparkplug the only factory to have this conflict within their female workforce. Betty Noe, an employee at Sheller-Globe, remarked, "I oppose it [women working men's jobs] in factories, unless that woman can prove that she can really do it. Because in some factories there are jobs that are not physically . . . women are not physically able to do the job." But not all women held these beliefs, and many would eventually challenge the division of labor with the firm conviction that women can do the same work as men, such as Ilene Christianson, who argued against the division of labor at Hinson Manufacturing: "because they figured a man could do more work than the women. But that is not true. Because I've seen a lot of women that can outdo a man sometimes out there."[28]

This gender inequality in the plant tied women together across all divides as they shared in the limitations placed on them. Some women absorbed this gendered inferiority, believing that women were not capable of working the more challenging and skilled jobs. But many more would begin to chafe at the constraints of working in the lowest-paid, most boring jobs in the plant and wanted more opportunities to make more money and take on the challenge of learning a skilled job. This will lie at the heart of the divide between working-class women regarding feminism and the fight for equality.

## Working Conditions and Shared Experiences

Women not only shared the experiences of unequal pay and limited job opportunities, they also dealt with harsh working environments in the factory. Women worked with dangerous equipment, harmful chemicals, and extreme heat or cold. Some plant operations were treacherous because a woman could lose a finger or a hand, or break an arm or leg on the machines they were running. Harmful chemicals emitted fumes that caused headaches or skin rashes. Repetitive tasks, which were common among female jobs, caused long-term ailments such as carpal tunnel syndrome and joint problems. Wilma Haynes was convinced she ended up with asthma because of her years working at IRC. "I have asthma now. I never had it before in my life," she remarked. "If you breathe those fumes all the time, that is dangerous." In addition to hazardous chemicals and fumes, workers had to deal with dust and dirt, which permeated everything. At Sheller-Globe, the mica used for synthetic rubber was everywhere. As Betty Noe described it, "There was mica dust four to five inches all over the place. Now, by mica dust, I mean it looks like a fine white sand. It sparkles in the sun, and it was on everything, tables, the people, the products they were working with, on the rafters. It would come down in showers on top of you." Noe eventually got dermatitis in her ear due to all the mica dust.[29]

At IRC, women worked with dangerous powders and chemicals. Haynes described working with a dangerous M-coat powder: "It's a powder, and they put it under tremendous heat, and it melts . . . around this resistor to . . . stabilize it. We have had so many people that was allergic to this and had to bid out of it." One worker who worked with chemical powders at IRC recalled that she "had to use several different kinds of chemicals that was harmful. I worked on it six months before I started getting a breakout, and then I got dizzy spells. And the swelling from being allergic to those chemicals would cause inner ear problems." But, according to Haynes, it was nearly impossible to convince company officials that conditions in the plant caused any serious health problems: "You couldn't convince the company that this was what was doing it. They blamed it on everything but there, which we all knew in our hearts that this was where it was coming from. They blamed it because you're getting older, you know. You're more susceptible to this stuff. But I'll never believe but it was from out of there. Because you've got this dust and these fumes through the factory."[30] At Amana, there were frequent issues with poor ventilation. In May 1955, a group of women complained about the excess smoke and odor in their work area caused by vacuum pumps. Leona Roberts complained, "We need a vent above the vacuum pumps to take away the smoke and odor. It gives me a headache, sore throat, and my eyes burn." Two other women complained about the fumes as well, and usually when workers complained together, they could persuade the company to make the needed changes.[31]

One of the most dangerous plants in the state was the IAAP in Burlington. The plant was known for an occasional accidental explosion, especially during the first years of operation. When Susan Rhum started working there in the early 1960s, the plant had a handful of explosions that took the lives of seven people along the component line. The plant built in precautions to ensure no significant damage was done in case of an explosion. According to Fern McCarthy, each assembly line was at least a mile apart so that an explosion would not set off a chain reaction to the other lines. They also had blow walls in between each wall to minimize the impact of an explosion. McCarthy described these walls as a "concrete slab going up as high as the building . . . and as wide as the building, so it might blow this way but the wall will stop it. All buildings that I know about were tin, so that when they blew, it would blow the lid off. . . . It'd go up and not out."[32]

Most women worked on the component line, making small detonators and fuses that went into larger weapons. The danger of working on the component line, as opposed to working on some of the larger weapons, was that "a big shell . . . might weigh a hundred pounds [but] was very unlikely to go off . . . and yet those little detonators and fuses were very touchy." IAAP also dealt with hazardous chemicals, especially tetrol powder, that could cause horrible rashes and irritated the nervous system. Susan Rhum described the conditions as poisonous and said, "A lot of people are allergic to it. They just become ill with it, broke out with [a rash]. The short time that I was in it, just a few days, I would develop a nosebleed from it. . . . They no longer use that. They've found other powders that are not so toxic."

The key to being safe at IAAP, according to Susan Rhum, was having a healthy respect for the materials. "You've just got to learn to respect that ammunition," said Rhum. "You've got to know what it can do and what you can do or can't do when you're working with it." And work together with your coworkers; as Alice Jackson stated, "You've gotta have trust in each other when you work out there or you'll never make it. There's been several good explosions that have killed several people, close friends on the shift before me. And to clean up the mess is not a pretty sight." Some women refused to work at IAAP because of all the dangers. Jackson noted, "When it [the plant] was going good I think a lot of the kids, or people, weren't aware of the dangers that could happen. And a lot of 'em were scared to death. And I mean scared. And unless you had confidence in yourself to the point where you knew you could handle it, they would quit." Workers pushed their employers to take worker safety more seriously, and later in the 1960s IAAP developed a safety program.[33]

Square D in Cedar Rapids also had a strong safety program that prevented many problems. Bev Clinton commented, "They're real good about taking care of 'em. We've had in the past some problems with the exhaust from the welding machines where they do that sort of thing." Some plants had safety committees who toured the plant to make sure everything was in safe and secure working condition. At Birtman Electric, the safety committee was given permission to shut down any unsafe operation to warn people about the consequences of carelessness.

Safety programs and union grievances promoted worker safety and provided ways workers could make suggestions about protective safety wear for their health and well-being. At Champion Sparkplug, women wore earplugs on the factory floor because it was so loud, and at IAAP, workers wore safety glasses. Most workplaces required proper footwear, such as steel-toed shoes. Some of these items did become useless and redundant over time, such as hairnets at Waterloo Industries. Marlene Kruger hated having to wear a hairnet, and she recalled, "At the time I started, you had to wear hairnets. Well, then the women complained that some of the men had hair as long as ours—why didn't they have to wear bonnets? So then they said the men had to wear bonnets too, or they had to get their hair cut. And so we finally worked our way out of those silly hairnets and bonnets. I guess it was to keep the hair out of the moving machinery, but it became moot after a while, and we don't have to wear them anymore."[34]

## Workplace Surveillance and Mutual Resistance Strategies

The mutual resistance to company control continued the process of building a collective consciousness. As soon as an employee stepped into the factory, they were under the control and supervision of the company. Workers also had very little downtime, or personal time, during their workday. Their days revolved around a system of buzzers and bells, which signaled when work began and ended. Workers needed to clean up their work area before clocking out at the end of the shift. At Waterloo Industries, workers wanted to ensure that everyone had equal responsibility for cleanup at the end of the day and had a series of discussions with company management about cleanup time. They stated, "Some welders have to work until the buzzer sounds and others are granted a couple minutes until cleanup . . .

and then are able to immediately leave the workstation when the buzzer goes off." After a long day of work, the unfair release time vexed employees eager to go home and rest.[35]

Workers also wanted convenient access to good drinking water and decent food, which became an issue workers fought for. At Amana, employees filed several grievances over dirty water fountains or poor-tasting water. In 1964, the company finally caved to the pressure and fixed the water fountains. The company also accommodated workers' desire for convenient and good-tasting food by installing several vending machines throughout the plant. In December 1969, a new hot drink machine was installed by the door line, and it served coffee, tea, and hot chocolate. There was also a Coke and milk machine by the maintenance department. The vending machines included pastries and sandwiches, and there were around four machines in each area. Even though these machines were convenient for a quick lunch, they also came at a risk. When three employees got sick from eating ham salad sandwiches from the vending machine, the union and the company made sure the vendors compensated workers for their illness. Over time the vending machines began to break down, and workers complained to the company about the inconvenience of broken-down vending machines. Management quickly put the blame on the employees and said they abused the machines and that was the reason for the machines always being down. Even though the company was willing to provide the machines, there was a limit to their compliance with workers' demands for convenient access to food in their workplaces, and management was unwilling to maintain the vending machines. The company did provide a cafeteria in the plant for workers to eat in during their half-hour lunch break, but the workers often complained of the cafeteria food. They grumbled about the food being gross, that it was cold and not well prepared, and that the prices were too high. Because of all of the complaints, the union asked the company to work on improving the quality of food available.[36]

Another issue was women's access to the restroom. Women were allowed to use the restroom periodically during the day as they needed. Sometimes companies attempted to crack down on restroom breaks, stating that employees abused this privilege and spent too much time away from their work areas. IRC, in the early 1970s, decided that women needed to start recording their personal downtime, "in order to measure and hopefully reduce loss of productivity." They made all employees record on their time sheets each time they left their workstation and when they returned. They argued, "Most of our production workers are not abusing the personal down time allowance, but a large enough minority is taking advantage of the situation, to the detriment of our overall productivity." After a month of this policy, production was up and the company sent a memo to employees thanking them for their efforts and to encourage them to keep their "personal time to a minimum" so they would not need to use time sheets in the future. IRC did have foremen continue to watch abusers and have them "record personal down time when it appears they have lost sight of the frequency or amount of time they spend on personal needs." The union did not necessarily approve of this policy, but they did cooperate, and the company convinced them that employees needed to self-regulate their personal time. Having employees become more aware of how they spent their time worked to increase production for IRC, but it was also a glaring reminder that the company had control over them while they were at work. By the shear act of clocking in, workers were subjecting themselves and their "personal time" to the surveillance and control of the company.[37]

At Amana, whenever the company attempted to crack down on excessive restroom use, women responded with a flood of grievances. On two separate occasions, foremen attempted to limit the number of restroom breaks their female employees were taking. In January 1957, the foreman, with the company's permission, issued warning slips to women in the liner department for excessive trips to the restroom. The company argued that while they would not deny someone the use of the restroom, warnings would be issued to those who habitually left their workplaces. The women in the liner department were irate. They balked at the company attempting, in any way, to cut into their easy access to the restroom. Leona Walters complained, "I was gone 12 minutes and when I got back I got a slip and I feel that I am not abusing the rules of loitering in the rest room. Nature takes its course and it should not be necessary to be given a warning slip." Dorothy Johnson argued, "We can't wait because if we do you will have some pretty sick people. How can anybody else tell if we have to go or not?" One of the biggest complaints women had was how difficult it would be to have everyone use the restroom at the same time. They suggested that it would be nearly impossible for all of the women to use the restroom during their fifteen-minute break periods during the day. Dorothy Rhinehart argued, “The only times you allow, as you say, for going to the restroom is 8:30 and 2:00 and then only five minutes. Did you ever try to figure out how long it takes for everyone in the plant to go to the restroom? We are doing you [a] favor.” Vivian Shaull stated, “It can’t be possible for everyone to go at the same time.” There was also a significant distance between the assembly line and the restroom, and it took several minutes just to walk to the bathroom. Vivian Shaull argued, “the distance we have to walk is too far for anyone to go if it wasn’t necessary.” Dorothy Rhinehart stated, “It is impossible for us to walk out there, go to the restroom, and be back in the time allowed.” She further argued that the foreman had no right to complain that the bathroom trips were an infringement on the production schedule. She criticized the foreman, saying, “I hope you don’t think E. Townsend [the foreman] does all the work back here. He’s too busy holding down the stool he sits on. It is not our fault that it takes so long to get out to the restroom and back.”

The company replied that if a worker had a medical issue and needed to use the restroom more frequently, then they could bring in a doctor’s note and receive an excuse for their frequent restroom use. Otherwise, the company felt justified in issuing warning slips since they believed “the foreman has a right to expect a fair day’s work from each one of his workers without regular daily interruption of his operations by people leaving for the rest rooms.” After meeting with the union shop committee, the company believed that they would not deny the ability of someone to use the restroom, but they would issue warnings to those who habitually left their work. The union succeeded in protecting the right of women to use the restroom, as long as workers did not abuse the privilege. This series of grievances demonstrated that women could work together to protect not only their basic human right to use the restroom but also their access to their gendered space within the factory.[38]

The issue of breaks and restroom use popped up again in 1967, this time in the coil department. The foreman told his workers in the coil department that he was going to cut down on their break periods. They would have only five minutes to use the restroom throughout the day, and if they were gone longer they would be issued a warning slip. The women believed this was not nearly enough time. Leona Wisnousky stated that the “time allowed us is not sufficient to attend to our needs.” Workers were encouraged to use their allotted break times to use the restroom, but as Leona stated, the workers viewed the break times as a time to rest, and they "should be able to do this with peace of mind." Orpha Barry also brought up an underlying issue that many women faced and a vital reason the restroom was important to them: "A woman cannot take care of personal needs in four minutes, and I don't think it is necessary to tell anyone when that time of the month is. I know when I have to go to the restroom, I feel we should have this privilege." The last thing a woman wanted to do was tell her male foreman that she was having her menstrual cycle. Women were very private about their cycles, especially around men. This feminine concern underpinned many of the issues of access to the restroom. This gender-specific concern helped women bond as they shared issues of female biology.[39]

The male foreman was another part in the mechanism of surveillance in the factory. Because of this, relationships with supervisors and foremen could be very tenuous, especially when a majority-female workforce had all-male supervision. Because there were so many women with only a few males in leadership, male supervisors often felt added pressure to reinforce the hierarchy in the plant through a gendered language of domination and control. In plants without union protection, foremen could reinforce the gender hierarchy by showing favoritism toward certain women. Foremen would move women they "liked" into good jobs, and keep the female workers they "did not like" in poor jobs with bad working conditions. Wilma Haynes commented, "As we used to say, 'If you was size 5 you had it made. If you was size 12 you didn't get nowhere.'"[40]

At times workers got along well with their foremen, while other relationships were rather tumultuous. Wilma Haynes had one of these roller-coaster relationships with her foreman, Ernie Mason, while she was the third-shift steward at IRC. When she began her new duties in early 1969, she and Mason did not get along at all. Especially in the first few weeks, they continued to clash over grievances. One particular fight really troubled her, and she recorded in her journal how Mason was mad and did not speak to her for about five days. Apparently he was quite moody and difficult to get along with and at times would avoid any social interaction with Haynes or the rest of the workers. Haynes recorded, "Ernie loves me so much he won't even speak when he passes out our checks." And on one shift, "Ernie walked around all night with head down not talking to any of us." When he was in a good mood, Haynes was sure to make note of it, recording in the day's log that he had been particularly friendly. He had similar cantankerous attitudes toward staff meetings, and at one meeting, he decided that it was only going to last as long as his two cigarettes. Haynes noted, "The section leader Margaret Burgus told us to hurry to the classroom for a meeting as Ernie only had two cigs [cigarettes]. When we got in there he informed us when his 2 cigs were gone the meeting was over." Later on, Mason did try to work on his attitude, and he remarked after a labor management training that he was "going to change his attitude." After working for a time on first shift, he told the third shift that "he had learned how to work with the union better" and was "going to have more meetings with stewards and [start] working closer with us." Three months after Mason's labor management training, he and Haynes had learned to work together and had actually become friends. Haynes wrote, "Ernie told Betty and all listening how . . . I hated him when I became steward but how good we were getting along now and how smooth a shift we had." The relationship between Haynes and Mason was indicative of the subjection of female workers to the whims and moods of their male supervisors, and even though Haynes protested many of Mason's actions, she was still under his authority and leadership. After a time, they learned how to work together, especially after Mason received some training on supervision and the union. But even though they had developed a rapport, she still desired his approval of her work, and she was still under his direct supervision.[41]

In addition to working under a male supervisor, women also had to adapt to working side by side with men. Interactions between men and women were more complicated than relations among women, as sexual tension infused many male-female interactions, especially among workers who were unaccustomed to working side by side with the opposite sex. At Waterloo Industries, as Marlene Kruger remembered, when the company first hired women, it was late summer and it was quite hot. The heat "caused some problems—the men had kind of gotten into the summertime [habit] of working without shirts, and some of the women that were hired in did not like some of those practices, and so the men had to start putting clothes on." The sexuality of half-naked men made some women uneasy, since many were unaccustomed to being near men who were not their husbands. Over time, women learned how to work with men and how to deal with increased sexual tension in the workplace.

Some women felt that there was very little tension between men and women, and that everyone got along very well. Edith Arendt recalled that the men she worked with "were all very courteous and nice. I could not have asked to have been more respected as a lady wishes to be treated than I was in the lathe department. I had no fault to find." She even remembered Art Collins, the head of Collins Radio, warning her that there might be some men who "would get fresh, me being the first lady or female. He said anyone lays a hand on you in the wrong manner, you report it to me, and they will be fired or suspended." But Arendt recalled that she never had to report any of her male coworkers.[42]

Most women did not remember relations being this good, and Arendt's experiences were perhaps a bit naive. It could be that the owner and founder of the company, Art Collins, was looking out for Arendt to ensure she would not be subjected to male harassment. Doris Peick, who also worked at Collins Radio, remembered things much differently, especially when she worked as a female inspector in a department with all men. She recalled that her position was "just unheard of," and her presence threatened the male-dominated gendered hierarchy within the plant. Peick recalled that the men "would pinch you and sometimes they would pat you, and sometimes they would tell off-color stories just to see how far they'd get with you," but Peick said, "[I would] really raise hell with them, I'll tell you. I had to learn to carry my own hard and fast." She remembered one incident when she tolerated no disrepect from a foreman:

> The men would say to you, you know, derogatory remarks. I had one foreman one time say to me . . . I worked morning shift at the time, and I'll never forget it. He said, "Boy, Doris, you look sharp." He came in at seven o'clock, and he was coming in on the day shift. He said, "Boy, Doris, you look sharp. I'd like to get in your pants." And I turned around very nastily, and I said, "That's nice, but there's not room for two buttholes in there." And he didn't speak to me for three days. But I didn't care. I put him down, and I put myself down along with it . . . because that's the type of thing I happened to put up.[43]

Even though women were subjected to unwanted sexual comments, as Peick illustrated, they found ways to deflect or resist sexual harassment. Unfortunately, the organizational infrastructure was not yet in place for women to file formal complaints and have the company take action on them.[44]

In smaller, family-owned manufacturing plants, relationships between men and women could become precarious, especially if only a handful of women worked in the plant and men felt threatened by their presence. Women could easily become victims of harassment in these workplaces, especially if the factory owners did not protect them. This could be even worse when the owners themselves were the perpetrators. At the Uchtorff Company, a family-owned, metal-producing company in the Quad Cities, two women filed a grievance with the National Labor Relations Board (NLRB) for unfair labor practices at the plant. The situation began in mid-1951, when Lois Stoneburg was transferred to the welding department to work with Doris Brickley, a skilled welder. Both women learned how to weld during World War II and were experienced welders when they started working at Uchtorff. The son of the company's owner, Richard Uchtorff, was involved in the business, and the son was determined to rid the plant of the IAM Local 388. In a severe abuse of power, he targeted Lois Stoneburg as a potential love interest and informant on the union. Richard Uchtorff would meander into the welding department, strike up a flirtatious conversation with Stoneburg, and then ask her for a date. At first she denied the request, but after he persisted, she finally agreed. Most likely she agreed to protect her job at the company. While on these dates, Uchtorff bombarded Stoneburg with questions about the union, wondering who the active members were and asking about Doris Brickley in particular. Stoneburg recorded, "He wanted to know about her Union activities and wanted me to tell him what went on in the Union meetings." When she tried to put an end to these dates, Uchtorff made her life miserable. Eventually both Stoneburg and Brickley lost their jobs due to Richard Uchtorff's unprofessional behavior and sexual harassment. They filed grievances with the NLRB in September 1955, but their requests were denied. The male leadership of the board presumably did not take the issue of sexual harassment seriously, as it was not until the push of the feminist movement in the 1970s that women's complaints of sexual harassment gained the attention they deserved.[45]

One way companies retained control over their employees was through a series of disciplinary warnings: first a verbal warning, followed by a written warning, and then a suspension or even termination. Written warnings were termed differently at each plant. At IAAP, workers received blue letters for any infraction of the rules, while at IRC, workers received pink slips. Women received warnings for a variety of things such as operating machines incorrectly or being slow in production. Foremen threatened workers with these warnings in order to keep production high. At IRC a foreman warned a worker "that if she didn't watch her capper she would have more pink slips than Younkers [a local department store]." On another occasion, the female supervisor scolded a worker "that she will either face the Mach. [*sic*] or be given a pink slip, and then to not to come bawling to her." One of the most common reasons for a warning slip was absenteeism and unexcused absences. Women who missed too many days in a month or a year were susceptible to verbal warnings and suspension. If their behavior continued over a long period of time, the company could terminate their employment. Sometimes these policies became an obstacle when women dealt with sick children or personal illness.[46]

If women believed warnings were given unfairly, they could file a grievance through the union. Grievance procedures were put in place to protect workers, not only for their safety but also to ensure that the company did not enact unfair labor practices. Grievance procedures involved a three- to four-step process. First a worker filed a grievance through the union steward, and the steward would address it to the foreman. If the foreman failed to make any changes, which was usually the case, then the steward would take the grievance to the head of labor management in the factory. If it was still not resolved, then a meeting between union leaders and labor management was held to discuss the grievance. If no solution was found after the third step, then it went to an outside arbitrator to resolve the conflict. Most grievances were settled in the second or third step. Filing a grievance gave women some agency over their position in the workplace hierarchy. For example, Alice Jackson received a blue slip because she had too many absences, but she had been very ill during that period because of the stuff she worked with at the plant. She stated, "If anybody works in loose powder, raw powder, you can become sick from it. It will cause lung problems, and I had bronchitis and pneumonia . . . and they accused me of missing too much work. And I filed a grievance over it."[47]

Not all grievances were valid, but the union usually supported workers in submitting a complaint. Shirley Herman at IRC was notorious for missing work, but she often believed her absences were justified. In February 1969, she got into serious trouble when she took a personal day without permission from the company and was given a three-day suspension. She believed it was unfair because she had asked permission for the day off and claimed it had to do with her second job. She wanted the pink slip removed and to be paid for the three days she was unfairly suspended. Her grievance went all the way to a third step, but it was still denied. The company argued that she did not have permission to take the day off, and her job at IRC should be her main priority. Herman is a good example of someone who often abused the company policies for absences, but the union at IRC choose to support her regardless. These union policies on grievances provided the support workers needed for job security and added another dimension to class consciousness.[48]

Companies also demanded strict discipline when it came to behavior toward superiors, and if a woman strayed from these understood codes of behavior, it could have serious repercussions for her employment. An infraction by Martha Reitz at IRC illustrated how one little slip-up could have considerable consequences. One morning in November 1974, Jerry Brook, an inspector with Western Electric Source Inspection, was visiting IRC in Burlington. During his inspection, he happened to grab a chair on the factory floor and was sitting in it when employee Martha Reitz returned to her workstation. When she saw a strange man sitting in her chair, she blurted out, "Who is the asshole in my chair?" While this could have been taken as a comedic mistake, Jerry Brook was extremely offended, picked up the chair and returned it to the workstation, and stormed to the office to report the incident. Reitz did not offer any apology, nor did Brook, nor did they exchange any words at all. It was not until T. Burton, the industrial relations manager, called Reitz into his office and informed her who the gentleman was that she realized her mistake. She quickly apologized and said that it was an honest mistake, but her apology was too late, and the company sent her home for a day and half suspension. She went home but immediately filed a grievance, saying that her comment was just a misunderstanding. The union agreed with her and took up her cause, but the male leaders of the company believed she had overstepped her boundary as a lady and as a female employee under the control of the male hierarchy in the plant. The union fought the grievance to the third level, but the company would not budge, and argued, "It is clear to the Company that Ms. Reitz's conduct was so inappropriate that it breaches a reasonable standard expected of all employees. A warning or reprimand or other less severe action on the part of the Company would have been inconsistent with the gravity of this specific incident." Even though they recognized that Reitz was extremely embarrassed by the incident, the company still punished her, stating that if "Ms. Reitz had exercised sound judgment and discretion in her conduct, no one would have been subjected to the embarrassment that has followed her breach." The company believed Reitz's comment was inappropriate because she questioned authority, acted out of order for the proper social code for a employees (especially female employees), and in this way subverted the gendered hierarchy in the plant. This is a good example of how companies maintained control over their workers by using disciplinary measures framed by notions of appropriate and inappropriate behavior according to an employee's class status and gender.[49]

Companies had other mechanisms of control besides warning slips. There were policies governing all sorts of things in the factory. It was difficult to receive personal phone calls at work since workers had to take calls in the office, and it was difficult to receive notice of a call while working on the factory floor. Sometimes important messages could get lost in the relay. Workers were not supposed to sleep on the job either, but long hours on third shift could become painful, and many women would drift off to sleep at work. If caught napping on the job, workers could possibly lose their job or receive a temporary suspension. There were even rules governing where to park, as many companies reserved spots for employees carpooling to work alongside spots for management. At IRC, the plant manager inadvertently stirred up trouble when he jokingly threatened to let the air out of the tires of all the cars parked incorrectly. He wrote a lengthy statement trying to retract his previous hyperbole:

> As a result of a recent facetious remark made by myself, there was some concern expressed about the disciplinary action the Company

might take as a result of unauthorized employees parking in the reserved parking places. I clarified our position by stating that in no way were we contemplating letting all the air out of the tires or towing cars away if they were found in unauthorized parking spaces. I would expect that employees would honor these reserved parking places in the same manner that I expect employees to honor other reserved parking places. Since most, if not all, of our employees are good citizens, I did not expect this to be a significant problem.[50]

Another policy concern that affected female workers was the length of maternity leave. Each plant and company had a different policy for maternity leave, and it usually depended on the number of female workers in the plant. Companies that had very few female workers or had just begun hiring women often had very poor maternity policies. Marlene Kruger argued that Waterloo Industries had a poor policy, and it took some time to even get maternity into the union contract. She stated, "[They] fought us on this [pregnancy] too. They said it wasn't sick leave, that they didn't have to pay. And I've had two children while working there, and they finally paid regular sick leave." Later, they had a clause in the contract that the company would pay a cash settlement to any woman who went home from the hospital the day after she had a baby. Kruger believed this was outrageous. "I personally thought the clause . . . had to come from a man because I couldn't imagine a woman who had had children wanting to go home the day after she had a baby. And they paid you so much for each day depending on which day you went home. They gave you money to encourage you to get out of the hospital and go home. Bad news."[51]

Most companies did provide some type of policy for women to take maternity leave. At Eagle Signal in the Quad Cities, women needed to request a leave of absence before the end of their fifth month. After the fifth month, women needed a doctor's certificate stating that they could continue to work after five months of pregnancy. Eagle Signal also allowed up to $120 for hospitalization, and at Birtman Electric, women had to have at least six months of employment before they could request maternity leave, and then they were granted up to six months' leave. Bev Clinton noted that women could work at Square D right up until the baby was born, and then women could take six to eight weeks of maternity leave. Ila Jean Bryne, at Globe Union in Fort Dodge, commented, "We've had ladies go out of there on second shift and have their baby born the next morning, that close. And then as long as the doctor tells you that you're not able to work, you're on medical leave. And then the company is pretty lenient about giving you a personal leave after that if you want to stay home a little bit longer."[52]

The shared pressures of the workplace provided the impetus for a collective consciousness. The common experiences of poor working conditions, company control, and the power of the foreman helped women bond in the workplace. It was also the unique experiences of women in a male-dominated space that added a gendered component to women's bonding. Fighting for access to the restroom, resisting sexual harassment of male foremen, and requesting better maternity rights united women through their shared experiences of oppression in a gendered capitalist system.

## Shared Spaces for Cultivating Solidarity

Despite shared experiences, women had few physical spaces in which to build a mutual commitment to each other and cultivate a class consciousness. Strong working-class neighborhoods once built class consciousness through the shared proximity of both work and living, as workers relied on each other within the workplace and at home. But during the postwar period and in places of industrial decentralization, those old neighborhoods disappeared. In places like the rural Midwest, companies gathered workers across a broad geographical space to fill the demands of production. Workers had to find new places and ways to build class consciousness and often looked to the factory itself as the place to start. Many women depended upon shared cultural norms to bridge the gaps of geographic distance, and they cultivated community building within the factory itself. Women were able to create class consciousness based on shared notions of work, gender, and family.

When women walked into an industrial workplace for the first time, it could be quite overwhelming, especially if they were accustomed to the quiet of the countryside. Pat Marshall, who came from a small town with a population of only 1,200, was completely overwhelmed by the noise and congestion when she first started at Collins Radio. Unaccustomed to all the people, she felt very small in her new surroundings. Pauline Fisher clearly recalled her first day at Ideal Manufacturing in Oskaloosa: "My first job was packing. Oh my, I wore some bad shoes, and it was hot weather, and oh! And there were two gals, well, one gal especially who helped me out 'cause I just had a terrible time. But she helped me out in the packing department, and I made out fine."[53] Even though walking into the factory for the first time may be daunting, women found comfort in female companionship and community within the workplace. This sense of togetherness and mutuality eased their transition into an industrial workplace environment.

Similar backgrounds and shared cultural norms helped create a sense of community, which is illustrated by a sample of twenty-five women involved in the Iowa Labor History Oral Project. Nine of these twenty-five women were raised on farms (36 percent), five grew up in small towns (20 percent), and eleven grew up in towns with a population over 10,000 (44 percent). Either their parents farmed or their fathers worked in working-class jobs such as tool and die making, railroad work, or construction. Their mothers usually did not work outside of the home and spent most of their time caring for their children, who ranged in age from two to seventeen. Most of the working-class women in the sample had at least a high school education, as nearly 90 percent of them graduated from high school. They also started working in the 1950s and 1960s, with a handful (20 percent) beginning during World War II. Forty percent of the women in the sample started working during the 1950s, and 32 percent started in the 1960s. The majority of these women were born in the 1920s and 1930s, putting them in their late twenties and early thirties when they began working.[54]

Once in the factory, women bonded over these commonalities and the cultural norms that came from their rural towns and communities. Institutional cultural norms dictated the ways women acted and behaved in social settings and informed their actions toward work, neighborliness, dependability, and civility. Above all others, the norm of hard work was a foundation of their identity as midwesterners, and it was understood that they were there to work. Earning a reputation for laziness could be detrimental and disgraceful to any worker. Edith Arendt, an employee at Collins Radio in Cedar Rapids, recalled learning from her father the value of hard work. She argued that "if you're going to live with your conscience, you want to feel that for the pay you have received, you have given good work and not wasted time or material." It also meant having a certain pride in your work. As Susan Rhum stated, while working at the IAAP, "I took pride in my work. I thought, well, if someone's going to have to use this ammunition, I want it to be the best ammunition. I realized it was a necessary evil, you might say. If someone's going to make it, why not here where we have good facilities, good people? I think people do take pride in their work out here."[55]

These women also shared a common ethnicity, as the population of racial and ethnic minorities remained below 5 percent throughout this period. In some urban areas minorities were a larger percentage of the population, but for the most part these women were white. The few Black women who worked in manufacturing were accustomed to their minority status and found ways to blend in as best they could with their female coworkers. Billye Smith Williams expressed this when she discussed her work at IRC: "I didn't feel ridiculous being the only black because I had been that so many times. I went to school where I became the only black. My sister died and my brother moved away. So I was by myself, black."[56]

Through years of working side by side with each other, women developed close friendships with their coworkers as they bonded over their shared identities as midwestern women, and they developed a sense of camaraderie in their workplace, creating a community among themselves. They shared each other's birthdays, gave bridal and baby showers, and used any excuse to have a potluck. Billye Smith Williams loved her time working at IRC, recalling, "I loved that place. . . . I think the people really took to me. Everybody was like a family there. They were really close, and everybody looked out for everybody. It was just a real nice place to work." Despite her race, she felt at home among her coworkers. Many women felt that work was similar to an extended family, as Ila Jean Bryne recalled about her time at Globe Union in Fort Dodge: "It was more of a family. . . . There was a lot more closeness between your foremen and yourself than there is today." Fern Klopp also reiterated these feelings when she reminisced about Turner Microphone: "It was just like one big family. They were very, very good to the people there." The workers got along with the company as well. As Klopp stated, "If we had any grievances or anything, they was very fair in trying to settle them. They would serve rolls. When I first started there, they used to serve rolls at our rest period. We had a rest period, ten minutes in the morning and ten minutes in the afternoon. Sometimes at noon they had a soup line."

The women at Clinton Garment cultivated a family-like atmosphere in their workplace as they worked side by side for many years. These women were typically the same age, married, and had children. Irene Vaughn, a worker at Clinton Garment, remarked that she "enjoyed it. Everybody enjoyed it. It was just like a club. Everybody liked each other, and you could talk as you worked. If you wanted to work hard, you made really good money." The apparel industry was a good opportunity for working women, offering women decent wages, a clean working environment, and fellowship with other female workers.

Workers also celebrated each other's birthdays and had potlucks to break up the monotony of the work week. Edith Arendt remembered, "If someone had a birthday, wedding, anniversary, or what have you, we would all take in a little basket, and during our noon hour we would have a surprise picnic for the fellow worker in our department." Workers developed camaraderie with each other and with foremen as well, and sometimes became a little rowdy, as when Ernie Mason, the foreman at IRC, told the steward to "put a bug in Kathryn's ear about not shooting rubber bands and about what he said about putting leads down his back." These lighthearted games and frivolities helped create a workplace culture that served to lift women's spirits against the quotidian drone of the work week.[57]

Women also developed ways of talking with each other, which fostered this shared identity as female workers. They talked about each other, the men they worked with, their husbands, children, recipes, or how they should fix their hair. Doris Peick commented that female workers "might talk about it within their women's group and say, 'Look at that dumb guy over there, pooping around. He's not doing a damn thing, and the boss never sees him,'" and they also discussed "a recipe or the kids or, you know, what color we want our hair to be next week, or whatever. . . . You know, women talk, which is definitely women talk." But despite the conversations that occurred throughout the day, women still worked hard. As Peick stated, "We work hard. Women know how to manage their time and how to manage their hands and can work and talk, for the most part, at the same time." Of course, women did not always get along with each other either, as there were often squabbles and melodramas going on in every plant, along with plenty of gossip. Joyce Burrows recalled some of the fights women had: "I mean we've had fights in the plant. We've had women literally throw scissors at each other."[58]

A good example of how women argued was a series of conflicts in the ultraclean room at IRC. In early September 1969, a group of women had a history of constant bickering and gossiping and not getting their work done. The foreman, Ernie Mason, and the third-shift steward, Wilma Haynes, called in each of the women to discuss what was going on in the department. The three women, Mary, Cita, and Shirley, blamed each other for what was happening. Mary and Cita ganged up on Shirley, saying she was not keeping up and was absent too much. Shirley said Mary was too bossy and wanted to know if the other two had been "bitching about her." Haynes, acting as arbitrator, believed Mary and Cita were to blame as well, and spent several meetings trying to resolve the situation. At one point, Haynes recorded, "Ernie and I met and evaluated what we had learned in the last 2 nites [*sic*] from talking to the girls and what we could do to limit the problem." Eventually Haynes learned the jobs in the department, so that she could help out if they got into a bind, and she recorded, "attitude of all girls will have to improve" and requested that they "don't be fussing if you get in a bind. Call Ernie and we'll get some help in there."[59]

Wilma Haynes recorded several incidents in her steward journal of women expressing irritation and aggravation at each other. For example, Haynes recorded that one woman, Shirley, wanted to receive back pay for an unfair suspension, and when Shirley discussed it with the head steward, Dorothy, Shirley got "real mad and huffy with her." Sometimes women got upset when their coworkers were making more money. Haynes logged that two women "got in to it about us making too much money. And hand spiraling not making any and us not watching our machines while they are running. Girls real mad because she said we were having a good time and making money 'while they worked real hard and didn't make any.'" When things were not going well, the bickering and gossiping only became worse. Haynes lamented, "Women were not happy, they were griping and complaining about things going on in the plant, and the supervision were having major issues with morale." The gossip could be too much for some, and many feelings were hurt by the behavior of coworkers. One woman became quite upset with how things were going in the plant, and complained to Haynes about her coworkers' behavior. Haynes emphasized, "I feel so sorry for her, she cried when I talked to her this morning after I got home from work." At times it even became too much for Haynes herself, as she lamented, "Punched out at 7:55. I came home and cried." Sometimes the gossip could really get under her skin, even when she acted like it did not: "Margaret and Doris walked to break together and were talking, stopped in aisle and talked and when I came along they stopped until I passed." Even though she made no explicit mention of how this made her feel, she did, however, record it in her journal, showing that it must have made an impression on her. Women in the workplace instituted cultural norms through gossip, validating proper behavior and ostracizing those who did live up to their standards. If a woman acted outside of these behavioral norms, she was ridiculed and chastised through the whispering conversations of gossip.[60]

Because women were constantly being watched by foremen and male management, women found physical spaces within the plant that were away from the male gaze. These fiercely protected spaces became the place within the plant where they felt comfortable sharing gossip, grievances, and other serious concerns with their fellow coworkers and friends. One of the most important places was the restroom, especially since it was off limits to their male supervisors and coworkers. The restroom became a restful place, with chairs, ashtrays, and decent toilet facilities. At Waterloo Industries, soon after they began hiring women in the late 1960s, the union requested that the company repair the female restroom. They added chairs, installed wooden doors for the stalls, and replaced the old, dingy curtains.[61] Women worked diligently to keep the restroom a restful place, and used the union to improve the conditions there. The union ensured that there were places to sit, tables with ashtrays so they could smoke, and plenty of paper towels to dry their hands. If the restroom became unsanitary or needed better ventilation, the union lodged grievances with the company to make improvements. At one point, women even set up little displays for their side businesses. They created displays for Avon products and their miscellaneous items, and someone even sold decorative ashtrays in the restroom. Because the restroom was a central location for women to congregate, it was an ideal situation to make a little side money. The company eventually put an end to this, arguing that the restroom was still company property, and that the "company is not going to run a general store in the restroom." Employees could still sell items during their lunch periods, but "they will not be able to set up displays as they have in the past and . . . no product shall be sold on company time." The company argued that the restroom was not a place for business. Despite the attempts of management to reclaim the bathrooms as company property, female workers saw it as their space, and because it was vital to the creation of worker solidarity, women fought to protect their access to it.[62]

Women also used it as place to discuss workplace issues because of its seclusion from the male foremen. At IRC, Wilma Haynes was frequently called into the restroom to discuss a grievance. For example, Joanne Wilkerson called Haynes into the bathroom to discuss being called out of her job classification when others were not. Haynes assured her she would look into it. Shirley Herman, who also gave Haynes all sorts of trouble, called Wilma to the bathroom one day to tell her that she never received her three-day back pay for her unjust suspension.

The home telephone was another convenient yet private way to discuss what was happening at work. The phone became a safe place for women to share gossip and resolve workplace problems within the privacy of their own homes. For stewards, the phone became a way to settle disputes, and Wilma Haynes spent many a morning on the telephone discussing situations with other workers and with Dorothy Warner, the head steward of the plant. For example, Warner called Haynes to inform her about a dispute in which they were both involved. Warner helped Haynes figure out some things she was confused about, stating, "Didn't know what she meant until Dorothy called tonight and told me Ernie [the foreman] had talked to her about the outcome of the grievance. He was mad and said he would never agree to it unless the company and the union made him and that Catherine and myself were liars and he didn't know how he could work with a liar. Did this ever make me mad! Called Catherine and talked to her about it. Went to work mad!" This situation was best resolved over the phone, since it dealt with sensitive material that could impede normal workplace relationships.[63]

## Conclusion

As Iowa women ventured into the factory, they connected with fellow female workers and overcame their fears about working in this new environment. The ephemeral process of developing a collective consciousness was forged through the crucible of the factory and through shared experiences in the workplace. Women formed bonds that would be set for life and would shape their identities as working mothers and wives. Women found common ground over limited job categories, crummy work environments, and a rural/midwestern culture that framed all of their interactions. Dealing with their limitations as women—lower pay, unskilled job categories, hostile male foremen, unwanted sexual advances, and the exploitative male gaze—placed additional burdens on female shoulders. These shared frustrations of gender and class molded a class consciousness that guided them on the path toward activism within the union. Through the union they would learn about their rights as workers and the role of activism in achieving those rights. It is on this foundation that women would begin to act in ways to improve their workplaces and see themselves as part of a larger community of workers.

# Chapter Four

## Negotiating Gender Roles in the Union

RUTH LUBERT, a working mother and union wife, loved being part of her union auxiliary, and throughout her life she relished her participation in it. She and her fellow auxiliary members decorated floats for the annual Labor Day parade and worked a booth at the local fair. Lubert found her lifelong friends in the auxiliary, and she maintained a devout faith that her activism supported her husband's local and the labor movement as a whole. Lubert grew up on a farm outside of Waterloo, and her parents raised her and her six siblings to appreciate the labor movement. Her father was a part-time farmer and full-time carpenter active within his union. He instilled within his children the value of hard work and the importance of labor in protecting your livelihood. When Lubert graduated from high school, she moved to Cedar Rapids and worked as a clerk in the local hospital. She did not stay away for long, however, and moved back to Waterloo after she met and married A. W., who worked at the John Deere plant in Waterloo. After her marriage, she worked for a short time at Black's Department Store, but after she had her first child, she quit working and stayed at home. They soon realized, however, that as a family they needed some sort of additional income to make ends meet, so she found temporary jobs such as working for the city directory, the census, and doing some house cleaning. "I went out after the kids got so I could . . . [and] had a child old enough to leave with them. Then I would go out and do housework sometimes if I could find a job. It was never any steady work." Despite taking care of her children and working part time, Lubert found time to participate in the Women's Auxiliary to UAW Local 838 at John Deere. Unlike many auxiliaries, Local 838's auxiliary was quite active and did a lot to support the union and their husbands. They served meals for the local's events and sold coffee and rolls to the men at their monthly Saturday morning meetings. She and her husband also sponsored a jive joint for teenagers that held dances for the teens and gave them a safe place for them to spend free time.[1] With both a working-class and a farm background, Lubert exemplified the experiences of many working-class women in Iowa during the 1950s and '60s. By embracing her role as the support to her husband, she embodied the traditional ideal of a working-class wife. She adjusted to the economic necessity of part-time work while maintaining the societal traditions of the submissive, supportive wife. She used unpaid labor to support her family and the union by fulfilling tasks that were acceptable to her position as a female in a patriarchal home. The ladies' auxiliary organization came to embody this ideal of the supportive union wife and defined the roles women could play in their support of the labor movement.

Women like Lubert learned to navigate these changes as both working-class men and women learned how to make compromises in the traditional separation of gendered roles, duties, and identities. As the old notions of separation between male and female became blurred, pushing the boundaries between what is feminine and what is masculine, both genders negotiated new roles and responsibilities through a series of incremental adjustments to their working-class identities. The first organizational space where these negotiations took place was within the auxiliary. Labor unions created the auxiliary for working-class wives, mothers, and daughters to support the efforts of men who belonged to the union. Labor leaders understood that to make a successful organization it needed to involve the entire family, especially the commitment of the worker's wife. As women worked in the labor movement, they learned the appropriate ways women could contribute to the local. This meant showing solidarity with the union while still retaining their domesticity and respectability as ladies. This unique combination of militancy and domesticity helped women formulate a personal identity that embraced their class status as well as their traditional roles as women under patriarchy. These working-class women were deeply committed to unionism and acted out their loyalty through traditional gender activities of cooking, sewing, and organizing social events. Women combined these traditional roles with solidarity with the labor movement, militancy on the picket line, and consumer organizing around the union label. Even though labor leaders often placed women on the fringes of the trade union movement—important in class struggle, but not essential to the class warfare waged through collective bargaining—women found ways to support labor while cultivating a distinctive identity as working-class women. In essence, the auxiliary acted as the wife to the union. The women's auxiliary cooked, made coffee, hosted fundraisers, and planned parties. These were roles women were familiar with through their involvement in churches, farm organizations, or community groups. In small towns and communities where organizational work was split along gendered lines, men were the leaders and women provided the unpaid domestic labor, and this gendered division replicated the division of the home.[2]

But working-class women's lives began to change when they started working alongside their male peers. Now women were the workers, and they were the union. Many women grappled with this new identity as it challenged the traditional ideal of the stay-at-home wife and mother. While economic necessity drove them into the workplace, they still felt uneasy with this new role and their infringement into male spaces within the workplace and the union. To cope, women formed women's committees to continue their support to the union in very gendered ways. They began to replicate the auxiliary by performing the domestic tasks of the union. They hosted fundraisers for charities, were active in the community, and sponsored potlucks and parties. Performing feminine duties within the male space of the union alleviated male fears about the encroachment of women into a previously all-male domain.

As women negotiated these new roles, the union itself adjusted to the socioeconomic changes of the postwar period. As the union began to switch its focus to politics as a tool for achieving pro-union goals and abandoned its reliance on the union label, so too did women's involvement switch to politics. After the devastation of the Taft-Hartley Act in 1947, labor needed allies in Washington who could help labor gain legislation beneficial to the working class.[3] Labor turned to women as a source of voluntary workers who could provide the long, tedious hours needed to achieve labor's political goals. The newly combined AFL-CIO created the Women's Activities Department (WAD) in 1955 to help wage war at the ballot box. The AFL-CIO hoped WAD could organize working-class women into a powerful political force. They gave women the responsibilities of voter registration and "get out the vote" drives on Election Day. WAD provided a subtle yet definite shift in how women's unpaid labor was used in labor's continual fight for their rights. As the AFL-CIO mobilized women through WAD, it became the role of working-class women to support organized labor at the ballot box and through volunteerism in political organizing. WAD was especially active in Iowa, as the Iowa Federation of Labor promoted WAD and hired Betty Talkington as the director. Talkington provided solid leadership of the organization for twenty years, mobilizing women all across the state into a powerful political force. Pushing women to support labor politics and encouraging women to become politically active, WAD provided yet another dimension to their gendered class identity. Women took pride in their political activity and valued their activism, incorporating it into their identity as working-class women.

As working-class families dealt with the changes of the postwar era, companies, unions, and families made adjustments to the new duties and responsibilities of shifting gender roles. This chapter highlights how working-class women negotiated these changes through incremental shifts toward greater female participation. Women's volunteer labor, which was conducted through the auxiliary, at first aligned with their traditional domestic duties. These are duties women learned through the reaffirmation of cultural norms and through churches, farm organizations, clubs, and other community organizations. But as more women entered the workplace, they continued to perform their traditional duties through the women's committee. This provided a nonthreatening way for women to participate in the union, as union men and women negotiated the blending of masculine and feminine spaces. The union leaders themselves envisioned a new role for women that included both the wives and workers through political activism. Women used their time to advance labor's cause and fight for the rights of workers without threatening male leadership. Women also learned how to use political mobility to achieve their goals—skills that would become useful when they applied them to gender equality. All of the negotiations, redefinitions, and subtle shifts opened the door for new roles that would promote gender equality in the workplace. Initially, however, most women relied on the old, traditional domestic roles they were comfortable and familiar with and believed this was the most beneficial way for them to support and fight for the union.

## The Women's Auxiliary

The numerous women's auxiliaries in Iowa helped working-class women conceive of their class status through a distinctive mix of gender and class identity. By stressing the importance of the union label and the auxiliary's vital role in providing food during a strike, the auxiliary taught women the importance of class struggle. But the auxiliary also stressed a distinctive vision of womanhood, which combined middle-class attributes of domestic efficiency, subservience to husbands, and charity work with a class consciousness of militancy on the picket line and female consumerist power through the support of the union label. Consequently, the auxiliary movement provided women with an unusual mixture of femininity and militancy, to create a gendered class identity that stressed the deportment and activity of a lady with the need for strength and resolve in class struggle. This gendered class identity was encouraged through the various activities of the auxiliary, which involved a strict observance of meeting rituals, numerous charity projects, and supporting the union.[4]

With the birth and development of the Congress of Industrial Organizations (CIO) during the 1930s, the labor movement grew rapidly, and working-class wives and mothers wanted to support their husbands and sons in the burgeoning trade union movement. Women organized auxiliaries to support their local unions, adding to the number of existing auxiliaries organized during the 1910s and 1920s. Both the national AFL and CIO saw the benefit of an organized auxiliary system and developed a structure that mirrored the national organizations. They created national, state, and local auxiliaries that fostered growth and provided guidance to women wanting to organize. In 1935 the AFL (American Federation of Labor) formed the American Federation of Women's Auxiliaries of Labor (AFWAL) and put the current two million auxiliary women in its fold. The CIO started its own national auxiliary—the Congress of Women's Auxiliaries—in the early 1940s. When the AFL and CIO combined in 1955, the auxiliaries combined to form the National AFL-CIO Women's Auxiliary.[5] In 1960, Iowa was one of a few states that had a state-level auxiliary, and the Iowa Federation of Labor (IFL) was very supportive of its auxiliary structure. In 1964 they passed a resolution at the state convention supporting the auxiliary and resolved that "every union man encourage and insist the eligible women in his family become members of the Auxiliary sponsored by his union or central body."[6]

Local auxiliaries emerged all across the state of Iowa during the 1950s and '60s, and they were most popular in heavily unionized areas such as Davenport, southeast Iowa, and Des Moines. In Fort Madison there were at least two different auxiliaries, and the nearby city of Burlington had three.[7] There were also auxiliaries in Charles City, Des Moines, Dubuque, Keokuk, Muscatine, Marshalltown, Newton, Ottumwa, and Waterloo.[8] Most auxiliaries in Iowa started between 1930 and 1960, with membership peaking in the 1950s. The auxiliary to the Tri-City Federation of Labor started in 1941, the Fort Madison Trades and Labor installed its auxiliary in 1954, and the Burlington Trades and Labor Assembly Auxiliary also started around 1950.[9] Even though most auxiliaries began in the 1940s and '50s, new auxiliaries were still forming late into the '60s and early '70s. The auxiliary to the Amalgamated Meat Cutters and Butcher Workmen (AMC&BW) Local 150 in Dubuque renewed its auxiliary in 1971, and a new meatpacking local in Spencer started an auxiliary in 1972.[10] One of the most successful auxiliaries in the state was the auxiliary to the Hawkeye Labor Council in Cedar Rapids, which began in the late 1960s. This auxiliary created its own successful catering business and was renowned in the Cedar Rapids area for its excellent food.[11]

The leaders of the AFL and CIO believed that if they could garner the support of the entire family, especially the wife, it would bolster the overall strength of the union, stating that auxiliaries were beneficial to local unions because they helped "wives, mothers, sisters and daughters get a better understanding of the benefits that strong labor unions bring to them and their families." The AFL-CIO also believed that auxiliaries promoted unionism in the community through charity work and the good reputation of its members, and as auxiliary women "rub[bed] shoulders" with other women's groups in the community they would bring a "sympathetic understanding of the AFL-CIO to non-labor groups." They also warned that "the enemies of labor fully recognize the importance of women's organizations and are constantly trying to influence their actions," and consequently labor needed to "counteract this anti-labor influence among women by building AFL-CIO auxiliaries."[12]

The AFL-CIO also supported auxiliaries because they became responsible for educating women on the importance of unionism. Ruby Hinrichs, who worked as a secretary for a building trades local in the Quad Cities, commented that on occasion members' wives "wanted to growl about" paying dues as they did not understand the importance of membership dues. Hinrichs would respond by explaining to them the importance of the union, commenting to a wife, "If you want your husband to go out and work for $3.50 an hour, that's your prerogative, but he could not command the wages that he has right now without belonging to the union."[13] Labor leaders hoped that auxiliaries would counteract misinformation women might have about unions. When Julie Fritz helped the auxiliary get started at the UPWA Local 31 in Fort Dodge, she hoped to educate other women about the union and emphasize their duty as a wife to their husband. She recalled, "We set up an auxiliary more or less to educate, bring the wives in and talk to them, and that they should stand behind their husbands . . . for the well-being of their husbands and their financial and physical well-being, because they were really working them hard."[14] Anna Kelsey, president of AFWAL in 1950, wrote in a memo to auxiliary women that auxiliaries strengthened the labor movement by teaching women about unionism, stating that "the union does more for the protection of the home and family life than any other affiliation," and that by learning about unionism women could join the "battle that the union must continue to wage in order to survive."[15]

Through the recruitment and education of auxiliary women, the AFL-CIO cultivated a group of loyal supporters, and as Dorothy Sue Cobble explained, "They defined themselves as an integral part of the labor movement, and many saw themselves as contributing as much to the success of the movement as the men."[16] They endeavored to achieve labor's success by exerting "women's influence" in politics, education, and most importantly, through their weapon of collective buying power of the union label.[17] The auxiliary of the Tri-City Federation of Labor believed that it was important for auxiliary women to work together for the common good of unionism, suggesting that if women would just "stop and think, that after all, what we represent is so much bigger than we are personally, we should consider it an honor and privilege to be able to belong to an union auxiliary."[18]

The AFL-CIO discovered how women's restless energy and willingness to volunteer could be a tremendous asset to the advancement of labor interests. The Women's Auxiliary of the Tri-City Federation of Labor argued, "Most women nowadays, do not stay in the kitchen, they are interested in civic affairs, world affairs, and they should be as long as they do not neglect their home." Consequently, the auxiliary was the perfect outlet for a union man's wife interested in supporting her husband in the labor movement, socializing with other working-class women, or pursuing volunteerism outside of the home. Labor men and women saw this as beneficial, as long as women did not neglect their household duties, which would violate the division of labor within the home and undermine the system of patriarchy and, in their minds, the foundation of the family.[19]

The AFL-CIO encouraged various trade union bodies to sponsor an auxiliary, and they were found at all levels of union organizations. In order to start a new auxiliary, a handful of union members and their wives needed the approval of the governing body. When a group of wives of the Plaster Tenders and General Construction Laborers in Cedar Rapids wanted to start an auxiliary, they contacted the local with their request. The secretary of the Plaster Tenders, John Evans, was quite surprised at this request, telling George O'Hara, a labor representative for the IFL, that he "visited with them for some time and found they were quite sincere. They stated that they had called about a dozen other wives and found they were very interested." Once the men and women forming the auxiliary had gained the approval of the union, the next step was to hold an initial meeting and to gather as much support as possible for the new auxiliary.[20]

The AFL-CIO national auxiliary encouraged the president of the sponsoring union to attend the first meeting of the auxiliary and give the local's official sanction to help women get started. During the auxiliary's first meeting, the union's president (or another officer) should "explain some of the foregoing details regarding the importance of organizing an active auxiliary," and express how important it was "for men and women to work together for the benefit of their families." At the meeting they needed to appoint a temporary president, schedule regular meetings, and gather membership cards with names, addresses, and telephone numbers.[21] The precise directions and the insistence on male oversight only furthered the idea that women needed male leadership and strengthened the hold patriarchy had over many of women's activities, especially when integrated with the male domain such as a labor union.

Before an auxiliary became official, it needed a charter from the National AFL-CIO Auxiliary. Several AFL-CIO unions, such as the IAM, had their own national auxiliary structure with its own bylaws and constitution, and the National AFL-CIO Auxiliary wanted all requests for a new auxiliary to go through the parent international union first. If there was no national auxiliary structure within the specific trade, then a new auxiliary could charter directly with the AFL-CIO. These auxiliaries were considered directly affiliated auxiliaries. To receive a charter, the auxiliary needed to send a letter of sanction along with the charter application and $2.00 application fee.[22]

Once the National Auxiliary had granted the charter, new members took the oath of obligation. Members pledged to obey the laws of the AFL-CIO Auxiliary, promote harmony in meetings, and to "do all in my power to bring about better conditions among the workers and their families." They promised to buy union label merchandise whenever possible and to "always conduct myself in a manner that will cast no bad reflection on the great movement I serve, the AFL-CIO Auxiliaries," which meant they needed to comport themselves as ladies in order to add respectability to the labor movement. Once they elected officers, they could begin planning their program. The National AFL-CIO Auxiliary moralized that "a busy Auxiliary is always the strongest and the one that renders the greater service." The National Auxiliaries provided new auxiliaries with material on how to conduct meetings, the importance of the union label, and the *Reporter*, a monthly newspaper of the National Auxiliary. Each new auxiliary also drew up its own bylaws and had them approved by the national office. Sample bylaws were given to each new auxiliary, but the National Auxiliary encouraged new members to "include anything that you think will help you to have a better auxiliary or anything that you think will work for better harmony in your group."[23] Auxiliary women believed maintaining harmony among themselves was a key attribute of a union wife. A woman could demonstrate her support of the union movement through a calm demeanor and by not creating interpersonal conflicts, which only caused a distraction from the auxiliary's main purpose—promoting unionism. A woman needed to be active within the auxiliary yet subservient to the general will of the group, as this was considered proper ladylike behavior befitting a union man's wife. This theme of harmony and good interpersonal relationships appears multiple times in literature published by the auxiliary leadership, and it correlated with the idea of solidarity and brotherhood in the union along with idealized visions of femininity.

The IAM auxiliaries also had clearly written rituals for initiations. New members had to pledge to commit themselves to the higher purpose of the labor auxiliary, but not without neglecting their "domestic duties." Members pledged to only purchase items with a union label, visit the sick, and "at all times do [their] utmost to relieve distress, lighten sorrow or anxiety, and to promote harmony between all members." Auxiliary ladies needed to do all this "without distinction of person believing this to be your duty because we are all children of the One Almighty Father." Once again, the theme of conducting business "without distinction of person" reinforced the notion of harmony and the need to work together for the greater good of the union. Newly elected auxiliary officers also had to pledge to adhere to the distinctive principles of the IAM auxiliary, as every installation service began with a prayer that asked God for guidance:

> We pray that Thou will give unto these Sisters who are about to become leaders in this Auxiliary for the coming year, faith in Thee, in our Auxiliary and its members. May they have the courage to always stand for Truth, Justice and Honor, remembering that Thy motto is to do unto others as we would have them do unto us. As they surround Thy Altar and assume the obligation of office may they realize that it is sacred in Thy sight. Dear Father may they have the hearty co-operation of every member and may only the things which tend to advance Unionism enter into the work of this Auxiliary and Thy name shall have the praise forever, Amen.

The prayer was followed by an address of the installing officer, which encouraged members to "let love, that divine attribute permeate and control your every action. Beautiful as the golden sunset, and as all-embracing, may purity of thought, work and action be ever present with you, shining forth with matchless splendor to refine and purify your lives, so that when your work is done, and your mission ended, you may look back in triumph on your official career, made illustrious by every obligation fulfilled."[24] Much of this language was outdated even in the 1950s, and relied heavily on Victorian ideologies of domesticity, religion, and fraternity. The IAM Ladies Auxiliary began in 1905 and borrowed the language of the women's club movement, which valued volunteerism, togetherness, and religiosity.[25]

The auxiliary's constitution also outlined the duties for each officer. The president was endowed with the duties of being a role model for the auxiliary and making sure all the officers fulfilled their particular tasks. She also needed to "treat all members alike" and be "impartial, tactful, and show no favoritism." She was to preside over meetings and ensure that all rules were followed and that a meeting was never "delayed because of some frivolous action or unnecessary talk." It was also imperative that the president not allow "personalities on the floor" to disrupt union business and to make sure that "the will of the majority is carried out."[26] Despite this stress on harmony, strong personalities did occasionally erupt, sometimes leading to the near collapse of the organization. The auxiliary of the Quad City Federation of Labor almost collapsed when a Mrs. Peterson took over in the early 1960s. Peterson let her personal affairs disrupt her leadership, causing conflicts within the auxiliary and among the membership. When her husband filed for divorce and took her son away, she disappeared from the organization, taking the secretary's books with her. The auxiliary became delinquent with dues and almost went under, but the Quad City Federation of Labor worked with the remaining women and managed to untangle the disagreements. This behavior was widely condemned by the women in the auxiliary as unladylike and not befitting a union lady.[27]

Once an auxiliary was up and running, they would plan a regular meeting schedule. Meetings were held at least once, sometimes twice, a month. The AFL-CIO national auxiliary proposed that auxiliaries follow Robert's Rules of Order to make meetings run efficiently, and every meeting opened with the Pledge of Allegiance and a prayer by the club chaplain.[28] Some auxiliaries had a clearly defined ritual for their meetings, such as the Machinists' auxiliary, which had an elaborate ritual that mixed religion and domesticity.[29] Before the beginning of each meeting, a Bible was placed at the president's station, and the meeting began with the divine blessing, which was a prayer for God to "purify our purpose, clarify our thoughts, and magnify our spirit of service." They requested that he "spread sunshine throughout the world until truth shall flourish and brotherly love rule everywhere." Following the divine blessing, they had a flag ceremony, then a presidential address and an opening ode that endorsed union principles: "Sisters let us dare do for our ideals high and true; let us labor on with union as our aim." Then they had the chorus, which reminded women to buy the union label and evoked a sense of urgency and militancy to their union mission:

> The world's awakening;
> let us buy the label goods. . . .
> We should work with might and zest.
> Teaching union to the rest.
> Who have silent stood while we have battled on.
> Let us draw them one by one.
> To our strong and mighty throng,
> then in union we will triumph and march along.

After conducting official auxiliary business, they had a sunshine drill, which was a collection of money, a closing song to the tune of "Auld Lang Syne," and a closing prayer.[30] To these auxiliary women, religion was part of their everyday existence, and it was acceptable and normal to mix religion with unionism. The language replicated the traditions of the women's club movement and projected the formality of middle-class respectability. Auxiliary women saw themselves as a worker's version of a women's club, and adopting formal language added to their identities as members of a ladies' organization.

Besides holding a monthly business meeting, some auxiliaries held an additional meeting to complete work on their various projects and to socialize. The IAM Auxiliary 262, Tall Corn Lodge, had two meetings every month. The first was a formal business meeting, where they conducted all of the official auxiliary business. The second meeting was social, including a dessert luncheon, with either a special speaker or a day to work on charity projects.[31] At times the auxiliary would sponsor a guest speaker to provide some useful and interesting information to the members. In 1951, the Tri-City Auxiliary had Chief of Police Claus Miller speak to them about narcotics, and the Meat Cutters Auxiliary in Dubuque had a handwriting analyst teach them how to analyze someone's handwriting.[32] Several times the auxiliary would sponsor a leader from the national auxiliary to visit their local organization and give them helpful advice and guidance. In 1951, the Tri-City Auxiliary had AFWAL President Anna Kelsey visit their lodge. Kelsey wrote to thank them "most heartily for all the kindnesses you extended to me, for the honor given me . . . the beautiful orchid, the banquet, for the patience the girls had in waiting for me at the airport . . . for the privilege of meeting all you nice people."[33]

While at their meetings, auxiliaries planned their activities for the year, which included advertising the union label.[34] They promoted the label by making each and every member promise to buy only union-made products. The Tri-City Auxiliary in Davenport encouraged all of their members to "spread the spirit of unionism" by asking for the union label whenever they went shopping.[35] The Tri-City Auxiliary also found a unique way of promoting the union label through union-made Christmas cards. They took great pride in their cards and took note when a certain local of the Tri-City Federation of Labor did not purchase them. When the Bartenders, Cooks and Waiters asked all delegates of the Tri-City Federation of Labor to only patronize unionized taverns, the auxiliary replied to the bartenders that they made "a practice of patronizing union places and buying union made goods whenever possible," but they were very disappointed that the "Bartenders, Cooks & Waiters did not cooperate with us in buying union made Christmas cards." The auxiliary advised that even though they "might cost a few cents more . . . the quality of paper and the workmanship is a great deal better, and by purchasing them you are helping a union co-worker."[36] The women of the auxiliary to UAW Local 838 in Waterloo promoted the union label by ensuring that all the women supported union-made goods. They also set up a booth every year at the Waterloo Cattle Congress to promote the union label. Leona Adams recalled that they displayed union-made goods and gave away union-made prizes. "We just tried to let people know what was union-made and what wasn't, like your cigarettes and your soap and different clothing, you know, and your food too."[37]

Another way the auxiliary supported the local was through support during a strike. Supporting a strike was seen as a basic role of auxiliary women, especially during the labor uprisings of the 1930s. As time progressed, however, the role of women during a strike began to wane, especially as more and more women became union members themselves, but it was one of the initial ways an auxiliary learned about class solidarity and militancy.[38] Women provided a variety of services during a strike, serving coffee and sandwiches to those on picket duty, manning a soup kitchen, or even passing out handbills.[39] The women in the auxiliary for UPWA Local 31 would go to grocery stores and various businesses in town asking for donations for those on strike. Julie Fritz believed that without the auxiliary, their strike in 1948 would never have survived. "Because it was through our efforts of making the wives understand that it was important for them to stand behind their husband that made their husbands feel like they were doing the right thing."[40] Supporting a strike was taught through the auxiliary, and it became part of their understanding of themselves as working-class women.

Even though auxiliaries were a valued asset during a strike, the union also valued their work in the kitchen. The kitchen became a place for working-class women to act out their class identity by fulfilling their gender roles in support of the local. Unions relied on the auxiliaries to play hostess during special functions, and the auxiliary was responsible for making and serving dinner, dessert, or coffee. The Burlington Trades and Labor Assembly asked their auxiliary to serve dinner for their special programs. They even bought $50 worth of fish one year and asked the auxiliary to prepare it for a fish dinner for the Assembly's delegates. The women in the Burlington auxiliary completely took over the kitchen in the labor temple, so that anyone who wanted to use it had to contact the auxiliary first.[41]

The auxiliary also typically performed other wifely duties such as sewing and decorating. The Burlington Trades and Labor Assembly auxiliary wanted to make drapes for the meeting room and asked the Assembly for money for the material. The Assembly authorized the expenditure and within a month the auxiliary had made drapes for the meeting room, all for a cost of $30.64. The Assembly gave them a "raising vote of thanks" for the drapes that they made and installed without charge. The Burlington Auxiliary also volunteered to take care of the sick committee and wanted the assembly to inform them when people were on the sick list.[42]

Part of the success of an auxiliary was its relationship with its parent organization, and if the local members were familiar with the auxiliary, or perhaps had wives who were active in the union, the two organizations worked well together and achieved their goals. Sometimes the union was unfamiliar with the auxiliary and was hesitant to use them or allow them to do things. When the IAM District 118 Auxiliary wanted to make drapes for their meeting room, which was one of the first projects they tackled, they wanted the district lodge to purchase the material. But the district told them no because they claimed the lease on the building was uncertain and it was impossible to spend money at that time. The district lodge did, however, have enough money to purchase new team shirts for their bowling team. The next year the auxiliary asked again for material and the district agreed to purchase it as long as they did the work and the price was reasonable. The curtains were done a month later.[43]

One of the more popular activities of the auxiliary was hosting dinners and potlucks. The potluck (where families brought food to share, such as vegetables, salads, desserts, or casseroles) was a favorite social activity where the entire family could participate. Potlucks were used to celebrate special events such as holidays or the auxiliary's anniversary. Sometimes auxiliaries sponsored annual dinners as a special event or as a fundraiser. The Tri-City Auxiliary had an annual chili supper where they invited all labor members in the Tri-City area (Davenport, Rock Island, and Moline) to attend. Sometimes auxiliaries even swapped tickets with each other to support each other's events. The Tri-City invited women of the nearby Auxiliary Local 248 to attend their chili supper, and the women of Auxiliary 248 invited the Tri-City women to attend their spaghetti supper, promising the supper would have "generous servings and well-prepared food."[44] The auxiliary to the Hawkeye Labor Council was a big event, especially after they became successful and renowned for their excellent catering business.[45] The auxiliary to the Keokuk Trades and Labor Assembly was also very busy around Christmas making dinners for various organizations, and during the Christmas season of 1967, they made six different Christmas dinners.[46] Auxiliaries stayed busy cooking and baking for other organizations as well as the union. The auxiliary to UAW Local 838 would make lunch for the United Way during their annual progress report meetings, and every year they got together and baked nearly a hundred dozen cookies for the Red Cross.[47]

Another key activity of the auxiliary was their commitment to fundraising and donating to charities. As working-class women aspired to achieve a sense of middle-class respectability, they wanted to emulate middle-class club women who were active in charity endeavors.[48] Auxiliaries raised money through a variety of ways. The auxiliary to UAW Local 838 in Waterloo sold breakfast at the monthly membership meetings.[49] The auxiliary to the Tri-City Federation of Labor held an annual bazaar where members sold their craft and sewing projects. In 1950, the membership made over $300 at their bazaar.[50] The Tri-City Auxiliary also bought union-made silk ties and sold them to union members.[51] The auxiliary's most successful endeavors at fundraising were bake sales and card parties. The Tri-City Auxiliary had two bake sales a year, and the auxiliary to the Burlington Trades and Labor Assembly had frequent card parties. They advertised the party as a way for women to socialize with each other and have fun. At a card party in 1955, the auxiliary raised $114.50.[52] The same auxiliary hosted an annual fundraising event for polio victims called Blue Crutch Day. They were able to raise around $500 every year for polio victims.[53]

Christmas was the most active time of the year for hosting parties and dinners and also for donating to charitable organizations. The IAM Loyal Sisters Auxiliary 315 in Newton gave Christmas gifts to their adopted girl at the Jasper County Home. They also filled "Ditty Bags" and stockings for the Red Cross to send "to our boys in Viet Nam" in 1967.[54] The Tri-City Auxiliary donated clothing material to the girls' home, "so they can make their own dresses and aprons," and they either bought or made enough clothing to clothe at least one boy at the Boys' Home, since the boys were not expected to make their own clothes.[55] The auxiliary to the AMC&BW Local 150 in Dubuque made Christmas baskets for needy families.[56]

Auxiliaries also helped workers on strike through food and monetary donations. When the Tri-City Auxiliary helped striking workers from a local factory, they remarked, "It made us feel so good when one of the men came and asked for our support."[57] In 1954 the auxiliary to the Burlington Trades and Labor Assembly held an event to raise money for fellow union members out on strike. Over two hundred showed up and managed to donate $100 to those on strike.[58]

Besides pursuing activities that supported the local union, women also enjoyed each other's friendship and created opportunities to socialize together. The auxiliary sponsored picnics, decorated floats for Labor Day parades, and hosted holiday parties throughout the year. They played bingo together and greatly enjoyed their card parties. Women sponsored dances for the union members and their spouses and even occasionally for their teenage children.[59] The auxiliary to UAW Local 838 actually published a monthly newsletter called the *Chit Chat,* which allowed women to keep up with the social affairs of its members. The *Chit Chat* reported where auxiliary members went on vacations, visitors they may have had, family members who were sick, or news about their various fundraising efforts.[60] This allowed members to keep up on the gossip about their fellow members and encouraged friendliness among each other. Women did form lifelong friendships in the auxiliary that they greatly valued. Mae Zinzer reminisced, "In these thirty years, I have found some good friends here, and I am sure that most of you can think of some pleasant and happy hours among these ladies."[61]

By the end of the 1960s, the auxiliary movement faded as women began to find greater interest in their workplaces and within the union itself. The IAM auxiliary, Tall Corn Lodge 162, began to lose membership during the sixties, and by the seventies had only thirteen active members.[62] Auxiliary women also lost focus on the more traditional activities of the auxiliary, such as the union label, and began to focus their energy on political activism. The Women's Activities Department was able to direct women's impulse for activism into voter registration. The decline of the auxiliary also created subtle changes in women's class and gendered identities as they began to view themselves not just as the wife of a laborer but as a member of the union.

## The Women's Committee

As women began to work in the factory, they also seized the opportunity to join the union. For some women, and for many men as well, this change in roles caused an uneasy blending of the sexes, and they struggled to adjust to the new economic and social realities of the postwar period. Some unions, namely the United Auto Workers and the United Packinghouse Workers of America, chose to address this tension between the sexes by creating an organizational space for women within the union. The women's committee was designed to increase women's participation, promote equality, and ease women's transition into the masculine spaces of the union and the factory. Many women's committees had a turbulent start as they wrestled with male hostility, women's hesitation toward union involvement, and the uneasiness surrounding women's change in roles. Union women began to see the women's committee as a way to bridge the gap between auxiliary status and full union member. By replicating the activities of the ladies' auxiliary, female labor leaders hoped their presence in the union would feel less threatening to both male and female members. They began to perform the domestic tasks of the union by hosting fundraisers for charities, sponsoring potlucks and picnics, and planning social activities. By relying on roles they were familiar with, women found a way to become active in the union, and through the blending of domestic femininity with class ideology, they found a way to act out their class identity.

The women's committee became a sacred organizational space for women. It was where women could share similar grievances, plan activities, and develop a sense of togetherness and camaraderie. The women's committee also gave them the social space where they could combine their traditional working-class gender roles with the principles of unionism in a way that was decisively different than the auxiliary. Within the women's committee they were official members of the union, able to vote for representatives, provide feedback during a contract negotiation, and bargain for their workplace rights. Even though women were still subjected to a gendered hierarchal structure within the union, they had a voice, even if it was limited. Women also learned how to fight for themselves as workers, and within the women's committee, union women could share their mutual concerns as workers and as women.[63]

Two of Iowa's largest unions, the UAW and the UPWA, had very active women's committees, and both unions wanted to help women integrate into the labor movement and accommodate their concerns as female workers.[64] The UAW was one of the first unions to accommodate the flood of new female members during the early years of World War II by instituting the women's committee, which helped women integrate into the union and taught them the main goals of unionism. By 1944, several active female members pushed the international to develop a Women's Bureau to demonstrate the UAW's commitment to women's concerns and help it address women's issues in the workplace. Once in place, the Women's Bureau—which became the Women's Department after World War II—provided the women's committee the advice and encouragement needed to address female issues in the workplace.[65] In Iowa, the UAW locals with a higher percentage of female members had a more active and involved women's committee. The women's committee at UAW Local 1237 became involved with several charity endeavors throughout the 1970s. However, not every UAW local in the state had an active committee.[66]

The UPWA was the other major union in the state to set up a women's committee program. The UPWA instituted the women's committee in the late 1950s to help women solve issues surrounding automation in the factory and the consequent layoffs of female workers. Ralph Helstein, longtime president of the UPWA, believed that a women's committee would help women gain equity in wages and ensure the local was hearing women's concerns. Helstein commented, "we operated on the principle that unless people were represented you couldn't be certain that their points of view would be properly presented." The UPWA left it up to the district and local levels how to institute the committee. Consequently, District 3, which included all the locals in Iowa, was slow to adopt the women's committee program. As Dennis Deslippe noted, "Attempts at the local level to build a viable women's program in District 3 foundered on the shoals of passivity and male hostility."[67]

It was in the UPWA District 3 locals where the most contentious relationships between male and female workers developed. Local 46 in Waterloo, as Dennis Deslippe noted, struggled to get their committee going, and only met occasionally and left few records.[68] The UPWA Local 3 (Cedar Rapids) had a similar story. It set up a women's committee in the early 1950s, with three officers overseeing its functions. Elections were held once a year to elect the chairwoman, vice chair, and secretary-treasurer. All officers had to be in good standing and active in the local. The chairwoman was responsible for presiding over meetings and ensuring that each participant in the committee had a proper voice, but Local 3 had difficulties getting women interested in the committee.[69] To garner support, the executive board allowed the chair of the committee to become an active member on the local's executive board, hoping that by allowing women more say it would help the women's committee become more active.[70] This attempt failed, so Local 3 moved the committee meetings to one hour before the regular union meetings. They hoped this more convenient time would encourage women to attend, but once again it failed to increase female attendance at the meetings.[71] The women's committee went through several chairs from 1955 to 1957, even paying the chair the same as a trustee in the hope that the chair would be willing to invest more time into the committee. In May 1956, the committee temporarily folded because so few women participated, and the secretary of the local reported "that the board . . . felt it necessary to recommend that unless sufficient interest was shown, the women's comm[ittee] remain dissolved."[72] The committee failed, either because women did not have enough time to become involved due to work and family needs, or because the committee failed to engage women's interest.

In 1957, the local gave the women's committee another chance with a new leader. Through her dynamic leadership, Darlyn Porter was able to get the committee going. Before officially restarting it, however, she informed the executive board that they needed to offer some sort of inducement to get women to attend meetings, such as having a monthly drawing.[73] Porter used creative ways to entice women to attend the meetings and created a social space where they felt comfortable sharing grievances, but also where they could work together to achieve the common ideals of class and femininity. One of the first things the women's committee hosted in 1957 was a breakfast at the park for the women in the local. The breakfast was free of charge for all members, but everyone needed to bring their own table service. In a letter to members, Porter encouraged everyone to attend, stating, "We feel this will give the women in the various departments a chance to become acquainted with each other and perhaps help to achieve a better feeling of unity. Please leave your name at the Union Office or contact me . . . if you plan to attend."[74] The women's committee began to work on charity projects and sponsor social activities for the union, but the committee also provided a space where they could express their feelings in regard to unequal wages, commenting to Porter that they believed the plant spent lots of money for good causes, but they still did not have enough to pay women a fair wage. Porter continued to encourage women to attend so that they could address these concerns.[75] Porter eventually stepped down as chair to focus her energy on other union affairs. Ruth Hopper took over in 1958 and fortified the committee into a lasting organization, which was an active part of Local 3 into the 1970s.[76] It was only by encouraging women to participate in activities that they were familiar with and comfortable doing that Local 3 was able to create a thriving women's committee.

Once UPWA locals in District 3 established women's committees, their activities often mirrored those of their auxiliary sisters, and even though women were union members and part of an industrial workforce, they still felt most comfortable fulfilling traditional gender roles of working-class women. They sponsored bake sales, special dinners, and fundraising for charity work. The women's committee of UPWA Local 1 in Ottumwa raised money for the union hall to get a new coffee pot, and the local's bulletin commented, "Orchids to the women's activities committee: What would we do without 'em?"[77] Local 1 sponsored a bake sale in the women's locker room.[78] They also sponsored another bake sale at the downtown J. C. Penney department store, and all the money went to the working men's Christmas party for needy children. The local's news bulletin reported, "This Bake Sale will be for a very worthwhile project, do your part and help buy some toys by buying from the Bake Sale for needy children that otherwise wouldn't have a very bright Christmas."[79] In 1969 they made homemade pies to raise money for the Ottumwa Police Department's program on drug abuse.[80] The women's committee of Local 1 pursued these activities in the late 1960s after a particularly nasty fight over the union's handling of the separate seniority system and its repercussions on the female workforce (see chapter 6). The women of Local 1 dealt with a tremendous amount of male hostility to any female leadership within the union, and no woman was ever elected to union office during the entire history of the local. It could be that these women turned to the more traditional roles of hosting bake sales in order to promote the union in the community without threatening male leadership. Ethel Jerred, who was at the very forefront on the fight over seniority, commented that she wanted the women's committee to "show the men that we wanted to do something for the union besides just yelling about our jobs."[81] Since the women of Local 1 could not fulfill leadership roles, and because there was so much strife in the union, they turned to their traditional gender roles as working-class women to help heal and restore harmony in the local.

The women's committee in Local 46 in Waterloo also pursued traditional gendered activities. In 1969 the women's committee of UPWA Local 46 helped the Iowa Federation of Labor organize and host the annual convention that was held in Waterloo. The women of Local 46 served as hostesses and helped the auxiliaries sell ribbons. Betty Talkington, the state women's activities director, wrote to Lyle Taylor, president of Local 46, to thank the women's committee for their help. She believed that "both tasks could not have been completed without their assistance."[82] The women's committee of UPWA Local 3 also sponsored a dance for teenagers. They thought that since "there have been numerous activities for our adult members, but very little for our teenagers," they should sponsor a dance for the young people. All the union members' teenage children were invited to attend, and each teenager was allowed to bring one friend. The women's committee chaperoned the dance and provided refreshments. A flier reminded members that "this affair is strictly for the kids" and they were sure the kids would "have a ball." They sent out fliers to all the members encouraging the teens to attend. These fliers pictured a figure of a teenager talking to another teen discussing the upcoming dance:

> As one teenager to another, there's going to be a real neat hop going on November 2nd. It's the soda pop hop. Sound Neat? It's going to be! Come and bring either your date or a friend. Dance your troubles away. Meet kids your own age. All teenagers 13–19, who have a parent or parents working at Wilson & Co. are invited. Nothing formal! Just wear what you'd wear to school. Skirts, sweaters, blouses, shirts and Ivy Leagues. Please no levies[*sic*]!!! So come along, join the crowd, have loads of fun. We'll be expecting to see you Nov. 2. Yours truly Johnny Teen."[83]

Whether the dance was a success is unknown, but it illustrated the type of activities the women's committee pursued to provide social activity for their members.

The women's committee of UAW Local 1237 in Burlington took a similar approach to their activities but did not face the underlying male hostility. At Champion Sparkplug in Burlington, women dominated the union itself, allowing them to express their grievances through the union structure. This left the women's committee open to fulfill its own agenda, and the women of Local 1237 designed it as an outreach to the community. Carol Carter stated that the women tried to work "with needy people in the community, addressing issues of community concern and helping our brothers and sisters in the community who are less fortunate than we are."[84] The UAW women's committee consisted of wives of workers, women in the local, and their children. They raised all of their money for charity through fundraisers such as dances, chili suppers, candy bar sales, and a yearly turkey raffle at Thanksgiving. Marlene Gerst described a cookbook the committee made one year when women in "the whole local . . . got their favorite recipes, and the women all got together, and they bound this up and made a cookbook. They sold it, and they made a lot of money on it." Gerst reiterated that all of their money for charity came from fundraising: "None of it comes out of union dues, and none of it comes out of anything like that. All that money that they raise is on their own. And that's done yearly."[85]

The women's committee donated to a host of local charities and worked closely with them to assist anyone in need. Carter remarked that they "worked with the social agencies in the county, and they have informed us when our help is needed," and most of those in need were outside of the union. Carter explained, "because in this area of the state these plants that are organized and are represented by a union are paid fairly well. Most of the people that have come to us for help have not been members of any union." This helped promote unionism throughout the community of Burlington and taught those unfamiliar with unions about organized labor and showed that they were there to help support the poor and the working class. The women's committee gave $25 every month to the Food Pantry, a local organization that distributed food to the needy in the city. They also sponsored canned food drives to help the Food Pantry stock up on nonperishable food items. They visited nursing homes and the county home where they distributed food, clothing, and games.[86]

At Christmas the chair of the women's committee actively called on different churches and local organizations to see if there were any families in need. One year they decided to help their retirees, because, Gerst remarked, "You know what it's like now to try to live on Social Security!" The women's committee got all of the retirees of Champion Sparkplug a fruit basket and a ham for Christmas.[87] During the year, if they heard of someone in need, they usually jumped in and tried to help out. If they heard of a family whose home had burned down, they tried to help with clothing and monetary donations. Dixie Bigger gave an example: "[If] a boy breaks his glasses at school and the mother can't afford to buy them and he has to have them, if it has been brought to our attention, we donate the money to buy his glasses." On one occasion, the women's committee was able to assist an elderly woman whose Social Security check was stolen. Dixie Bigger recounted:

> The president [of the women's committee] was at the grocery store and . . . this older lady was ahead of her, and she had only bought some potatoes and soup and a can of canned milk. When she left, the checkout girl told Anne she really felt sorry for that older lady. She was just robbed of her Social Security check a day or so before and she had no money. What she had bought then, that was the money she had. So we kind of checked into it, and she lived by herself, and she was up there at a pretty good age. Anne went and talked to her and asked her if there was anything she needed, and she needed groceries. So Anne went and bought what she needed and went over, and she cleaned out her refrigerator and stocked it for her. She said she had a son that did live near here, but she hadn't seen him for years. He very seldom came around. She really had no close relatives since her brother had died a couple years before. We bought her some groceries, and Anne went over there and checked on her several times. Last year some time she had died. But, you know, cases like that, where nobody really is interested in, we try to help.

By devoting so much time and energy to their charity work, the women of Local 1237 exemplified the ideals of gendered class identity. Using the organizational structure of the union to pursue their rights as workers in the factory, they were able to use the women's committee to pursue their own passions as female workers. For these particular women, it meant generously giving back to the community of Burlington.

While many women found traditional roles suffocating, especially toward the end of the 1960s, many more found them a natural fit. Women's committees built on the concepts of femininity and class that the auxiliary laid down. Through sheer persistence, however, the door to greater equity in the workplace was slowly opening. Once women learned the language and ideology of rights, they applied them to their workplaces and began the difficult task of creating true equality between men and women.

Meanwhile, women learned the language of workers' rights through political activism, and women embraced a new role within the organizational structure of labor.

## The Woman's Activities Department

The political mobilization of women provides yet another dimension to the formation of a gendered class consciousness. When both the AFL and the CIO began to align politically with the Democratic Party in the mid-1940s, they enlisted women to fight for labor at the ballot box. The AFL-CIO created the Women's Activities Department (WAD) to utilize women's political power to labor's advantage. They desired to teach women about political activism and workers' political rights. WAD created a bridge between women in auxiliaries and female union members. By uniting in a common cause, women forged class solidarity as they fought side by side for political gain. Working-class women also formed a new understanding of rights and some would begin to apply their political activism not only to workers' rights but also to women's rights. Labor's new focus on political activism also effectively switched women's role within the labor movement from exercising their purchasing power through the union label to practicing their political power.

WAD began in 1955 when the AFL and CIO merged and the leaders of the two groups combined the AFL's Labor's League for Political Education with the CIO's Political Action Committee to form the Committee on Political Education (COPE) to serve as the nonpartisan, political arm of the AFL-CIO. Labor leaders designed COPE to report facts about candidates, follow the voting records of public officials, and help educate members about politics. After the disappointments of the Taft-Hartley Act in 1947, the AFL-CIO wanted to ensure that no other legislation would cause as much damage to organized labor, stating that they had "learned through bitter experience that the gains won at the bargaining table can be whittled down or wiped out by decisions of Congress." They believed that COPE could be the "means through which AFL-CIO members exert their collective bargaining strength to obtain good government [and to] create good laws."[88] To get more people involved in COPE, the AFL-CIO developed WAD, which would open the arena of political action to a worker's entire family, especially to women. The directors of COPE envisioned WAD as a way to "achieve full participation of women trade union members, and the wives, widows, sisters, and daughters of trade unionists in the development . . . of COPE."[89]

WAD was developed as a subcommittee of COPE and remained under the supervision of all COPE directors. It was structured similarly to COPE itself, with a national director, a state director, a divisional or regional director, and then a city or county director. At WAD's national level, there were two directors, since they wanted to keep chairs of both the AFL and CIO women's committees. They split the country in half, making a Western Division with an office in Oklahoma City and an Eastern Division with an office in Washington, DC. States and central labor bodies were encouraged to appoint their own WAD director. The WAD director was then under the supervision of the chairman of the Central Labor Council and was given a set of duties such as taking charge of the WAD work room, presiding over WAD meetings, and representing WAD at all local labor council and COPE meetings.[90] WAD developed quickly, and during the early 1960s there were approximately 448 WAD groups across the country, which employed about twenty-nine women as full-time directors and organizers.

Labor leaders saw women as a potentially powerful political force both at the ballot box and in mobilization efforts. They argued that "one reason for the growing importance of women in politics . . . is . . . that potential women voters now out-number potential male voters by nearly four million."[91] It was no wonder then that union leaders began to view women as a large pool of political activists, stating, "We have a virtually untapped reservoir of political power in women workers and the wives of union members. We MUST utilize this power. We MUST provide educational programs for women. We MUST let them know they are a very important part of the trade union movement."[92]

Labor leaders in Iowa encouraged women to participate in WAD, and many unions in Iowa had strong programs. The UPWA Local P-1 in Ottumwa advocated the importance of women in politics and argued that women helped labor achieve workplace safeguards. They reasoned that "one of the more important reasons why the lady of the house should be in politics, is that when she is interested, she has proven to be the best means as yet found of making sure that the breadwinner is a registered voter."[93] They later encouraged union members "to carry the labor story home to their wives and sweethearts" and argued that "if this were done, and we could get our women-folk aroused, we would be able to do something about these restrictive laws. It has been proved that once women get involved in political action, they can and will do a job."[94] The Iowa state WAD informed male union leaders that women were quite capable of performing tasks outside of their traditional roles and warned them not to "get into the habit of thinking this is the only thing they can do."[95] Clearly male union members needed a friendly reminder that women were useful outside of the kitchen as well as inside.

Iowa's WAD program was quite successful, in large part due to the organizational skill of state WAD director Betty Talkington. Talkington was familiar with both labor and politics, as she was actively involved in IBEW Local 1362 at Collins Radio in Cedar Rapids, where she worked during the early 1950s. It was there that she became active in the Democratic Party in Linn County, working as a secretary for the Linn County Democratic Central Committee for several years. In 1962 the IFL invited her to become head of the WAD, a position that she held for twenty years. It was through her exhaustive efforts that WAD grew as she traveled extensively to different locals and city labor councils helping them set up the WAD program. Talkington and the leaders of the IFL set up an advisory board to the state WAD composed of all the WAD directors at the local level. For example, the IFL had twenty-two central labor councils, and all of them had both COPE and WAD programs, with fifteen of the WAD groups staying quite active. Six out of the twenty-two groups had a program set up but then failed to find a director.[96]

Even though the national and state AFL-CIO stressed the importance of women's involvement, some male union leaders found the transition of women from dutiful housewife to political powerhouse difficult to accept. When the IFL asked district COPE chairmen to write essays on the theme "why women should be in politics," James Couch from Ottumwa put it this way: "The wife who cooks your meals, bears and rears your children, washes your clothes, empties your pockets, saves your pennies, spends your dollars, nags a little, cheers you a lot, has another important role, 'A political role' and not just as a voter. She is aroused to action on the 'Political Front.'" Even though Couch admitted that women had a political role, he still spent most of his essay describing her role as a "wife."[97] Donald Lewis,

Seventh District COPE chairman, wrote a very glib essay, stating, "Women ought to be involved deeply in politics because the average woman is a homemaker who spends the majority of the breadwinner's pay. By being involved in politics she would know first hand why her buying power is in the condition that it is." Once again, women's role was still connected to the home and to her job of supporting labor through her purchasing power. Lewis then wrote a separate tongue-in-cheek letter to Betty Talkington on what he really thought women should be doing: staying at home, having babies, cleaning the house, and then having more babies. This may have been a joke, but the tone of his reply came across loud and clear: Women had limited abilities other than keeping a home and raising children. According to these men, women were most valuable for their free domestic labor and reproductive capabilities.[98]

Despite some hesitation toward the new role for labor women, the leaders of the AFL-CIO viewed women's political power as an important asset to their new battle at the ballot box. Once WAD was in place, all they needed to do was to get women involved. Their first step was to recruit, and they developed methods for coaxing women into becoming volunteers. Some unions started with a small committee composed of interested women, who began to recruit other individuals to join them, which was very similar to how the auxiliaries recruited new members. Other unions held a family social night or a husband-and-wife night out to teach both spouses about WAD and COPE. More often the Central Council president sent a letter to each local union and asked the local's president to "name at least five of the wives of union members (or union members themselves if there were women in the local union) who will serve as the WAD Committee." The COPE leaders also encouraged the WAD director to attend local union meetings to recruit volunteers, and with the permission of the local's male leadership, she would give a short talk about the values of WAD and COPE. At the meetings, the WAD director would pass out cards for volunteers to fill in with personal information and their availability to help. These cards were then collected, filed, and followed up with a personal phone call. If a male union member was attending without his spouse, he was "urged to put his wife's name on the card and to speak to his wife when he goes home, telling her that one of the coordinators will be calling and asking for her help."[99]

WHO ARE WE?

We're dues paying union members, the wives of union members, and the friends of union families. We're members of the Women's Activities Department of the AFL-CIO Committee on Political Education. **We're proud to belong and we'll tell you why:**

We COPE WADs work to make our city, state and nation **a better place to live.**
We work to win **better** schools for our children, **better** housing, **more** security and health care for the elderly.
We wish to **protect** hard-won bargaining gains against anti-labor legislation.
We work to elect Congressmen and state and city officials **who are concerned with the welfare of working people.**
In short, we COPE WADs work **at** politics so politics will work **for** us.

**We believe that political action and political education are just about as important to the welfare of our family and friends as anything.**

WHAT DO WE DO?

HAVE YOU REGISTERED ?

Do you want to be in on something interesting and exciting? **Politics can be** all this and **fun**, too. Don't get us wrong. It's hard work. Just like getting ready for a party, there's lots to do and sometimes you think there just isn't time to do it all. But you get it done and **get a real feeling of satisfaction.** Some of the projects include . . .

Help to get people registered so they **can** vote and then work to make sure they **do** vote.
Help **inform** people about the important issues in an election and about the voting records of candidates.
Help raise **voluntary dollars for COPE** so it can carry on its important work at the local, state and national level.

Of course, all our efforts point to Election Day and we're busy then, too. We baby sit, give people rides to the polls, man telephones and distribute literature at voting places.
When it's all over we start right in again analyzing the vote. **Just like housework, there's always something to do.**

WHAT ARE THE REWARDS?

You know, one of the best things about being a COPE WAD is the **sense of belonging** you get, the feeling that you're among good people trying to do something useful for your families and your community. Let's put it this way . . . the warm feeling that you're among **friends.** There's something else, too. It's knowing that you're doing your part to **build a better life** for yourself, your family, friends and neighbors.

**In short, it's the feeling of being a good citizen.** Try it. Phone the president of your Central Labor Council to find out when the council's next COPE WAD meeting is. Plan to attend the meeting. Then you'll know what we mean when we say, "We're WADs, and we're proud of it." **When you're a WAD, you'll be proud of it, and earn awards, too.**

WHAT ARE THE AWARDS?

Along with the sense of belonging, and knowing you're doing your part, you can also earn recognition for your hours of service. The awards are presented by different sections of the labor movement, and consist of a pin and certificate at each level.

Check the stairway on the last page of this brochure for further information.

Committee on Political Education
WOMEN'S ACTIVITIES DEPARTMENT
of the
IOWA FEDERATION OF LABOR
AFL - CIO

C. L. DAVIS, Pres.
J. B. MINCKS, Director

"Meet the Iowa WADS," ca. 1970, Des Moines, Iowa.
Iowa Federation of Labor Collection, SHSI, Iowa City.

The Burlington Trades and Labor Assembly was successful in attracting volunteers to their WAD program and were active throughout the 1960s. This was in large part due to the leadership of Lucy Golliday, who had inexhaustible energy when it came to volunteer work and organizing. Golliday was head of the ladies auxiliary, and she easily switched focus from the auxiliary to WAD. In 1958, she suggested that the Trades and Labor Assembly throw a New Years' party for delegates and their wives to get them interested in COPE.[100] They also sponsored a "covered dish" dinner, and Margaret Thornburg (chair of the West Division of WAD) was to give the principal address. They distributed a flier with a picture of a woman holding a telephone to her ear, prominently displaying her wedding ring, to encourage delegates and their wives to come to the dinner. The flier urged them to at least try to come hear the "important message by a very talented speaker."[101] The turnout for the dinner was good, with a fair number of delegates and their wives making an appearance.[102]

The last step in creating a program and getting women involved was showing appreciation. As they noted, "Every effort should be made to get the council officers to show their APPRECIATION of the volunteers." Council officers should "drop in on one of the workrooms once in a while just to say how proud they are of the WAD volunteers. See that the volunteers are acknowledged at a meeting when their husbands are present. Try to arrange social affairs during the course of the year in their honor."[103] WAD also gave out awards in order to keep up morale among the most active volunteers. They believed that the awards were meaningful, as they noted that WAD women received and wore them with pride. Women received several different levels of awards, as there was a lapel pin for 100 hours of work, a lapel pin in Lucite for 500 hours, a gold bar for 2,500 hours, and an Elgin watch with the WAD seal for 4,000 hours of volunteer work. WAD directors were encouraged to keep a book of hours, so that the women could be awarded appropriately.[104] The Iowa state WAD gave fifty-four 100-hour pins between 1959 and 1963. In 1967 alone they gave thirty-five 100-hour pins, eight 300-hour awards, fourteen 500-hour, nine 1,000-hour, six 2,500-hour, and two women received a 5,000-hour award.[105]

The main activity of WAD was the voter registration drive, as they strove to register as many union members as possible. They did this by comparing union membership lists against registered voters and by making a triplicate copy of registration files. They kept an expansive card catalog of voters and sponsored a regimented canvassing drive targeting unregistered voters. Their biggest push, however, was a get-out-the-vote drive held during any major election. WAD set up a COPE headquarters in every precinct, often in someone's home. On Election Day they had an elaborate system prepared: checkers to check off those who had voted, messengers to transmit lists of those who had voted, babysitters to watch children, drivers to take people to the polls, someone to hand out leaflets, and even a person to drive a sound truck. Women also needed to fulfill the domestic role by providing plenty of snacks, as the WAD directors recommended: "The workers will get tired so WAD should be prepared to have sandwiches and coffee ready to serve whenever and wherever needed."[106]

The WAD sponsored other activities as well. They held a variety of conferences and workshops discussing the duties and functions of the program. Women could serve on different committees, such as organizing, registration, absentee ballots, visitation, legislative action, and "get out the vote." They used their homes for coffee klatches and neighborhood meet-the-candidate gatherings. Women were responsible for keeping meticulous records of all of their activities and maintained a massive central card file on all their contacts. WAD also promoted trips to the state capitol to see how the legislative process worked, and in Iowa, WAD groups visited the capitol in Des Moines, talked to legislators, toured the capitol building, attended both houses while in session, and even ate lunch in the cafeteria.[107]

Women appeared to respond positively to their participation in WAD, and some enjoyed the new opportunities and the fellowship with other women. One pamphlet advertised WAD as a good time, enticing women, "Do you want to be in on something interesting and exciting? Politics can be all this and fun too. Don't get us wrong. It's hard work. Just like getting ready for a party, there's lots to do and sometimes you think there just isn't time to do it all. But you get it done and get a real feeling of satisfaction."[108] Some treated it as an extension of family, stating, "You know, one of the best things about being a COPE WAD is the sense of belonging you get, the feeling that you're among good people trying to do something useful for your families and your community."[109] Ethel Jerred perhaps stated it best, when she wrote to Betty Talkington about an upcoming award ceremony, and how she felt receiving her own awards. "I know the girls will be just as proud of these as I was. Driving back home that evening, I was thinking of the closeness that we girls have had working on all of these projects together. These thoughts are what this pin represents to me."[110]

WAD provided the bridge between the auxiliary and the women's committee. It pushed the boundaries of acceptable women's work to include political activism. Both the auxiliary and union women worked side by side to get out the vote on Election Day. Women learned important skills working on election campaigns, including essential administrative skills, the language of political rights, and the ability to organize and mobilize people toward a common goal. These skills provided the needed know-how to work toward the goal of gender equality and workplace rights.

## Conclusion

As women became active in the union they struggled to find their place in an organizational structure that had been dominated by men since its inception. Men also needed to adjust to the female presence in both the workplace and in the union hall. These relationships were often tense due to the awkwardness of blended gendered spaces. Both men and women struggled to adapt, and women found themselves pushed into gender roles that were familiar and comfortable to both of the sexes. Participating in the union in these familiar ways opened the door for further activism within the union. The embrace of political activism through WAD exposed women to the world of politics and the role of legislation in protecting workers' rights. These skills became essential in the fight for women's equality and equity in the workplace. As women adopted the language of rights, they would apply it to improve their position in the union and the workplace.

# Chapter Five

## An Education in Workplace Rights

Carol Carter learned the importance of organized labor from her father, an ardent union man who worked for the railroad in Burlington for forty years. The first thing she did when she began her full-time job at Champion Sparkplug was join the union. She remarked that the union "embraced [her] own very deep feelings about equality on and off the job and justice for workers in this country." This feeling motivated her to pursue an active life in the union and in her community of Burlington. When she first joined, however, she found it difficult to be involved in much of anything. She had young daughters, was working forty hours a week, and still managed the care of her home and family. Maintaining the balancing act of work and home absorbed all her time, and despite her enthusiasm for the union, she had very little time left for any active involvement. As her daughters grew, the demands of the home lessened, and she devoted more of her time and energy to UAW Local 1237. It was not long before she emerged as a pivotal leader of the local. She not only served as the local's president but also participated in the Community Action Program, became a mobile registrar, and served in numerous organizations including the Southeast Iowa Fair Practice Council, the Iowa Citizen Labor Energy Coalition, and the Democratic County Central Committee. Carter approached her activism with tremendous enthusiasm, while still working forty hours a week. She believed it was the union that got her involved in community activism, stating, "I started getting active in politics, really through my union, and then from there I worked in the community."[1]

As women joined the ranks of organized labor, they learned the principles of unionism and the importance of workplace rights. In return, the union, as a democratically organized institution, learned how to accommodate the specific needs of their female workforce. Women discovered ways to achieve their goals in the workplace by expressing militancy in their demands and fighting for goals that were important to them. As more women began participating within the union itself, they saw themselves as deserving equal treatment in the workplace. The more they learned about unionism, the more they began to apply the ideas of fairness, equality, and rights to themselves. They wrestled with how to reframe their identities as female workers and began to embrace the tenets of feminism.[2]

The first step on the road to a strong class identity was education. Even though women bonded in the workplace over shared cultural values and grievances, they lacked knowledge of how to act out their class consciousness. Many Iowa women had little experience with unionism, having spent most of their lives in rural farming communities. Union leaders often used trial and error to find the best means to educate women. In Iowa, union leaders learned to frame their methods of unionizing in ways that would appeal to the cultural norms of a rural and small-town workforce. Sometimes unions had very steep learning curves on how to relate to a female workforce (especially in small towns), but once they adjusted their message to accommodate female fears about membership, unions achieved more success. From their first encounters, women shaped and defined the union and their message while the union educated them on their rights as workers.

As women grew as leaders and activists, they sought greater influence within the union but found themselves stymied by male opposition. There were more opportunities for women in female-majority unions, where they could pursue their desire for activism without the hostility of male members. In male-dominated unions, however, women were continually thwarted by a masculine hegemony of the local, and their activities were limited to what was deemed appropriate for women. The persistence of a few female members began to adjust the organizational priorities of the union to accommodate women's particular needs and concerns.

Women also participated in strikes and were active on the picket lines, even acting out violently by hitting strikebreakers with their handbags. As women exercised militancy through an authorized strike, a wildcat strike, or a workplace slowdown, they learned how to work together to achieve their goals. Women experienced the power of their collective voice, which they would eventually use to achieve gender equality in the workplace. As women wrestled with their identities as workers and as women, they found a way to bridge the competing ideas of activism and femininity.

## Organizing Strategies for Female Workers

For many women in Iowa, an organizing campaign was their first introduction to unionism. Even though some working women grew up in union homes, just as many did not. Union organizers often started with the basics in educating a female workforce, which meant organizers needed an awareness of the regional and gendered assumptions regarding unionism. A successful unionizing drive was a reciprocal relationship between a workforce that was ready to organize and union organizers who were able to connect with its particular concerns. An effective union demonstrated what they could do for a workforce and educated female workers on how they could belong to a union and still retain a sense of femininity. An unsuccessful drive resulted in a failure to connect with women and their gendered interests. Women feared the loss of employment or the slandering of their reputation and a loss of respectability within their communities. Joining a union was fraught with uncertainties, as the cultural norms and assumptions of proper female behavior in small towns did not include activism in male-dominated spaces such as labor unions.[3]

The first step to an organizing campaign was a desire on the part of the workforce to seek union representation. Women sought the benefits of collective bargaining for the same basic reasons most workers around the globe decide to organize: better job security, higher wages, and good benefits. Edith Arendt commented that the workforce at Collins Radio was successful in organizing with the International Brotherhood of Electrical Workers (IBEW) because "in the changing times . . . we felt if we were unionized in the IBEW we would have more protection in case of cutbacks or discrimination."[4] Women in Iowa also fought for several gender-specific improvements such as maternity leave and equal pay with men. For example, female workers at Federal Prescription in Madrid, a small town northwest of Des Moines, decided to unionize when the company denied their request for a five-cent raise, even though the women were only making minimum wage ($1.60 per hour) with no benefits or paid vacations.[5]

The workers at Sheaffer Pen in Fort Madison organized after the Textron

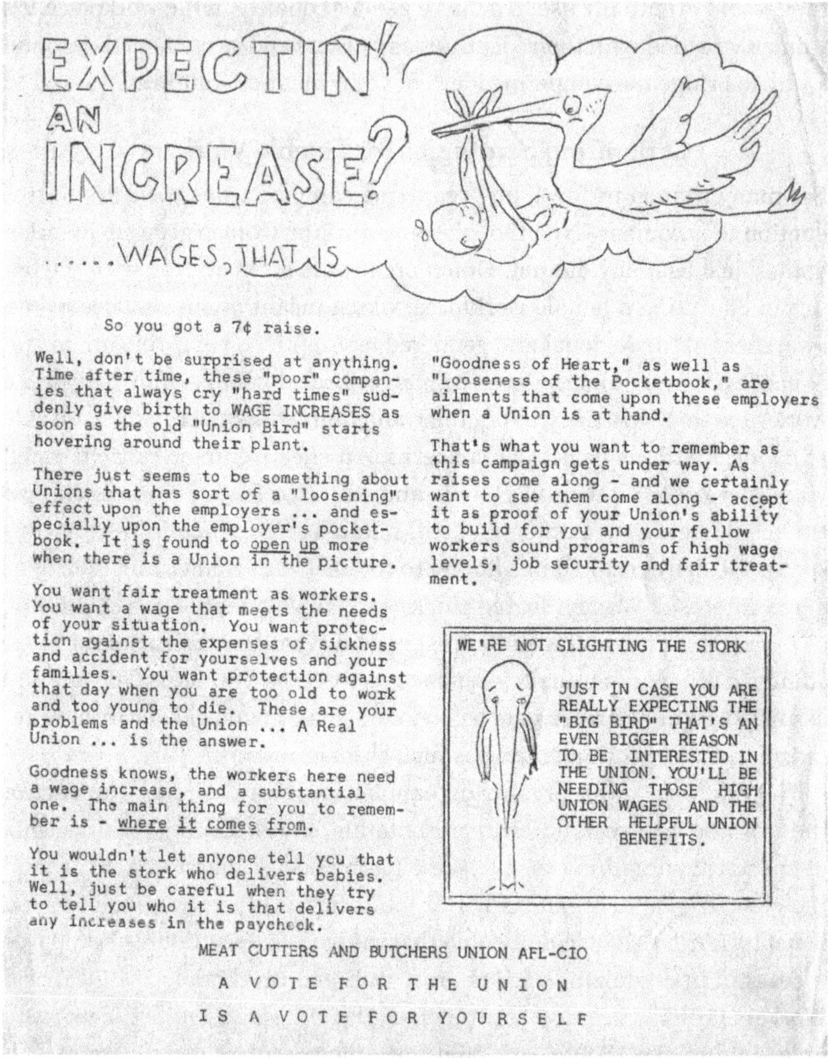

EXPECTIN' AN INCREASE?

.....WAGES, THAT IS

So you got a 7¢ raise.

Well, don't be surprised at anything. Time after time, these "poor" companies that always cry "hard times" suddenly give birth to WAGE INCREASES as soon as the old "Union Bird" starts hovering around their plant.

There just seems to be something about Unions that has sort of a "loosening" effect upon the employers ... and especially upon the employer's pocketbook. It is found to open up more when there is a Union in the picture.

You want fair treatment as workers. You want a wage that meets the needs of your situation. You want protection against the expenses of sickness and accident for yourselves and your families. You want protection against that day when you are too old to work and too young to die. These are your problems and the Union ... A Real Union ... is the answer.

Goodness knows, the workers here need a wage increase, and a substantial one. The main thing for you to remember is - where it comes from.

You wouldn't let anyone tell you that it is the stork who delivers babies. Well, just be careful when they try to tell you who it is that delivers any increases in the paycheck.

"Goodness of Heart," as well as "Looseness of the Pocketbook," are ailments that come upon these employers when a Union is at hand.

That's what you want to remember as this campaign gets under way. As raises come along - and we certainly want to see them come along - accept it as proof of your Union's ability to build for you and your fellow workers sound programs of high wage levels, job security and fair treatment.

WE'RE NOT SLIGHTING THE STORK

JUST IN CASE YOU ARE REALLY EXPECTING THE "BIG BIRD" THAT'S AN EVEN BIGGER REASON TO BE INTERESTED IN THE UNION. YOU'LL BE NEEDING THOSE HIGH UNION WAGES AND THE OTHER HELPFUL UNION BENEFITS.

MEAT CUTTERS AND BUTCHERS UNION AFL-CIO

A VOTE FOR THE UNION

IS A VOTE FOR YOURSELF

"Expectin' an Increase?," ca. 1961, Des Moines, Iowa.
George O'Hara Collection, SHSI, Iowa City.

Company took over in 1967. This was part of a nationwide trend of large companies buying out small, family-owned businesses and industries. The Textron Company ended the lucrative pensions and profit-sharing plans that the Sheaffer family had implemented for their workforce, and to protect their pensions, the women and men of Sheaffer decided to organize with the UAW.[6] This was not the first time a union attempted to organize Sheaffer Pen, as the International Association of Machinists had tried several years before, but the IAM was unable to convince the workforce at the time that they needed a union. The UAW was able to connect with the mostly female workforce by promising them better wages and by demonstrating their commitment to maternity leave. The UAW showed the women at Sheaffer Pen its contract with Champion Sparkplug in Burlington, only twenty miles north of Fort Madison, which contained a maternity leave of one year with the right to return to their old job and a minimum of $70 per week in maternity benefits.[7] They also educated the female workforce at Sheaffer about unionism. Tom Cale recalled that most women in Fort Madison "just didn't know anything about unions,"[8] and the UAW was their first introduction to unionism. With patience and empathy, the UAW successfully organized Sheaffer Pen in 1968.

Because so many women in Iowa were like those in Fort Madison, union leaders often wrote handbills and fliers to encourage women to join. These fliers utilized highly gendered language and imagery directed at the specific concerns of female workers. When the Amalgamated Meat Cutters and Butcher Workmen (AMC&BW) targeted two glove manufacturers in Des Moines, they used gendered language and imagery to persuade women to vote for the union. The Lindfelt Glove Company and the Des Moines Glove Company both made leather gloves and employed mostly women.[9] One flier had a picture of a stork carrying a baby asking whether they were "expectin' an increase? Wages, that is." The flier then encouraged women to join because it would increase their wages and, in turn, help them support the children they had or would have. This also reiterated the idea that part of being a responsible mother was providing for her children, which meant working for good wages. The bottom of the flier stated, "Just in case you are really expecting the 'big bird' that's an even bigger reason to be interested in the union. You'll be needing those high union wages and other helpful union benefits."[10] A different flier empathized with women, asking them how they could support their families "on your small salary." They reminded the workforce that some of their fellow workers were widows, some had sick husbands who could not work, and some had "small kiddies to support." They all needed to vote "yes" for the union in order to help themselves and their coworkers.[11] They further argued that "Smart Girls Join the Union" because "without union security women become second class workers." The union could "guarantee the best possible job rates backed by a Union contract, grievance machinery that gives you the ability to protect yourself" and "security without regard to sex."[12] They also warned women that "IF you do not vote YES—you will betray yourself, your family, and your fellow workers. Those fellows behind the big desks will not worry about your welfare—The Amalgamated will."[13] In other words, to be a good wife, mother, and worker a woman needed to work for union wages so that she could support her class alliances while supporting her family. This strategy worked for the AMC&BW, as workers at both Des Moines Glove and Lindfelt voted to join it in 1963.

Organizing was definitely not easy. Organizers also had to dismiss workers' fears about losing their jobs due to union activity. These fears were often legitimate, as some women did lose their jobs for organizing. At Des Moines Glove, two female employees were fired for union organizing, but after the union won the election, they were rehired with back pay.[14] Things did not always end well either, and at Federal Prescription in Madrid, the company fired nine employees for organizing. When the union failed to win the vote, these nine employees permanently lost their jobs.[15] Organizers also fought with companies trying to persuade their workforce not to organize. In a long rebuttal to the union, which was sent to all employees, E. G. Freund, the plant manager at Des Moines Glove, argued that the union's "interests are purely selfish" and they offer "pie in the sky promises" that can "only have a negative effect on the competitive position" of the company.[16]

The case of Marcella "Sally" Foley demonstrated how union activism could have serious repercussions. In 1958 the AMC&BW organized the Carroll Egg Company, which was owned and operated by a man who was known to be incredibly resistant to unionizing. The plant manager discouraged women from organizing and even threatened them, warning that they would lose their jobs if they unionized: "If we get a union organized in this plant you girls will be out of work." He told them that he believed in a "good union" but that "a union would be no good in a plant like this," and that they were all there to work, so they needed to keep the union out.[17] Marcella Foley was very active in organizing and hosted union meetings in her home. When the plant manager learned of her union activity, he changed his attitude toward her and began harassing her, even stalking her to the dressing room. She recalled that one morning, "I went to the dressing room, which I usually did every day about that time. When I came out of the dressing room, Mr. Webber was standing at the door. Two other girls walked out ahead of me. Mr. Webber let them go by and stopped me. He told me, 'Sally, we're here to grade eggs and not to spend any time in the dressing room. Check out and go home and think over this business of the Union the rest of the week.'" When she returned to work the following Monday, the plant manager's attitude continued to be "very unfriendly."[18]

Later that month she was called into the office by the plant owner along with three other workers. He blamed the women for not grading the eggs correctly and gave them all a two-week layoff and told them to go home and practice grading eggs. A few days later when they protested their suspension, he fired Marcella Foley, telling her, "No employee of mine is going to call my assistant manager, Mr. Headley, an s.o.b. and get away with it." Foley swore she never called Headley anything like this and appealed to the union to help her get her job back. Foley's experience demonstrated the perils of organizing and how women were held to a high standard in the workplace. Even though they were working in an industrial setting, they were still expected to act as ladies, which meant refraining from foul language and disrespecting a supervisor. In Foley's case, the manager used slander to smear her reputation and have her fired for unladylike behavior.[19]

Some unionizing attempts were completely unsuccessful, as union organizers often encountered difficulties in connecting with Iowa women's cultural norms. When the Machinists tried to organize the McGraw-Edison Company in Centerville in 1972, they encountered staunch resistance from the company and the community, and they failed to connect with the female workforce's regional concerns. McGraw-Edison, which made electronic appliances for Toastmaster, moved into Centerville in the late 1960s and was part of the industrialization of the state during the 1950s and '60s. The company employed mostly women from the region, and by the early seventies, several of the female workers wanted to unionize for better wages. Burdine Mulder, who had an excellent work and attendance record, was fired for allegedly removing material from a company bulletin board. She believed it was for her unionizing activity, and two male coworkers also lost their jobs.[20] The company tried a smear campaign against the IAM organizers, accusing them of going to bars and getting drunk. The night before the union election, company officials publicly accused the union organizers of getting drunk and being chased by the highway patrol for drunk driving. Several of the pro-union workers believed this smear tactic had serious repercussions on the way people voted, as the plant superintendent was seen and heard spreading this rumor the day of the election.[21]

The community was also very hesitant to embrace unionism, especially since they were isolated in south central Iowa, a poor section of the state with little industrial development and little familiarity with unions. They were fearful that if the IAM unionized McGraw-Edison, the company would leave the region and destabilize the local industrial economy.[22] The Machinists organizers did their best to dispel this belief, arguing that unionizing does not force a company to leave and that strikes were rare since the union preferred to negotiate and bargain over contracts rather than to strike.[23] But many workers in the community still feared unionism. Hazel Cichosz was especially outspoken in her disregard for the union, publically criticizing the union organizers in an editorial. She also criticized the three employees fired for unionizing, claiming that one of them "frequents the taverns and I might add a gambler. He laid $100 on the table at the shelter house wanting to bet us ladies on Union matters." The second worker was a "trouble-maker who runs around telling lies on the company along with lying about the management. And last but not least, the lady was discharged for taking something from the company bulletin board to give to Union representatives." She was "glad we don't have people like these employed here any longer." She also felt that the union organizers did not respect the female employees at McGraw-Edison, and that she "attended the meeting at the shelter house only to be called everything except a lady by the union leaders." In a second editorial she expressed her ire at those organizing, stating that the organizers were "at the gates holding up traffic pushing their junk (in my eyes) and at the employees. They don't have enough sense to give up. It's too bad we can't get rid of this bunch before it wrecks what we have fought to build up in Centerville. I know how unions operate and from a meeting I attended I never heard so many lies and bull in my life. They can really spread it good."[24] In the case of McGraw-Edison, union organizers were unable to connect with the social and cultural assumptions of the mostly female workforce. They failed to convince the community of Centerville that a union would not cause

McGraw Edison to leave, nor would it jeopardize their economic growth. The company successfully used slander and disinformation to paint the organizers as a dangerous and immoral threat to the community. Using inuendo and malicious gossip, the company convinced enough women in the community that associating with the union and its organizers would damage their reputations. Midwestern culture in rural areas valued morality, honesty, and good citizenship, and the last thing a woman living in a small town needed was for her name to become fodder for gossip.

In contrast to McGraw-Edison, a successful union drive at IRC in Burlington demonstrated how union organizers did successfully connect with their female workforce. It took three tries to organize the women at IRC. The first two attempts were made in 1962 and 1963 by the International Union of Electrical Workers (IUE), but the women at IRC did not feel comfortable with the IUE organizers, and both drives were unsuccessful. Letha Alliman believed that at that point in time the women were satisfied with the company and believed they did not need a union. She remarked, "The people were basically satisfied because it's a nice clean factory. It was all women. It's not like other factories I've worked in, because it was air conditioned and, you know, they were just kind of happy, even if they didn't make the most money on earth. So we kind of had to really rile them up for the election."[25] Wilma Haynes also believed that the organizer sent by the IUE was not very effective in getting the women organized. She recalled, "He wanted to organize at the bar. Our people were not this type of people. Of course, he was chasing a few of the girls! And he didn't make an impression with them."[26] It was rather ironic that the IUE was not more successful in organizing an all-female workforce, when the international organization had a strong women's program by the 1960s and was one of the first unions to host an annual women's conference.[27]

After the two failed attempts by the IUE, several women began to think that trying to organize with the IAM would work better. The Machinists had a local nearby at the Iowa Army Ammunition Plant, and the women were familiar with the union. The Machinists also had a strong presence in Iowa while the IUE did not. Letha Alliman recalled why they went with the IAM: "Well, my personal opinion was that, number one, the Machinists had a business agent that we could go to right here in this area, where the IUE, he was in St. Louis, and he would come in maybe once every two months or whenever we really, really had a big problem." When several women began talking about trying to organize again, Lynn Maxson, a local business representative for the IAM, introduced Lee Parker to the women of IRC, and Maxson and Parker conducted most of the organizing. Letha Alliman liked the Machinists, not only because they were nearby, but in her personal opinion, she said, "The two guys that were trying to organize us, the guy for the Machinists was Lee Parker, and he was a sophisticated gentleman, you know? And the guy from the other one was meeting them in the bars and, you know. That plant just isn't that type. I think that had a big bearing on it."[28]

By 1967, the women were also ready and willing to unionize because the company failed to grant a significant wage increase and re-timed several of the piece rate jobs so that it was harder for women to make money. Haynes commented that they were tired of "being pushed and shoved." Even though women were ready to organize, they were still anxious about the process and were afraid they would lose their jobs. Haynes commented that they "tried twice to have meetings. People wouldn't come. They were scared the foreman would see them. Seemed like we had enough tattletales that it always got back to the company who was there and who wasn't."[29] Lynn Maxson and Lee Parker decided that a better strategy for organizing was small meetings in people's homes. This would add an element of privacy to the meetings, and women could meet without fear of the foreman and plant manager spying on them. Maxson asked Haynes whether she would be willing to host some of these small meetings and invite a handful of women to come over for morning coffee, so that Maxson and Parker could discuss the union with them. Eventually Haynes had ten to twelve women come to her house in the morning, where she gave them coffee and cookies and discussed unionizing. This strategy seemed to work well, and they kept the first few meetings in the women's homes. The women at IRC needed a private and feminine space, such as a living room, where their femininity was not questioned nor their reputation under attack and where they could comfortably address their workplace concerns. Over the course of a couple months, twenty to twenty-five women hosted these union coffees. All the hostesses would then meet with Parker to discuss how the organizing was going, and in this way Parker could get a feel for how the women were leaning. He would ask the hostesses, "How do you think we're doing?" or "How do people feel? How's the company accepting it?" The company did learn of the organizing and sponsored meetings with the employees to counteract the union. The company informed the workforce of all the good things they did for them and that they did not need a union, but it did not influence the workforce the way it did earlier. Women would come out of these meetings laughing and joking about the measly ten cent raise they received that year. Haynes commented that they knew at this point that they were ready for an election and were confident they could win.[30]

Part of the strategy was promoting the IAM inside the factory. IAM stickers were plastered everywhere, on the ceilings in the bathroom, up the railings, even in the rolls of toilet paper, so that when you unrolled it a "vote IAM" sign would flutter out. The company allowed the signs, and the women were allowed to put them anywhere in the factory except on the product. They finally sponsored an election in 1967, and Haynes volunteered to watch the polls that opened at 5:30 in the morning. She spent the entire day in eager anticipation of the union vote. They met that night to learn the election results and found out they won. Once they had won the election, the IAM helped them negotiate a contract that provided seniority, paid holidays, and a re-timing of some of the piece rate jobs.[31]

## Female Activism within the Union

In the dialectical nature of democratic institutions, the unions were as much influenced and changed by their female members as women were influenced by the union. After women had organized and joined a union, they were often eager and excited to begin participating. The union taught women about their workplace rights, how to defend themselves through the grievance structure, how to work together through collective bargaining, and how to use militancy in order to achieve their goals. Women began to see themselves as class actors with the right to fight for their rights in ways similar to men. This new spirit of activism met several challenges as women confronted deep-seated sexism in union locals.

Before women became active in their locals, there were several obstacles to overcome. The first was women's general lack of knowledge about unionism. For example, before Pauline Fisher started working at Ideal Manufacturing, she did not know much about unions because, as she stated, she grew up on a farm and had little interaction with unionism. Her coworkers told her to join the union, so she did. Pat Marshall had a similar story, commenting that she and her husband came from "farming communities with no industry," and when they started at Collins Radio their coworkers told them that joining the union "was the thing to do," so they joined. Even though Lila McAlister's husband belonged to a union, she knew very little about unionism before starting work at the Amana Refrigeration Company. She commented that she "knew that they were very important as far as the workers were concerned" but other than that she was unfamiliar with them. Her husband instructed her when she started work, "when they ask you to join the union, you join," and so she did. Some women needed some coaxing, but they usually gave in to the peer pressure. Harriet Erzinger did not join the UPWA Local 1 immediately, but once several people began asking her to, she gave in and joined.[32] Lack of knowledge was quickly overcome by women's eagerness to appease their coworkers and maintain workplace camaraderie.

Second, and one of the most challenging obstacles, was women's responsibilities in the home. As Carol Carter remarked, when her daughters were young, "my time was limited with working a full forty hours in the plant and caring for my home and family." Bev Clinton, who was very active in the Machinists local at Square D in Cedar Rapids, knew several women she wanted to get more involved, but it was "hard to do when they still [had] families and stuff to take care of." Marlene Gerst raised nine children and waited until they were older before becoming involved in the union. She wanted to be at home during their formative years and believed, "you can't raise nine kids and dump them out on society and have a bunch of kids that really aren't going to contribute anything. . . . I think they need their mother, and I kind of thought that was my priority at that time." Some unions provided childcare for women who wanted to attend meetings. At a woman's conference in the early 1960s, the UPWA discussed how the lack of childcare prevented female involvement. Union meetings were also held at inconvenient times for women, and many could not afford to pay a babysitter so that they could attend the meeting. The UPWA suggested that locals offer free childcare to women who wanted to attend meetings.[33]

Even though some unions attempted to accommodate young women with small children, responsibilities at home usually trumped any sort of activism. "My time was limited," Carol Carter recalled. "I just kind of gradually started going to the union meetings. As my girls got older, I could devote more time to that sort of work." Letha Alliman got involved in the Machinists Local at IRC because many of her coworkers were too busy with their families to get involved. She remarked, "Well . . . I mostly got involved because no one else would! Isn't that a terrible reason!" But she realized that most of her coworkers were busy with their families. "They won't hardly go out of town at all because most of them are married and have families and they've got to get home and fix supper and this sort of thing, and they can't leave their husbands." In fact, she herself did not have time to get involved until after she was divorced, remarking, "When I was married, I didn't go either. I never really got involved until after I was divorced." It was not until women were middle-aged with older children that they really started getting involved. Marlene Gerst commented, "We're getting at the age where our families are grown. We don't have any kids to worry about. What better thing to do than working with the union for the betterment of it?" Marion Klaner got involved because she was divorced and so she had time. She commented, "If I was married, I'd never spend the time."[34] Women believed it was their duty and cultural expectation to care for the home and family. These maternal roles within the patriarchal family were so ingrained that it was unfathomable to set aside their duties at home to be out and active in the union. Women who were divorced, widowed, or single had more freedom to pursue labor activism, since they were not under the control of their husbands, nor were they pressured to succumb to submissive roles under patriarchy. Older children could manage themselves and no longer needed the strong maternal influence of their mothers. This slow release from maternal duties also allowed women to pursue other activities and interests outside of the home. It was rare (and incredibly brave) for a woman with a husband and small children to resist societal pressures of conformity to gender roles. Nonconformist women found themselves fodder for gossip and their reputations ruined through slander. They were often met with hostility from family members and even their coworkers.

A third obstacle was hostility of male union members. In unions with a majority male membership, women had difficulties getting involved due to men with discriminatory attitudes. The UPWA realized that locals and union meetings were often dominated by men, which made women uncomfortable about getting involved. During a UPWA women's conference, union leaders wondered, "With women making up such a large number of the employees in our industry, almost one-fourth, why don't they participate in union activities?" They came up with several reasons: Business meetings were "designed for and by men [with] no attention given to women's problems," leaders made "no real effort . . . to get women out," and the general atmosphere was unappealing to a lady, as meeting halls were dirty, and men used "foul and vulgar language." In this environment, men made "women feel inferior," using "slander, gossip, petty bickering, and attacks on women's morals." Last, they believed husbands did not trust their wives since men used "union meetings as an excuse to get out of the house," and so they worried their wives would do the same.[35] Female presence in male-dominated spaces such as union halls could be seen as threatening to a man's sense of masculinity, and they often resorted to underhanded measures to keep control over the union. Some of these measures included making women feel inferior during meetings or implicating they did not maintain a proper home.

Because of the male dominance in most unions, women usually resorted to more traditional roles in the local. As discussed in chapter 4, women often served on committees viewed as appropriate for women, such as the activities committee or the sick and welfare committees. Women helped plan activities like picnics, bowling teams, skating parties, and Christmas parties.[36] When women started serving on the UPWA Local 3 welfare committee, they complained that the union's cards for the sick in the hospital were "unsuitable" and "they needed to find new ones." Until they found more suitable cards they would send flowers instead, but only at a limit of $2. Three months later they found suitable cards and had an improved program of visiting the sick.[37] Males (and female members as well) viewed these types of activities as acceptable and appropriate duties for women to perform as they allowed women to serve in the union without threatening patriarchal views of male superiority and dominance in these traditionally masculine spaces.

It was in majority-female unions where women were more likely to serve as leaders.[38] Both the Ideal Manufacturing company in Oskaloosa and Turner Microphone in Cedar Rapids employed a majority of women in their workforce, and women served in most elected offices in the union.[39]

The IAM had many women in leadership positions, and even though the national organization did not start a women's program until the 1990s, the IAM was flexible when it came to women serving in local leadership. For example, IAM Locals 388 and 2087 in the Quad Cities had almost all female officers in the 1950s.[40]

It was much more difficult for women to be chosen for leadership in male-dominated unions. Women who sought leadership positions in male-majority unions had to balance the threatening nature of female leadership with reaffirmations of their own femininity. To run for office, a woman needed a sterling reputation as both an effective leader and a good housekeeper, wife, or mother. Marion Klaner thought the success of women within the labor movement was all in "how women carry themselves. I think for one thing men can get by doing so much more than women. . . . You have to keep your personal life, or you got to carry yourself probably in a little different manner than men, to be able to carry on. And I think a lot of women have failed just that way."[41] Ethel Jerred aptly remarked that the male members "would let us cook, and they would let us stand on the picket line, but when it came time for a woman to run for an office . . . all you've got to do is look down through the history of the union and see how many women have served on the board."[42] UPWA Local 1 in Ottumwa was notorious for preventing women from holding office. Ethel Jerred ran several times and never won. "I got defeated," she recalled. "I don't know what they were afraid of unless they were afraid a woman's going to be a little bit more effective than they were."[43] The national UPWA encouraged women to run for office, as they were well aware that the number of female officers within the UPWA was woefully inadequate. Ethel Jerred attended these conventions where she felt challenged to run. "I've come back from conventions where they would say, 'Well, you women get out. Run for office,'" but, she noted, in Local 1, "You're dead before you start. All you got to do is put your name up for nomination, right away they're starting things against you."[44]

Local 1 was not the only local with this problem. UPWA Local 38 in Mason City had no female officers until the 1970s, and UPWA Local 31 in Fort Dodge had only a few female officers in its entire history. Jane Burleson kept running for office in Local 31 even though she rarely won, remarking, "I always did run for office in the union. Used to run just to give the guys opposition."[45] One way men kept women from running was to spread damaging rumors. Florence Jones remembered that if a woman was elected the men "just drove her out of office," spreading rumors that "she went with the guys," and "they got up every meeting and said that there were different reasons why a girl should not have this office, and they didn't want her in there." Sometimes it was difficult for women at union meetings to say anything at all because they were teased or ignored. Florence Jones remembered, "Now, women were never treated equally at the union meetings because it was mostly the men who were in most of the key jobs, and that was what the union meetings was about. They'd probably kid you a lot or catcall or something if you'd get up. It was never a mean kind of . . . they were friendly. I don't how to say it except they just didn't take you seriously as they could."[46]

Women learned ways to break through male hostility by serving in positions that did not carry as much responsibility. It was in steward positions that women often began their activism. Bev Clinton worked at Square D in Cedar Rapids for only a couple of years when she was asked to become a steward. One of the business representatives noticed her, and he involved her in one of his "gangs" and encouraged her to go to leadership schools to learn more about the union.[47] Mickey Lockhart became a steward in UPWA Local 3 because, as she remembered, she "kind of stuck up for" herself, and earned a reputation of pursuing her rights as a worker.[48] Marlene Kruger had a similar reputation of being a loudmouth, and she did not cower when she saw "people . . . doing people wrong." Even though "a lot of people [didn't] stand up for themselves," she "would stand up for them." Kruger's reputation for sticking up for people pushed her into a steward position, and she liked being a steward because she believed it gave her more protection: "Once you're a steward you've got a little bit more right to be able to talk back than you would just as a worker."[49] Pat Marshall became a steward when Al Meier, the business manager for the IBEW at Collins Radio, noticed her leadership potential. She recalled, "[He] came out and asked if I wanted to be a steward. I said I didn't know. I didn't know much about unions. And he said, well, he had observed me and thought that I was level-headed and would probably make a good steward . . . so he twisted my arm, and I became a steward." Once a woman became a steward, she received stewardship training from the union and learned how to pursue grievances and how to protect workers' jobs. Serving as a steward gave workers a crash course on unionism, and it often pushed women into serving in other leadership positions. Pat Marshall believed that "once you start being a steward, you learn more about unions, and the more you learn, the more you become involved. It's just been a growing process in unionism ever since."[50]

Other elected positions open to women included serving as a delegate to the county or city labor council. The Hawkeye Labor Council in Cedar Rapids had several female delegates, and several women held positions within the council itself. Doris Peick served as the recording secretary of the council for many years and became a prominent labor leader in the Cedar Rapids area. The Burlington Trades and Labor Assembly also had several active women throughout the 1960s. In 1963 Lucy Golliday became the recording secretary, and by 1965 several women were serving the assembly.[51] Women also commonly ran for recording secretary or treasurer. These positions were often deemed appropriate for women, since it allowed them to have some leadership within the union but did not directly challenge male control.

Although women usually served in the secondary offices, women did occasionally serve as president, especially in female-dominated unions. In the UAW Local 1237 at Champion Sparkplug, women dominated the union and had several female presidents. Marlene Gerst served as president for many years, and Carol Carter was very active as well.[52] Under rare circumstances, women were elected to the office of president in a majority-male union. When Aggie Nemec was elected president of the AMC&BW Local 62 in Omaha, Nebraska, just across the Missouri River from Iowa, the Omaha newspaper, the *Morning World-Herald*, printed an entire profile on Nemec, remarking on her achievement in a male-dominated union at Wilson Foods, which had 900 men and 250 women. The article assured readers that she still took care of her home, despite her leadership position, and that she had the full support of her husband. The article gave a report of her day, which started at seven in the morning "when she [left] her neatly kept home . . . to report for work in the smoked meat department at Wilson's." Her husband, a retired packinghouse worker, supported her, and Nemec praised the "man in her life" as she commented, "Louie has been a great help. He's also a good cook. He almost always has dinner waiting for me when I get home."[53] Nemec's role was indicative of subtle changes in attitudes toward gender and gender roles that began to percolate throughout society by the 1970s. As the women's movement began to challenge the assumptions of patriarchy, it became easier for women to serve in the leadership roles of president or vice president, where women demonstrated that they could be effective union leaders without losing their femininity or threatening men's masculinity.[54]

Unions helped women overcome these obstacles to activism through conferences and leadership schools. These conferences became places where women learned and where they could air their specific concerns as female workers. It also gave unions the opportunity to learn more about women's concerns and add them to their main agendas. The UPWA was especially active in promoting women's conferences. They sponsored them at the national and district levels, and national UPWA leaders encouraged locals to send their female delegates to the women's conference. The women who attended reported back to the local what they learned and discussed.[55] At the conferences, UPWA leaders would discuss some of the common problems women faced in the meatpacking industry, the biggest of which was the differential in pay. Many locals were actively hostile to women, and conference leaders tried to tackle men's attitudes. One conference report from the early 1960s summed up men's attitudes: "the historic and traditional concept of women as servants—to cook, to sew, to raise the children, to satisfy sexual needs, etc. But now they must also be the breadwinner in effect, perform two full time jobs. The overpowering amount of resistance and resentment they meet from men leaves women without the slightest doubt but that they have a second-class status in union activities."

In order to address the problem of female inactivity they wanted to provide women plenty of opportunities to express their concerns. They stated they wanted to provide "opportunity and means through which women can demonstrate constructively and concretely the very great contribution they can make to the life of this union, the entire labor movement, and all humanity." They devised a program to help women workers feel more comfortable participating in the union, and they wanted women to become members of all the regular committees. They suggested that locals allow time at their regular meetings for women to discuss their problems, and they published newsletters with articles and memos of special interest to women workers.[56]

The 1960 annual UPWA district women's conference was held in Cedar Rapids and was hosted by Local 3. The local was excited about this opportunity and spent a great amount of time planning and preparing for the conference, even getting the mayor to give the opening address. The mayor of Cedar Rapids noted that "women play an important part in our economy and government today, in which case it is well to keep in touch with them."[57] Local 3 sponsored twelve official delegates to the conference, but the entire membership was invited to attend. Other UPWA locals in Iowa sent delegates to the conference; Local 31 sent two, Local 38 sent two, Local 1 sent three, and Local 46 sent thirteen.[58] The conference ran for two days and broke up into a series of workshops. Workshop A discussed the need for stronger women's activities committees, and they suggested they write handbills that would acquaint women with the women's activities and address the "personalities between women" that had "stymied the women's activities committee." They also called for greater participation of men in solving women's problems, because "no plant problems are strictly men or women's." They said, "[We need to] wake up membership that certain things didn't just happen, that we have to get together and iron out our problems with unity between men and women."[59] A different panel discussed the effects of mechanization and the combining of jobs that led to the loss of female jobs. They suggested that educational programs be set up "to acquaint the entire membership with the seriousness of the problems raised and prepare them for whatever action may be necessary to remedy this loss to our Union of our female members."[60] They suggested that the next women's conference should be spread over four days instead of two in order to address all of the issues that might arise. The Cedar Rapids conference illustrated the commitment of some unions to addressing women's workplace concerns.

As women became more involved, their relationship became reciprocal in that union activism changed women and, in turn, the women changed the union. With the increase in the number of female members, unions began to address the needs and concerns of their female workforce. They questioned the validity of separate seniority lists and recognized some of the challenges women faced in becoming an active union member. Women began to apply the principles of unionism to their own lives and to fight for their rights as both women and workers.

## Gendered Expressions of Militancy

One way women acted upon their knowledge of unionism, workplace rights, and solidarity was through militant action. Women expressed militancy by going on strike, showing solidarity on the picket line, or even staging workplace actions to maintain control over particular issues. By exercising militancy, women learned how to fight for their rights, which would give them the tools they need to fight for gender equality as well.

The most effective weapon when negotiating for a new contract was the strike. Unions went on strike to fight for a wage increase, better benefits, or improved pension plans. The women at Sheaffer Pen in Fort Madison went on strike in December 1975 because their contract had expired and the company failed to grant them a pay raise in the new contract.[61] The workers at Globe Union in Fort Dodge went on strike twice for seniority rights, improved job bidding rights, and better wages.[62] Sometimes the company even consciously forced a strike, hoping that the strike would break the union. This was precisely what happened at Norwesco in Grundy Center, a small firm that had only around one hundred female employees. The company hired a contract consultant who was known for breaking unions to rewrite the entire contract to reduce the benefits for workers so that they would go on strike and then break the union by refusing to negotiate.[63]

A successful strike needed solidarity on the picket line, community support, and the determination to see their goals put into a new contract. Maintaining the picket line was of utmost importance, and sometimes extreme measures were necessary to ensure that no one reentered the workplace and broke the strike. The women at Sheaffer Pen, during the strike of 1976, employed aggressive picketing strategies to block the entrances to all the plants. They harassed women crossing the picket line, spread roofing nails across the parking lot entrance, and then assaulted managers while they were picking up the nails. They also threw eggs at strikebreakers, and one union member took a baseball bat to a strikebreaker's car.[64] Sheaffer decided that the melee outside their doors had become too contentious and requested an injunction to limit the number of pickets at the plant's entrances. The court decided in favor of the company and limited the pickets to five, and consequently, the amount of conflict subsided. The women in UPWA Local 3 showed similar animation on the picket line, especially when a group of female picketers grabbed two women trying to sneak through the picket line and then beat them with their pocketbooks. Jeannette Haymond called it "a free for all!" and commented, "Yeah, there was some violence." But over all, "it wasn't too vicious, not too bad. But there was some."[65]

A successful strike also needed the strong support of a community. During the strike at Sheaffer Pen, the community of Fort Madison sponsored a rally in support of the union. Nearly two thousand members and supporters from all across southeast Iowa came to the rally at the Fort Madison high school gym.[66] Other locals in the state donated money, and the AMC&BW Local 3 (formerly UPWA Local 3) in Cedar Rapids donated $200 to the strike.[67] Fort Dodge, also a strong union community, was very supportive of the women at Globe Union when they went out on strike. Other union locals and businesses in the community donated food for sandwiches and snacks for those on picket duty. The company, Globe Union, imported workers all the way from Milwaukee, Wisconsin, because they knew no one in Fort Dodge would cross the picket line.[68]

Women also showed resolve during the final negotiations of a strike to ensure that they achieved at least one if not all of their strike goals. During the UAW strike at Sheaffer, the company wanted to keep the ability to punish employees for alleged "unlawful acts" during the strike. This would allow them to fire those women who were the most militant while out on the picket line. In an open letter to the public, published in the town's newspaper, the *Democrat*, the union argued, "Under our system of justice only the Courts can punish a citizen for an unlawful act," and "if the Company has evidence that any Union member has violated the law, that evidence should be presented with the appropriate authorities for prosecution. The Union leaders have not and will not condone unlawful activity."[69] Even though the strike had already lasted nineteen to twenty weeks, the members of UAW Local 1551 were determined to achieve what they wanted. When the strike officially ended, Sheaffer was not allowed to fire workers who had been arrested during the strike.[70]

Strikes were not always successful, nor did they always have community support. Women at the Universal Producing Company in Fairfield, about twenty miles north of Fort Madison, not only met with fierce resistance from the company but did not receive support from the community or their union. The Universal Producing Company employed a majority of female workers, and in March 1971 they took aggressive action to disband the union. The women of IAM Local 1293 went on strike because the company refused to negotiate a new contract with them, and then refused to meet with the union once the strike started. Floyd McIntosh, the financial secretary of the District Lodge, commented he could "not believe all the harassment this company has handed out." By May, McIntosh wanted to begin soliciting donations from other IAM locals to help them win their fight.[71]

Fifty women stood picket seven days a week at the main plant and at three warehouses. Leah McCracken, who commuted to Fairfield from the small town of Keosauqua, complained about the unfair labor practices to the international president of the IAM, charging that the local union was not supporting their strike or their efforts to get a better contract with the company.[72] The five other IAM locals in Fairfield did not offer support, and the women claimed that IAM members of fellow locals were allowing their wives and daughters to cross their picket line. "Some even bring them to work and pick them up. We had one woman stand picket with us one week, write a note why she was quitting the Union and go back to work. Now they tell us there is nothing we can do about it. We need your help in trying to get the NLRB to act in our favor and to quit messing around and letting our President appeal and reappeal."[73]

In a letter to Jarret Molen, a special representative to the IAM, Gilbert Brunner, general vice president of the IAM, wrote, "it is my understanding that at the time of the challenge there were 175 employees in the plant. It is my further understanding that at the present time we have 115 people in the plant working and approximately 25 people on the picket line who are housewives and picket for a few hours and are attempting to keep the strike going so they can continue to draw the $40.00 a week out of our strike benefits." Even though they appealed to the NLRB, Brunner believed:

> the National Labor Relations Board will dismiss our charge against the company. Naturally, if we push we could keep the strike going but we are fighting a losing battle. Therefore, I recommend that we notify the company that all of the pickets are ready and willing to return to work forthwith. It would appear to me that this would be the better

> way to go rather than to leave these 25 militant people think[ing] that they could eventually win that strike. I recommend that this action be taken at your earliest opportunity.[74]

This letter demonstrates the union's lack of commitment to effectively communicate with the women at Universal and their dismissive attitude toward the female workforce. The international simply saw them as mere housewives milking the union for strike benefits when they had husbands who were working. The women lost the strike, and eventually the local at Universal fell apart.

The Machinists were not always so dismissive or unsupportive of their membership, and a strike at IRC in Burlington demonstrated their commitment to a strike that had more of a chance for success. After the women at IRC voted in their union in 1967, they wanted to maintain the status quo and used their union mainly for its grievance procedure and seniority protection. By 1974, however, after they had received virtually no pay increase and very little improvements in benefits, they decided to go on strike for dental insurance, eye insurance, a prescription drug plan, and an improved pension plan.[75] IRC had also sold the company to TRW in 1973, who then tried to force women to work mandatory overtime two weekends a month. (A very similar merger happened with Sheaffer Pen.) With so many of the female employees taking care of children and families, they begrudged the extra time at work. In a letter to the editor, Mrs. Nyal Thomas wrote, "We are a factory made up primarily of women . . . with families and all with homes to keep. Who wants to be forced to work their weekends!!" She also commented, "through the years we have fallen further and further behind the other major plants in this area in wages and benefits."[76]

Nearly seven hundred women walked out of the IRC plant on May 1, 1974. These women had never gone on strike before, and it was a tremendous step for them, because, as Letha Alliman commented, "They don't seem that strong union people. But yet we really stuck together." The strike started at midnight, and when the clock struck twelve, the entire night shift ran out screaming. They had already set up strike trailers across the street from the plant, and as Haynes noted, "The whole plant was there to greet them. The first night I expect near every one of us walked. At every shift change we were all out there." The first two weeks of the strike were

Strike headquarters at IRC, 1974. IAM Local Lodge 2303 Collection, Iowa Labor Collection, SHSI, Iowa City.

fairly peaceful. Women maintained an orderly picket line, the company did not try to sneak in strikebreakers, and community support for the strike was very high. Husbands were especially supportive and would visit, even during the night shift. Letha Alliman recollected, "We had a trailer that was our strike headquarters, right there by the picket line, and a lot of times their husbands would come out and visit in the trailer." Alliman also noted, "Of course, a lot of the girls, their husbands belonged to the union, which I would imagine had . . . you know, they went home and talked to their husbands, and their husbands had a big part in it [going on strike]." The local formed a strike committee that made sure that there was enough food and supplies in the strike trailer, formed a welfare committee to make sure everyone's bills were still being paid, and made their own picket signs. The women did a lot of things themselves. They had some help from the business representative with the District Lodge, but they maintained the picket line on their own.[77]

At the beginning of the strike, IRC was uncooperative, refusing to negotiate, and would not even meet with the union for three to four weeks

Women of IAM Local Lodge 2303 on the picket line at IRC, ca. 1974, Burlington, Iowa. IAM Local Lodge 2303 Collection, Iowa Labor Collection, SHSI, Iowa City.

after the strike began. The company then began advertising for replacement workers. One of their strategies was to get students on summer break at the University of Iowa to work for the summer.[78] They also encouraged the women out on strike to come back to work, and even threatened them, stating that they would lose their seniority unless they went back to work. The company eventually chose to smuggle workers into the plant, which caused serious turmoil as workers crossed the picket line and threatened the success of the strike. The company had the foremen and the office personnel running the machines, and they even had the wives and girlfriends of the foremen working.[79]

When the company began hiring strikebreakers, conflict erupted. Police began patrolling the area during shift change to ensure that there were no serious conflicts, but as Letha Alliman remembered, the police would not take the side of the picketers. "They would really get nervous. The police really didn't handle it very good, and I can see why in a way, maybe." Most of the conflict erupted at shift change. Women on the picket line threw eggs and Christmas bulbs with paint thinner in them. "One morning the whole bunch of them just picked up a little car." The police arrested one of the male strikers for running down a strikebreaker. Letha Alliman described the event:

> We had a kid that crossed the picket line on a motorcycle. It was a foreman that worked there, his brother, and he was very, very nervous, and he tried to get out everywhere on that motorcycle except going out the drive. So one night, some of us knew he was going over toward Church Hill, so a bunch of us got over there, you know, and he came out on the motorcycle just charging right through all of us. Of course, we run. But this one guy in our bargaining unit run toward him to grab him, but the motorcycle fell over before Mike ever got to him. But the police still charged him for doing great bodily harm or something, you know, and I don't think Mike ever even touched him. But they took him down to the jail, and all of us went down there, hollering.

They eventually went to City Hall and talked to the City Council about how the police were handling the situation and were not treating those on strike fairly. They succeeded in limiting the number of police on patrol to two patrol cars per shift.[80]

Despite the trouble on the picket line, the women stayed strong throughout the eleven-week strike. Letha Alliman was impressed by her union sisters' solidarity, remarking, "It was really amazing to me." They also had the support of the Burlington community and all the union locals in the city. Other locals donated food and money to help support the women while they were on strike. Grocery stores in the community also donated food to the strikers. After ten weeks of limited production, IRC was ready to negotiate a new contract. At first they agreed to all the terms of the contract, but they wanted to accept the women back according to seniority. This became a sticking point, as the women were afraid if they did not return according to seniority the leaders of the strike would lose their jobs. So they voted to reject this proposal. The company eventually capitulated, and the strike ended in mid-July. In the new contract they received a prescription drug plan, four paid holidays, a wage increase, and new pension benefits. The union's relationship with management did not improve immediately after the strike, but that could be because of the plant manager whom, Letha Alliman believed, the company had hired for the sole purpose of breaking the union. He eventually left, and relations began to improve, but as Alliman commented, "Boy, right after the strike it was . . . you could see when you'd go in a room with them. You could just feel it, you know."[81]

Organized and preplanned strikes were the most effective at accomplishing long-term goals, but short-notice wildcat strikes achieved more immediate goals. Material culture became a motivating factor for these types of militant actions and expressed women's priorities. The best example of this was a walkout at Champion Sparkplug during the early 1970s. During the hot summer months women wore shorts to work to stay cool, but management began to think that their shorts were too short and implemented a new dress code that shorts had to be knee length. The outraged women believed the company had no right to tell them what they could wear. Marlene Gerst noted that the women felt like the company had gone too far and that they were pushing them around. When the company asked several women to go home and change because their shorts were too short, the women staged a walkout. They decided that if some had to leave, they were all going to leave. They made picket signs and broke up into groups, with two groups at one end of the plant and a group at the other end, and set up their pickets. They also called their union representative, Bob Roberts, who was in Des Moines, and informed him they were out on strike. He recommended that they return to work, because the wildcat was in violation of the contract.

Marlene Gerst remembered going out and talking with them and convincing them that they needed to go back to work the next day. She commented, "We talked to them, and there I was probably seven months pregnant, and here I am talking to all these girls. I understand. You made your point, you know. They were ready to go back." They went back without getting the dress code changed, and they did comply with the new regulations for a while. As Gerst noted, "Some of them wore the same shorts. They just made big ruffles on the end of them, you know, sewed them on the end of them and came in." Over time the women began wearing shorter and shorter shorts until they were at the length they wanted them, and the company had learned their lesson and never said anything about shorts again. As Gerst stated, the strike illustrated that the women believed the company did not "have the right to dictate to us what we should wear."[82] The wildcat strike at Champion demonstrated that women were willing to fight for their rights and that they were able to use the ideas taught by the union to achieve their workplace goals. Even for something as simple as wearing shorts to work, women were willing to fight for their rights.

## Conclusion

Despite these limited gains in leadership, old notions of women's gender roles trickled into the actions of union women. Some women felt uncomfortable serving or even belonging in the union, fearing that they might be violating the primacy of their husband's leadership in the home. For example, some of the women at Hinson Manufacturing wanted to pay their union dues in cash since they did not want their husbands to know they were in the union.[83] Despite their achievements in unions and the workplace, bridging the divide between home and work remained a precarious endeavor.

Iowa women found ways to embrace their working-class identities while maintaining the balance of patriarchy within the home and the union. While their presence in predominantly male spaces was unsettling to both men and women, unions adjusted to the change. Union locals altered priorities to accommodate female concerns, and women found in the union an institution that could give them job protection. The transition was not easy, as men viewed women as a threat to the primacy of the male breadwinner ideology, and while women were accepted as workers and fellow union members, the fight for full gender equality in the workplace was still a serious challenge. By the mid-1970s, many women in the union were ready for this challenge and began to demand gender equality, using the arguments of the feminist movement to achieve their goals.

# Chapter Six

## Encounters with Feminism

BETTY TALKINGTON, an influential leader in the labor movement in Iowa, began working for the Iowa Federation of Labor in the early 1960s as the Women's Activities Department director. Even though her initial job was mobilizing working-class women across the state into political activism, Talkington eventually became an active leader in the feminist movement. She helped plan and organize countless conferences, workshops, and public hearings throughout the 1970s. She fought for the concerns of working women such as childcare, maternity leave, and better wages. She also served on the Governor's Commission on the Status of Women, was a founding member of both the National Organization for Women (NOW) and the Coalition of Labor Union Women (CLUW), helped plan the state conference for the International Women's Year in 1977, and organized an annual conference for union women in Iowa. She believed that one of her greatest achievements was helping union women form a permanent women's committee in the IFL in 1974. Talkington demonstrated how the identity of working-class women could change over time. Even though she began her career encouraging women to become politically active and support labor through the fulfillment of their gender roles, she ended her career embracing labor feminism and helping union women in Iowa strive for gender equality. She endorsed a working-class feminism that encouraged women to seek justice and equality through the organization of their union and supported women as they fought for a democratic union that listened and responded to their needs and concerns.[1]

As the feminist movement surged in the late 1960s and into the 1970s, its efforts to improve the lives of working women found working-class women eager to achieve equal treatment with men in both the workplace and the union. Union women easily adopted the feminist language of rights, as they were already familiar with the concept of workplace rights. Feminism began to change the ways working-class women thought of themselves as both workers and women. This encouraged women to pursue leadership roles in the union, to break down barriers surrounding higher-paying jobs, and to question the assumptions underpinning sex-based job categories. Even though many women embraced working-class feminism, old notions of women's place remained, especially among women who had embraced unionism in the late 1950s and early '60s. These women had difficulty adjusting to labor feminism because it challenged their notion of what it meant to be a female participant in the labor movement. These types of generational differences on women's proper place led to a divide among working-class women.[2]

The rise of the feminist movement coalesced with the trend of women fighting for equal rights within the factory and the union. These two movements merged to form labor feminism, which focused on the particular needs of working women. Several trends emerged to help women form a working-class feminist identity. First was a series of conferences and committees that helped women learn more about feminism and the needs of working-class women. Second was a movement within the workplace for women to break down barriers and begin fighting for greater equality in the workplace. Last, as women began working in male jobs throughout the factory, they gained a sense of pride in themselves that they could do these types of jobs.

Despite the tremendous move forward in terms of equality, male hostility remained a challenge to many union women. Some women chose to challenge sexism directly, and the fight for equality was fraught with acrimony and discord, but in the end, they were rewarded with more equal treatment in the workplace. The negative consequence of this fight was a split with female union members who would rather maintain the status quo and accept their place within the patriarchal system. These women were fearful of the changes implemented by the feminist movement and clung tightly to the notion of women's work and women's place. Feminism became a symbol of the erosion of the traditional household and the cause of economic uncertainty in the 1970s, the ideology upon which the working class could blame the dramatic social-political changes of the decade. It was the reluctance of these union women to embrace full gender equality that stymied the rapid growth women had achieved in their pursuit of workplace equity.

## The Emergence of Feminism in Iowa

As the feminist movement in the 1970s reached every corner of the nation, feminism permanently altered the landscape of American society. From consciousness raising to workshops and seminars, women worked to end discrimination and achieve equal rights. Women such as Betty Talkington ensured that feminism addressed the needs of working women.

Other feminist groups and leaders turned to union women to help them address the needs of working women. The Governor's Commission on the Status of Women was one of the initial bodies to tackle the growing concern over women working outside of the home. Following the example of President Kennedy in 1961, who set up the President's Commission on the Status of Women, governors across the country established commissions in their own states. Iowa Governor Harold Hughes was the first governor in the state to establish such a commission in 1964. He appointed a handful of women and men, including Betty Talkington, to study the issues of concern for the female population. The commission spent two years on their study and published their first report in November 1964, which included recommendations on employment practices and state labor laws. The following year the committee thoroughly studied the report and set goals for the future, such as increasing occupational training for women and encouraging the state to adopt minimum wage laws and pursue equal pay for equal work.[3] After the initial two years of study, the commission lay dormant until Governor Robert Ray relaunched it in 1970.

Governor Ray picked thirty-two women and men to serve for one year on the commission. After studying issues and holding workshops, Governor Ray's commission made several policy recommendations. They acknowledged that "women feel it is necessary to go back to work as a supplement to the family income" and that once a woman "re-enters the working world she often will stay there." They argued that by the 1970s things had changed: "We are living in a different world today. It has become more natural for women to go back to work. Although her concern is still for the home, she still wants to do well on her job."[4] To accommodate this trend of women in the workforce, the commission created programs for women who wished to return to work and to make the workplace more equitable for them. They pursued multiple avenues for greater equality and looked closely at Iowa labor laws to ensure they were not discriminatory and pressured the state legislature to amend the Iowa Civil Rights Act to make discrimination by sex illegal.[5] They encouraged businesses and federal contractors to stop listing job wanted ads under "male" or "female" classified columns, and published job hiring guidelines for contractors so that they could create personnel policies against discrimination.[6] The commission also strove to increase awareness about maternity and suggested that companies give women "time off from work to have babies" and provide better maternity benefits.[7]

The commission recommended that the governor pursue affirmative action as well, to "reaffirm the State's policy of equal rights for all citizens."[8] Alice McKee, a member on Governor Ray's commission, recalled how difficult it was for women to obtain nontraditional jobs: "They'd work out on highways. You see them all the time now, but then it was rare. They did not provide toilet facilities for them and tried to make it as uncomfortable as they possibly could."[9] McKee noted that companies ostracized women in these jobs by not providing restroom and locker room facilities. Members of the commission believed better affirmative action policies would reduce the difficulty of obtaining these jobs and to improve working conditions for the few women already working in nontraditional jobs.[10] To create more awareness of affirmative action programs and increase the number of women in skilled trades, the commission started a project to educate women and employers about apprenticeship programs. The Iowa Commission on the Status of Women had a workshop in June 1979 at the University of Northern Iowa in Cedar Falls to train women on applying for and receiving apprenticeships. Because the project was initiated in the Waterloo area, the workshops focused on apprenticeships in Waterloo, including opportunities at John Deere. They also informed the attendees of the types of nontraditional job training available at the local community college, Hawkeye Institute of Technology.[11] They sponsored a conference in October 1979 to help both women and employers learn about federal regulations in hiring women as well as equal employment opportunities.[12]

These policy recommendations began to have some effect on workplaces across the state. More businesses were recognizing discriminatory practices against women, but the commission saw several remaining challenges to making an equitable workplace. In its Second Annual Report, the commission recognized that "women, in general, do not know how to file a complaint regarding sex discrimination. It is difficult for them to ascertain, easily, whether their complaint is valid and to know which agency can best assist them."[13] In the Third Annual Report, they requested additional funding to support a study on the underemployment of women and used the data to develop projects that would counteract the factors limiting women's employment.[14] Last, the commission encouraged the state to pursue more research on employed women in Iowa, including the types of jobs they worked, their yearly income, and the size of households.[15]

The other key focus of the commission was to plan several workshops and conferences on the employment of women, including two major workshops on anti–sex discrimination laws and the need for improved and more accessible childcare. In a report, the commission stated, "Women now have legal protection against unfair hiring practices. They now need similar protections against unequal promotion, the lack of opportunity to advance, and unequal pay."[16] The commission formed a subcommittee on employment status and planned a workshop in 1969 to "acquaint employers with the new anti-sex discrimination law, the value of hiring women, and the need for industry-supported day care centers for the children of working women."[17]

The leaders of the project kept track of the women from the Introduction to the Trades workshop to see how they were succeeding in finding jobs. The project leaders at one point wanted the women to be aware of an apprenticeship opening with the bricklayer's union in Waterloo. They contacted the women and suggested they prepare for the opening by "going to the library and contacting the union for any materials that would help [them] anticipate and respond to the . . . interview questions." By following up with the project enrollees, they were able to help women find jobs and also celebrate the successes of some of them. They learned, for example, that one woman got a job working at Chamberlain in Waterloo (a metal-finishing manufacturer), another woman found a job as a plumber, and one woman, according to Louise Lex, the project director, "had the courage to insist on being included in a meeting with her co-workers that was held in the factory men's room."[18]

Besides the Governor's Commission (which later became the Iowa Commission on the Status of Women in the 1970s), other feminist organizations in the state worked to help women achieve greater equality in the workplace. The YWCA worked to promote women's rights and sponsored a meeting with the Iowa Commission on the Status of Women to help women find better employment.[19] The American Association of University Women promoted awareness about discrimination toward women on maternity leave.[20]

Other women's organizations continued to develop programs to help women get better jobs with higher pay. The League of Women Voters (LWV) distributed information stating that Iowa working women only made $.55 for every dollar made by men in 1975. The LWV also pressured the Iowa Civil Rights Commission to do more to address the complaints of female workers. The commission, which was created by the Iowa Civil Rights Act of 1965, had a large caseload of employee complaints, especially on sex discrimination.[21] The LWV believed that the state should grant "the commission power to require employers and unions to keep records that the commission considers necessary in enforcing the law, similar to the power of the EEOC to require record-keeping."[22] By 1972, the Iowa Civil Rights Commission had 238 formal complaints based on sex, 34 percent of all 690 complaints. According to a memo published by the commission in 1972, "the variety of subjects in sex discrimination complaints received by the Commission is almost infinite, covering the broad spectrum of recruitment, hiring, promotion, seniority, benefits, equal pay, protective restrictions, weightlifting, advertising, and so on." The first complaints submitted to the commission regarded discrimination in hiring, job orders, and sex-segregated want ads, but by the early 1970s, according to the commission, "a larger percentage of the Commission's time is being spent dealing with problems in the area of promotion, upgrading, and maternity policies." The practice of hiring women to work in stereotyped female roles also began to grate on women who desired higher-paying jobs within the factory. The commission commented, "This paucity of promotional possibilities and under utilization of women has drawn a good deal of the Commission's attention in the last several months as it seeks to remedy these patterns of exclusion for the whole class of women."[23]

The commission also heard several cases regarding maternity rights. They noted in 1972 that a "current focal point of many sex discrimination charges concerns the rights of pregnant women" and "the vast majority of these decisions have broadly defined the rights of a pregnant woman to work as long as she (in consultation with her doctor) desires to and feels she is able." Employers also had to grant women a reasonable period of leave to have a child and guarantee reemployment on their return. One particular case they heard dealt with the rights of women to maternity benefits under a health care plan. This employer had a health plan that gave coverage only to the wives of the male workers and to women who were the primary wage earners in their families. This left women who were not the primary wage earner without health insurance or maternity benefits. The commission decided that "because pregnancy is unique to women, any health or benefit system which fails to provide pregnancy benefits to all women has a disparate impact on the whole class (women) and is discriminatory."[24]

One of the most important events for the feminist movement in the state was the Iowa conference in honor of the International Women's Year of 1977. Part of the national celebration was a series of statewide conferences where state representatives elected delegates and approved a list of recommendations for the national meeting. State conventions were held from February through July 1977. The Iowa conference was a three-day event in June celebrating women in Iowa. Several of the leading feminists in the state planned the meeting, including Betty Talkington, who ensured that the conference would discuss the concerns of working women. The meeting had four major goals: to promote women's concerns, recognize women's achievements, develop a plan of action, and elect twenty-two delegates to the national conference in Houston. Participants came from across the state, with the largest number (402) coming from Des Moines.[25] Union locals, such as UFCW Local 3, endorsed the conference and sent delegates.[26] The conference sponsored forty-eight different workshops that discussed anything from widowhood to alcoholism, inheritance rights, health care, land use, finding jobs, or employment discrimination. There were also workshops on assertiveness training and job hunting.[27] At the end of the meeting, they suggested that "unions should review the impact on women of all their practices and correct injustices to women" and "called for a pledge of support for the women in unions in Iowa who are working through their unions to improve the status of women and to enhance employment equity for all the women of Iowa through their up-front work in the union movement."[28] The International Women's Year acknowledged all that union women had accomplished for women's rights and provided resources for working women to continue the quest for equity in the workplace.

The feminist movement in Iowa provided working women an important advocate in the fight for workplace equity and fairness. Organizations like the Governor's Commission provided the resources and organizational support as well as institutional momentum for the continual improvement of women's rights. While the feminist movement as a whole often neglected the particular needs and interests of working-class women, it was the collusion of feminism and unionism that would give women the language and the courage to directly challenge sexist male hostility. These skills were essential to break the stranglehold of inequality in the workplace.

## Challenging Male Hostility at the John Morrell Company

The fight against automation in the meatpacking industry illustrated how women applied the principles of unionism and feminism to achieve gender equality in the workplace. It also showed the subtle changes occurring within the female workforce by the end of the 1960s and the growing rift among female workers as some embraced the ideas of feminism while others did not. Women pressured male-dominated unions into fighting for their job rights just as they did to protect men's jobs.

The female workforce in the packing industry suffered a significant number of layoffs in the 1960s because of job mechanization, especially within the female departments. Because of the dual seniority system within the packing industry, with separate tracks for men and women, women could not transfer to men's jobs when laid off because they were not eligible for those jobs. This caused women to remain laid off for months at a time, even if they had several years of seniority. David Hart, a business representative for District 3 of the UPWA, remarked that some of the laid-off women had as much as sixteen years plant seniority.[29] At a UPWA International Convention in 1958, the women's activities committee noted that on average three women were laid off to every man.[30] The International UPWA set up task forces to study how to ameliorate the effects of mechanization in the factory, and by 1960, they began to set aside a fixed percentage of dues for retraining those affected by automation. Betty Talkington, in a speech for the IFL, stated that "the establishment of this fund . . . is a real step forward."[31] They also set up an automation committee to counteract the repercussions of mechanization, and negotiated contract provisions that would allow them to bargain over job combinations and preserve some jobs for women.[32]

The separate seniority lists, which had divided jobs in meatpacking since the inception of the industry, was no longer practical by the 1960s. When women in meatpacking saw men with less seniority still working while they were unemployed, they began to clamor that they could perform several of the jobs the men were doing. After all, during World War II, they had done those exact same jobs. Betty Talkington reminded her audience during a speech for the IFL that "during the war, women served as welders, truck drivers, lathe operators, riveters, blast furnace topmen, railroad section men, and in other occupations previously considered unusual for women."[33] Ethel Jerred lamented that as jobs began being cut in the women's departments such as canning and bacon, the company refused to give them a chance to switch to the kill and cut departments, places they worked during the war.[34] Even though the UPWA made efforts at the national level to address automation, at the local level, many women felt that the union was not doing enough. They began to question the efficacy and equity of the separate seniority system and pushed the union to create a single seniority system. While this fight over automation and separate seniority reached all UPWA locals in the state, it was in Local 1 that the biggest fight erupted, and it was there that women would use the principles of unionism to fight for their rights.

Local 1 had a long tradition of a labor militancy, which crystallized during the struggle to form an industrial union at John Morrell in Ottumwa. Historian Wilson Warren stated that Local 1 had a "militant brand of industrial unionism," which was formed through a generation of organizers who, against great odds, organized a union at Morrell during the 1930s. This older generation of union leaders took a hard-nosed stance toward the company, and their militancy was reinforced by a deep-seated masculinity.[35] This militancy meant protecting men's jobs, since they believed that providing for their families was one of the most important endeavors of the local. Jesse Merrill, president of the local during the 1960s, commented, "Basically . . . I've always been a believer . . . that if the man's head of the house, he should have the job." No one espoused these ideas of working-class masculinity better than Virgil Bankson, the chief steward and prominent leader of the local. Bankson's wife did not work, and neither did he want her to. He believed, "If I couldn't make a living for her, I shouldn't have married her." When Morrell eliminated Harriet Erzinger's job due to technological changes, she went to the union to complain. Bankson told her she should just quit because her husband had a good job and she did not need to work.[36]

During World War II, Bankson argued that the female workers should not earn seniority because then they would want to stay in the plant after the war, and thus rob returning soldiers of good jobs. His ardent beliefs put him into a heated debate with another prominent union member, Ed Filliman, who argued that women paid dues and therefore deserved to earn seniority. Bankson was dismissive of Filliman's arguments, and according to Bankson, the two became bitter enemies. Bankson argued years after the war that women "got seniority, and that created problems, too. I know this. . . . There's more divorces over women taking men's jobs than anything else." Bankson seemed to be threatened by women working, claiming that women started "running around" and that one particular woman got "very independent and bitter" and that "she thought she was a wheel, you know, and she was trying to climb the ladder and get control of the union." Bankson's ideas and attitudes about women's proper place—in the home—permeated the union's leadership and the male culture of the union.[37] Ethel Jerred, who became the leader of the women fighting for their jobs, described this male culture within the union as a "clique" with Bankson in charge, and the other male leaders reluctant to "buck" Bankson's leadership. She described Bankson as "antifemale unless it was his female that he liked at that moment," as Bankson would pick "pets" and play favorites. The bitterness between Bankson and Jerred became deep-seated due to the battle over seniority and colored their recollections of each other. There was much truth to Jerred's description of Bankson's views of women in the workplace, and one could easily surmise that Jerred was the female "wheel" that Bankson described as trying to take over the union.[38]

The women of Local 1, who constituted about 15 percent of the workforce, also embraced the militant tradition of the local. One active female member recalled that "anytime they had a walk-out or a slowdown, anyplace in that plant, the women was right there beside 'em." Women also served as stewards in the bacon and sausage departments and had received rigorous training in the local's militant traditions. Women were not afraid to voice their opinions or to fight for their workplace rights. When they began to be laid off in large numbers they relied on the grievance and steward system. Virgil Bankson's journal was filled with accounts of women and men being laid off during the early 1960s, and the local did make some efforts to try to get women their jobs back.[39] In 1962, the local's *Bulletin* commented that the "Company, in our opinion, is trying to do away with the women in this plant by combining jobs and making them so they think women will give them up. In our opinion this is underhanded and the Union has ways of handling things when a Company starts taking advantage of them." They also changed the wording in the 1962 union contract that would allow the union to bargain over the combination jobs and whether a new job should be done by a man or a woman.[40] They also suggested that new job descriptions be written for each job in the plant, and consequently whether it was a male or female job could be reevaluated.[41] Despite these efforts, the women of Local 1 felt that their grievances were being ignored by Bankson and his cohort. As Ethel Jerred recalled, they wrote grievances on discrimination, but "they were throwed in the wastepaper basket. Because I had another union official over there tell me, who was a secretary in the union, that when I'd walk to the door they was tore up by Virgil Bankson and throwed in a wastepaper basket."[42]

Rowena Hornbeck and Ethel Jerred emerged as leaders of the frustrated women and sponsored informal meetings at each others' homes to discuss strategies to solve the issue of disappearing jobs. Their first plan was to approach the union's leadership and continue to file grievances. They took their complaints to Chief Steward Virgil Bankson as well as the women's committee. While the union held meetings and tried to assuage the fears of the displaced women, the union leadership also failed to take direct action.

The local did sponsor a special meeting in November 1963 to discuss the issues of seniority and decided to form a committee of nine women, one from each department that had suffered from the cutbacks. The committee visited other packinghouses to see how they handled the situation. By the end of November the union wrote a proposal to address the situation. In this proposal, distributed in early December, all male and female jobs were to stay the same, unless jobs were combined. Then the jobs would be posted as dual jobs and would be open to anyone in the department with the highest seniority, regardless of sex. This was supposed to create more jobs within the department, but it still did not solve the women's issues because they were limited to a few departments in the plant. The union held another special meeting in January 1964 to discuss "the women's problems" and seniority issues, but after this, the issues were momentarily dropped. Ethel Jerred and Rowena Hornbeck continued to encourage the women to fill out grievances and attend union meetings to raise their concerns. This was no easy task. As Hornbeck recalled, the men tried to shut out the women at union meetings: "We was always out of order every time we opened our mouths. It was old business, new business, unfinished business, then we was just plain out of order." Even when they were heard, the men's responses were often, "That's the way it is. It's good enough for you."[43]

The status of women's jobs thus remained in limbo until the 1964 Civil Rights Act gave them new hope. Title VII of the act prohibited discrimination on the basis of race and sex in all matters of employment and gave companies until July 1965 to comply with the new rules and regulations. John Morrell and Local 1 began thinking of how to make the necessary changes as early as March 1965 but waited until July to begin taking the Civil Rights Act seriously and put their plant in compliance with the law.[44] Company officials and leaders of the UPWA sat down to find a solution to the problem. Needless to say, they had a difficult time coming to an agreement, and in a series of letters between UPWA representative Dave Hart and company representative Harry Hansel, the plant and the union blamed each other for not finding an official solution to the problem of compliance. They both agreed that the dual seniority system would have to go, and that more jobs should be open to women, but the sticking point was that the union wanted the ability to bargain over the elimination and combination of jobs. The male leaders believed that if they could just stop the elimination of female jobs, then the women would go back to work in female jobs and they could keep male jobs open for men. But the company was absolutely resistant on this point and stated in a letter that they were "unwilling, solely for economic reasons, to give up our right to combine jobs."[45]

By November 1965, they finally agreed to adopt the Swift plan that included plant-wide seniority, department seniority, and the ABC system of job categories. The ABC system broke down jobs according to physical aptitude: A was typically a male job, B was a female job, and C was open to both. The union was still hesitant to adopt this plan because it would put more men out on layoff, since both seniority lists would be combined. The union officials knew that eventually having more men laid off would cause a commotion among the male workforce. They formed a committee composed of company officials and union members, including Ethel Jerred and Rowena Hornbeck. The company gave them a guide on how to categorize each job, and it suggested that jobs should be based on the "normal" capability of men and women to perform the job, and not what was "unusual" or "exceptional," but what the committee believed was average. The handout also included a job content analysis that listed a rating form on physical demands such as handling, body motion, physical effort, and dexterity. Many of these criteria were unspecific, undefined, and highly subjective, and as the committee went through the plant, they often had to guess haphazardly at which category to place each job. Ethel Jerred commented that they "went over department by department, job by job, to see whether it would fit into an A category, B category, or C category." It took an entire month to complete the process. Once it was done, they submitted the report to Dave Hart and Ed Filliman from District 3, and they met with the company to go over the results.[46]

By February, they were ready to restart the plant under the new system. Workers could bring at least five years of seniority into their new departments, and men and women could "bid" on any of the A, B, or C jobs. Ideally, the men would bid on A jobs, the women on B, and either men or women could bid on C. But technically, the workers could bid on any category of job, and once they were on that job, they must be able to physically complete it, or they would be laid off. This stipulation caused serious trouble once the new categories went into effect. The union called a special meeting to explain what was going on and how seniority would be affected, and, as expected, the male members of the union were not happy with this new system. They feared that women would be venturing into their departments, stealing their jobs, and, in essence, eroding their sense of masculinity. As Virgil Bankson remembered it, "There's a lot of men that were bitter toward women coming in their departments and taking jobs away, so there was men that would bid on the B jobs, which were women's." And that was exactly what happened. Embittered men bid on B and C jobs, and since men outnumbered the women, it caused women to bid on A jobs. Some of these jobs were physically demanding, and many women could not adequately perform them, plus a handful of men either sabotaged the jobs or failed to instruct women on how to do them. The same day the new policies went into effect, the women were back out on the street. Ethel Jerred commented that the men intentionally did this and had bragged to her that "they'll be called in at six o'clock Monday but by seven o'clock they'll be back on the street."[47]

Ethel Jerred was furious at what the men had done. She had devoted much of her time and energy over the past two and a half years trying to get women back into the plant and was outspoken at union meetings in defense of the women's rights. Because of her zealous devotion, she began to receive threats from anonymous union members. They threatened her physical safety and even the safety of her young daughter who was in elementary school. Someone smeared ketchup all over the walls of her new home in the country. They also, as Jerred described, dripped "paint . . . all over the new carpeting in the living room. Had ripped the drapes off of the living room." She never reported the damage to the police because, as she put it, she was too proud. "I never did ever tell anybody how much damage was done to the home, because my pride wouldn't let me. Because I wasn't about to let anybody know they were going to get me down."[48]

The company and the union decided to sponsor a meeting at the Holiday Inn in Ottumwa, to try to smooth things over and get the new seniority system to work, but this meeting failed to resolve anything. Jerred recalled that they "walked out of that meeting with nothing." Virgil Bankson recalled a meeting, most likely the same one, where he exploded at Rowena Hornbeck and at Ethel Jerred:

> So this one woman . . . she thought she was really cute. She pointed her finger at me, and she said, "That guy there wants us to go down and drive hogs and cattle." I said, "You don't have no trouble doing it out on your farm, do you?" Cut her feet right out from under her! But she lived on a farm, and she drove the hogs and the cattle. "Yeah," I said, "What's wrong with you driving the hogs and the cattle? You ain't no different than a man. You want a man's job, don't you? What's the matter with that?" And that started it off. Of course, I shut her up. . . . I was cutting up.[49]

Banksson's attitude at this meeting clearly revealed his unwillingness to seriously fight for the women's right to their jobs. After this disastrous meeting, Ethel Jerred decided to meet with Ed Filliman and other leaders in the UPWA to get some help getting the women back to work in the plant. She and her husband drove down to Kansas City to a UPWA conference, and she pulled Filliman aside, telling him they needed to talk. She told him what happened and how the women were back out without any jobs. So Filliman agreed to come back to Ottumwa and try to find a solution. When Filliman arrived, he met fierce resistance from both Bankson and the male members in the local. Bankson recalled that he told Filliman, "Ed, it won't work. These people, you can't keep them from bidding. They got seniority." Filliman replied, "You got to protect these women." Bankson replied, "I know, Ed, but it ain't going to work." Bankson then commented that Filliman "thought he had it all worked out. He was there a week. He went back to Chicago, and he told Ralph [Helstein], he says, 'Everything's worked out.' Very next day she blowed, right on the hog kill [floor]." Indeed, the case was not fixed when Ed Filliman returned to Chicago, and it fell apart on the first day it was implemented. When the system started again on March 28, the *Bulletin*, the local's weekly newsletter, put in a plug for all the workers to follow it, and argued, "We feel they are entitled to these jobs because they are a member of your union and pay the same amount of dues as anyone else. This new program can work if everyone works together." But the program still did not work, and when the women were back on the street for a second time after the installation of the ABC system, they decided to sue.[50] Bankson described what happened: "The men bid all the C jobs, and there wasn't no B jobs. There wasn't nothing left but A jobs, and every time a woman would try to take a job, some bunch of guys would talk an older guy into bumping her out, and the first thing you know, they're all out on the street again. There ain't no jobs for them." Shortly after Filliman's return to Ottumwa to help with the seniority system, he died of a heart attack, and the women of Ottumwa lost a strong advocate of gender equality in the workplace.[51]

After Filliman's death, several women decided to sue the union and the company. Twenty-one women pooled their resources, traveled to Waterloo, Iowa, and hired attorney Dave Dutton to sue the union and the company for their failure to comply with the Civil Rights Act. Dutton was an activist in the civil rights movement in Waterloo and had filed a similar suit for female packinghouse workers at the Rath Packing Plant. The women trusted his decisions, and Dutton filed a suit with the Federal District Court in Des Moines. He sent a notification to the company, the local, and the International UPWA headquarters, listing the egregious examples of how the union and the company failed their female workers. Perhaps the most alarming was how men working in the plant failed to adequately explain the new jobs and warn women of their potential dangers. Dutton stated, "On numerous occasions my clients have barely escaped serious injuries because of this lack of instruction." The women asked for wages back to the July 1965 Civil Rights Act compliance deadline and a guarantee of job protection. The suit did not last long, however, as the judge dismissed the suit because of a technicality. He gave John Morrell Company an extension in order to work out a new system, and by July 1968, the case came to an official close when the court found John Morrell in compliance with the law. The company also agreed to give each of the plaintiffs $450 and reimbursed Dave Dutton for his work.[52]

While the suit came to an uneventful end, the situation in the plant remained tense, and the battle over the ABC system left numerous scars. The women who had filed the suit were harassed by the men in the plant. One of the grievances in the lawsuit stated, "Union members have been officially advised not to speak to them or to associate with them in any way. Signs have been posted that ridicule the plaintiffs and that subject them to scorn and harassment." Harriet Erzinger commented, "Everybody hated each other almost. It wasn't like it was when I first started in 1940." Ruth Morrow, who had met with some of the women earlier, decided not to join the suit because she thought it would be inconvenient. She noted that the women who sued had to walk into the plant together and stay close because of all the harassment. Many women did not agree with the ABC system and liked the old dual seniority system better. Laura Major commented, "I thought it was better the other way." Harriet Erzinger definitely did not want to venture into the male departments. She noted, "I didn't want a man's job. I wanted a job that was easy enough that I could do it. I didn't want to learn how to use a knife. I didn't want to carry a hundred-pound bag . . . or whatever I had to do." Some women lost dear friends over it. Ethel Jerred noted that she and another union-minded coworker, Sue Smith, stopped talking to each other because of their disagreements.[53]

By 1968, however, things in the plant began to settle down, and male workers learned to work side by side with their union sisters. Some even realized that women could be just as good at their jobs as male workers. Dorven Bride commented in the early 1980s, "I think they've accepted them [women] as equal, especially on knives. We got a lot of women using knives . . . and they do a real good job. Matter of fact, they probably do as good a job or better than the men on the knife." Jesse Morrill, who was president of the local at the time, realized that "most women in there was no different than us. They was down there to make a living." He regretted his actions and the union's actions during the time of the suit, even realizing that "they probably had just cause to sue, because we needed something done. We should've sat down and worked something out. The union should've been on their toes and done something about it." Even Ethel Jerred noted the change in attitude from many of the male workers. "In the long run, before it was over, I think the women had proven to the men that we came up there as ladies. There was more women on the cut and the kill and down through there, and they were holding their own."

The battle in Ottumwa illustrates the importance of the male breadwinner ideology within the industrial workplace, and how men and women resisted changes to the gendered hierarchy. In Ottumwa, it took a handful of courageous women to challenge gender inequality at John Morrell to make male workers understand that women were workers too, and just like the men, they wanted the opportunity to earn a living. And much to their surprise, men found women to be good coworkers, capable of performing the same work.[54]

The change to a single seniority list at Morrell was needlessly complicated and acrimonious, as other UPWA locals across the state achieved their goals without major conflict. The historical literature on the move toward a single seniority list has shown how women fought for gender equality and how the struggle pushed them toward feminism. This was precisely what happened at both Morrell in Ottumwa and Rath Packing in Waterloo, but what scholars have glossed over was what happened at Wilson Foods in Cedar Rapids, which saw a very different reaction to the decline of sex-based jobs.[55] Instead of fighting to change the system, many women at Wilson wanted to keep the separate seniority list so that they could keep their current jobs. These women did not want to work in male jobs because they were afraid they would not be able to handle them physically. They stated repeatedly that they had no desire to work a man's job. Wilson began to eliminate women's jobs because of an increase in mechanization at the same time as other meatpacking companies. When it was first addressed by the union in 1955, Darlyn Porter, an instrumental female leader in the local, immediately argued against combining seniority lists. The union's leaders decided that they were going to freeze women's jobs so they could not become men's jobs.[56] By the late 1960s, Wilson did adopt the ABC system of jobs with a single seniority system, but there was not the type of trouble Morrell had. For the most part, the women and men at Wilson kept to their traditional job categories, and the men did not try to push the women out of the plant.

When the courts declared the ABC system in violation of the Civil Rights Act and required meatpacking plants to dismantle it, the women of Local 3 filed a suit with the Equal Employment Opportunity Commission (EEOC) to keep the ABC system—not because they thought the system helped women earn more money, but because it was protecting women by not placing them in male jobs that they could not physically perform. As Elizabeth Smith remarked, "And there was jobs that they put in, women's jobs that really were men's jobs, like hanging bellies. Women had no business hanging bellies . . . when they'd be that big!"[57] This sentiment toward job categories was part of an older system of protectionism established to guarantee women's work and to keep them safe in the workplace.

In 1974 Local 3 tried to re-envision the intent of the ABC system, because it caused women to be removed from female jobs. The issue began because the union believed the company was being unfair in the ham boning department when more men than women were placed on light jobs.[58] President Schriner called a women's committee meeting in July 1974 to resolve their problems. At this meeting, they decided to protect the ABC system. They wrote two resolutions for the IFL annual convention. Women visited other plants to see how they were handling the seniority system, and Esther Kadlec and Marion Klaner visited AMC&BW Local 150 in Dubuque to present their problems with dismantling the ABC jobs. They also visited Quaker Oats and Collins in Cedar Rapids, and according to Marion Klaner, they wanted to see how women at these plants responded to the "equal rights law." The reaction they got was not what Kadlec and Klaner were hoping to hear. Klaner commented, "Their attitude was, gee, what are you guys talking about? Why wouldn't we want to change?" Klaner believed their attitude was different because of the type of work they did, and she knew these women did not have to worry about working a job that was too physically demanding.[59]

Even though the meetings with other locals did not provide the type of support the women of AMC&BW Local 3 were hoping for, they continued their quest to protect the women in the plant. Esther Kadlec wanted an amendment that would "protect the women's jobs in packing plants and heavy industry or any undesirable jobs for women due to difficult, heavy lifting and dangerous aspects in these industries and plants throughout the country. With ABC job classifications and proper policing of all jobs, we feel that in the packing plants and other heavy industries, this procedure is more non-discriminatory than without these classifications. Women will be eliminated from these plants and industries because they are unable to perform these jobs."[60] Both the women's committee and the executive board endorsed this proposal. Kadlec asked for the support of Dave Hansel, a district representative to the AMC&BW, commenting, "We hope to enlighten your members and acquire your support in this amendment that we are striving to have presented and passed in Congress."[61] They also wrote to the EEOC to try and reinstate ABC jobs, and there was unanimous approval. They wanted an EEOC representative to sit and discuss the ABC jobs in heavy industry, and the EEOC officials came to the plant in November to observe the situation. After this the EEOC did not pursue the case any further, and the ABC system remained obsolete. This case demonstrated that in some situations women did not want to challenge the separate job category system because they viewed the job protection it provided more beneficial than a three-tiered system.[62]

What caused such a different reaction between Morrell's and Wilson's workforces over the decline of female jobs? One explanation could be the acute sense of masculinity cultivated at Morrell, which led to dire misunderstandings between male and female workers. Even though many men at Wilson had sexist ideas about women working and did not support equal pay for women, they still believed women had the right to keep their jobs on the basis of seniority. Wilson decided to freeze all women's jobs, and the local would screen any new job that the company set up to determine whether it was a male or female job. The men at Morrell saw the female workers as a threat to their job security and a source of erosion of their position as head of the family.[63]

The perceived threat to men's right to work turned into a hysteria that was directly fed by the cult of personality around Virgil Bankson. He had established a position of authority within Local 1 through the early union battles at John Morrell, and few members of the local wanted to cross him. His rigid ideas of the patriarchal household made it virtually impossible for women to deal rationally with the decline of female jobs. Bankson's belief that women should stay at home and their husbands should be working had a direct influence on the rest of the male membership and made them unwilling to adequately address the loss of female jobs. This type of intense masculinity and sexism pushed women into suing the local and into the embrace of feminism. Women who did not confront this type of intense sexism were more likely to maintain their traditional belief that women could not perform men's jobs and wanted to remain in female job categories. Women at Wilson believed that separate seniority gave them job protection and physical safety. This old ideology of protectionism meant more to them than achieving full equality in the workplace.

## Betty Talkington and the Women's Committee to the IFL

The UPWA was not the only union to deal with acrimonious fallout over women's pursuit of workplace rights. It was embedded in the IFL as well. When the Women's Activities Director, Betty Talkington, attempted to create a women's committee to the IFL, she faced a wall of male misogyny among the prominent labor leaders. One of her proudest achievements was finding a way around the blockade of male hostility and getting a resolution passed during the IFL's annual convention. It took ingenuity and courage to work around Hugh Clark, a leader among the building trades unions in Dubuque and the long-serving president of the IFL. He was quite sexist and outspoken in his views about women's place in society. When Talkington and a handful of women first approached him about creating a women's committee in 1972, he was incredibly resistant to the idea. In fact, Talkington described his reaction as completely "horrified." She was undeterred, however, and gathered a handful of women to convince their union to propose the resolution to the convention. When the resolution landed on the president's desk, Talkington commented that "the roof almost went off the building." Clark told her that "these resolutions wouldn't pass and he just didn't want to waste the convention's time or his time as chair of the meeting trying to discuss these things." Clark then tried to kill the resolution by giving it to the convention committee with a "don't pass" response. He also threatened her job, telling her that if she "worked for these resolutions when they hit the floor" that she was gone. She would lose her job. So she gathered her female friends and told them what happened and what to do, but with the "don't pass" report from the committee and very few female delegates to the convention, the resolution failed. Talkington then felt that her hands were tied and that she dare not press the issue, but in 1974, several prominent union women wanted to try again.

This time Talkington took a behind-the-scenes role and had very little direct involvement. There was also more help from male union members, so the resolution had more broad-based support. When she went to the convention, she knew "the boss was madder than hell" at her, and he assigned the resolution to a committee he knew he could influence so he could tell them to kill it. When the women and men started coming to her for advice about how to get the resolution out of the committee without a "Do not pass" stamp, she wanted to remain under the radar, telling them, "I have to stay clear of it. I just can't stand the strain." But when the committee did mark the resolution "Do not pass," she advised them to get a committee to bring it out. So they worked on the committees until they found one willing to bring the resolution out on the floor to be voted on.

Betty Talkington. Louise Rosenfield Noun Papers, Iowa Women's Archives, University of Iowa Libraries, Iowa City.

Talkington recalled, "When the chair of the convention committee took the podium and read the resolution, the president immediately left the platform, and I saw him go from vice president to vice president, and I knew what was happening." The president tried to convince all of the vice presidents to vote against it, but those in favor of the resolution took aside each vice president to pressure them to vote for it, and by "the time the debate came, there were about eight people for the resolutions, and three stood firm against them." They finally won their standing women's committee for the IFL. It thereafter met annually at the convention with the members appointed by the president.[64]

But the committee continued to have difficulties dealing with Hugh Clark, as he was incredibly dismissive. Clark asked five women to join the committee, with Erma Wiszmann, a leader in the Communications Workers in America (CWA) in Davenport, as president.[65] In 1976 Wiszmann wanted to call a meeting in the spring to discuss the Equal Rights Amendment (ERA) and put together some questions for political candidates wanting a Committee on Political Education (COPE) endorsement. She also wanted to have some input on the IFL's annual women's conference in July.[66] Clark responded with a condescending letter that he felt a meeting in May was not necessary. Betty Talkington was handling all the preparations for the annual women's conference, and all the COPE endorsements were handled by the central bodies, according to the COPE rules and regulations. He also did not understand why they needed to discuss the ERA since it was "resolved in the state of Iowa sometime ago." His main reason, however, for not wanting the meeting was "the cost of calling the people into Des Moines. Our budget is very limited due to the unemployment that many of our local unions are facing, and that curtails our income on per capita tax." He concluded that "any problems that have to be resolved by our Women's Committee can be taken care of when they meet . . . at the convention."[67]

Wiszmann was not going to be that easily dismissed and responded to Clark informing him that even though she had been "involved in labor for a long number of years," she needed "to know things, like, exactly what is the process by which a political candidate gets a COPE endorsement." She was unsure if all the central bodies came together to decide or if this was done at the convention. She wanted to know, "How does a member or committee get their views considered to possibly be included as part of questions for screening?" Most likely, she wanted to ensure that COPE was taking into consideration working women's rights when endorsing a candidate. She also wanted to clarify that the committee wanted to work out their viewpoint on the ERA because there was an effort in the state legislature to rescind their ratification. Even though Iowa was the fourth state to ratify the ERA, she remarked, "I am concerned because nationally on this, we are so close, yet so far. I believe, for example, a candidate's attitude to ERA ought to be a question to which he, or she, must respond on favorably to gain COPE endorsement even though our State has long ago passed it."[68] Even though female labor leaders had succeeded in getting their women's committee to the IFL, getting the leaders of the IFL to take them seriously was still an uphill battle. Over time, however, the committee became an important organization promoting union women's concerns.

## Labor Feminism

The women's committee to the IFL was one of many accomplishments for labor women in Iowa. Scholars have called this combination of gender and workplace rights labor feminism, and it was an instrumental force of change in the industrial workplace. The most powerful voice for labor feminism was the Coalition of Labor Union Women (CLUW), a nonpartisan organization formed in 1974 to help working-class women voice their concerns. Treva Doggett, a founding member of CLUW, stated that the organization was intended to "deal with the specific problems facing union women in particular and working women in general." During the founding conference there were thirty-four workshops discussing how to create an organization and set up principles and guidelines. Doggett stated that "the primary purpose of the national Coalition is to unify union women in a viable organization to determine, first, common problems and concerns, and second, to develop action programs within the frame-work of our unions." Some of the main areas of concern were unionizing unorganized women, getting women more involved in their union, and better affirmative action policies in the workplace.[69] Several women in Iowa attended the founding conference, including Esther Kadlec and Dorothy Cooper of AMC&BW Local 3 in Cedar Rapids and Erma Wiszmann, who was president of CWA Local 7117 in Davenport.[70] Wiszmann recalled that it was "just a tremendous experience." She went back to the Quad Cities and tried to start the first local chapter of CLUW in Iowa, but even though her local had sponsored nine women to attend the national CLUW conference, she had a difficult time getting enough support for a local chapter. The first local chapter actually started in Cedar Rapids, under the direction of Pat Marshall, who was then president of the International Brotherhood of Electrical Workers (IBEW) Local 1362 at Collins Radio. Both IBEW Local 1362 and AMC&BW Local 3 had a large number of female members, which made it possible to open a CLUW chapter. Wiszmann said she was "green with envy" that she was not able to get the first chapter open.[71] The policy measures pursued by feminist organizations like CLUW had a direct impact on the workplace, and it helped women break down sex-based job categories in the factory.

Betty Talkington, who supported CLUW and other feminist initiatives, started an annual conference for union women beginning in 1972. The conference was an all-day event held in Des Moines, and the cost was $5 to attend. The day's events included coffee and rolls, a luncheon, and special speakers. At the first conference they had Mary Manning, from the U.S. Department of Labor, Women's Bureau, come and talk, along with Jeanne Lambie, a business representative for AFSCME, Helen Hensler, cochair of the Wisconsin AFL-CIO's Women's Committee, and Catherine Conroy, a representative from the CWA.[72] The next year, the format was the same, and it still cost $5 to attend. In 1973, they were able to get Marguerite Gilmore, the chief regional director of the Women's Bureau, to come and talk. They hoped that at this second conference women would have a chance "to learn more about the structure of unions and their allied organization and the laws concerning working men and women."[73] The third conference, in May 1975, was planned by the newly formed women's committee. Unions across the state encouraged women to attend the women's conference and often sponsored women to attend. For example, AMC&BW Local 3 in Cedar Rapids sponsored a carload of female members to attend in 1973.[74]

The IFL was not the only organization to sponsor women's conferences, as the University of Iowa Labor School held several workshops for working women. In 1975, the University of Iowa sponsored a workshop on discrimination against women and minorities, stating, "This conference will present to union members the latest information on court cases, arbitration awards and legal interpretations of specific provisions covering all aspects of discrimination. This two-day conference will be divided into 'discrimination and women' on March 18 and 'discrimination and the minorities' on March 19."[75] In April 1977, the Labor School sponsored a large Trade Union Women's Seminar, and many women attended. AMC&BW Local 3 sent two members to the seminar, and Nadine Klaner later reported that it was an "excellent seminar with well-versed speakers."[76] The seminar discussed women workers, politics, and the law, and it had workshops on women in labor history, "organizing women workers, and women workers and their families." A brochure for the seminar stated that it would "help working women arm themselves with up-to-date accurate information concerning their current status in the world of work, politics, and both as individuals and as union members."[77]

The government provided a tremendous boost to gender equality in the workplace by implementing affirmative action policies. These policy changes forced employers and some trade unions to change their apprenticeship programs to ensure that women were being admitted. Clinton Corn, which had a long history of excluding women within their plant, finally adopted affirmative action policies. The state pushed the company to achieve 20 percent female participation, and to achieve this they needed to change the qualifications for the apprenticeship programs. They developed a point system so that all minorities received extra points on apprenticeship applications, but they only gave them out when "apprenticeship statistics indicated an underutilization of minorities and females."[78]

Despite Clinton Corn's notoriety for sex discrimination, after the Civil Rights Act and the government's policies of affirmative action, the company had to begin hiring women. Because of Executive Order 11248, which went into effect June 12, 1978, Clinton Corn had to provide the government with statistical information about the number of women in the plant. They also had to disseminate more information to organizations to increase the number of female employees.[79] By 1976 and 1977 more women were working in the plant, and they even had enough women to form a women's bowling league called the Honeybees.[80] The process of adding women did experience some hiccups along the way. Michael Krajnovich, a leader of the American Federation of Grain Millers Local 6, noted that the company tried to get around the order to hire more women:

> They had some quality control labs in the plant, so they hired two or three women and put them in the quality control lab and said, "We got women working in the plant." In fact, the personnel manager told me when I was [the union's] business agent, back in 1976, that he was going to do his utmost, his very best, to keep women out of the plant. He absolutely would not hire a woman to work out in the plant until the federal government absolutely demanded that he do so. He was going to do everything legally and everything possible to keep women out of the plant. In 1977 the federal government came down there and did a complete check of personnel records and where the people were

working, and demanded that you [the company] hire women into the plant the next time you hire, or go to court. That's when they started hiring women in later 1977.[81]

Even though Clinton Corn began hiring, women often did not stay long, because foremen and male coworkers made it tough on them. Because of how the seniority system worked, women started in some of the less desirable jobs in the plant. Krajnovich commented, "It was a little harder for a woman to, say, work the chute job in the sugar house, where you're catching hundred-pound bags off of a chute and walking down to the end of the boxcar and loading the boxcar with hundred-pound bags. They used to sort of chuckle about putting a woman out there and watched her get knocked on her hind end with that hundred-pound bag, then walk off the job, you know."[82] The company also encountered other problems due to the increased number of women working. They had to change their maternity leave policy and provide more maternity benefits on their insurance plan. They also addressed the issue of not having showers for women in the starch department of the plant.[83] By 1979 there were around fifty female employees out of a workforce of 720. According to Krajnovich, the opening of Clinton Corn to women was a real boon to female workers in the community, as the company provided high-paying jobs.[84]

The new affirmative action policies in the early 1970s also allowed women to get jobs in other factories where they had been previously excluded. Women began working in greater numbers in farm equipment and grain milling. More women began working at J. I. Case in Burlington. As William Brown recalled, when he first started working at Case in 1962 there were very few women there, but by the mid-1970s the company began hiring more women due to the changes recommended by the EEOC.[85] These changes also encouraged women to push through barriers within the workplace and begin working on jobs that were previously assigned to men. At the Amana Refrigeration plant, women started working in areas where previously only men worked. Tom Larkin said, "[Women] worked everywhere that we worked. By the time I got there they made no distinction between men and women. You were hired, and if there was an open job they just put you in there." Even though women began working in the stock department, there were still very few electricians, maintenance workers, or tool and die workers. Larkin mentioned that a few women worked "in construction as outside laborers. And an outside laborer is basically a utility person. They do whatever needs to be done." If a woman wanted to work in these male-dominated jobs, she would have to prove that she could handle the work. Larkin commented,

> If a woman wanted to get in there, she'd have to be real good at what she did, because there are no women down there in those positions right now, and she would get a magnifying glass. You know, everything that she did would be scrutinized, and the first time she made a mistake it would be like, "See that, there you go." So it would take one person who was great at what she did to go through that. . . . It would make it a lot easier for somebody else to do.[86]

Women took advantage of these changes in the workplace. Darlene Croft began working in male jobs at Wadco Foods in Estherville in the 1970s. She felt, "If I could do the work and handle the work, I was gonna do it. As long as I could handle it, why I was gonna get paid for it. I feel if I can do the work then I'm entitled to get paid for it just as much as that man is."[87] She was able to prove to herself and her coworkers that women could perform the heavy jobs in the plant.

Cheryl Benson recalled the difficulties she had in breaking into a male-dominated department within Ideal Manufacturing. She recounted that all job openings in the plant were to be posted and then workers could bid on them, and the worker with the highest seniority got the job. After working there for six months, she decided she wanted to try working on a punch press, which she thought would be more interesting than packing, which was her job at the time, and working a press paid a lot more. She kept waiting for a job opening to be posted so she could bid on it, but no opening was posted. When she noticed that a couple of men had been hired to work on the presses and no job bid had been posted, she took the issue to the president of the union. The president told Benson that they were not posted because "nobody wanted them." Benson replied, "Well, you can't do that. . . . You can't give my rights away without my permission." So she informed the plant supervisor that she wanted a job working on a punch press. He told her no one wanted those. She responded, "I do, and I'm somebody, and I want the job bid or I'll file a grievance." So they started posting the jobs, and it took her four or five bids to get the job because of all the women bidding on it.[88] Even though Benson was proactive in breaking down barriers, other women at Ideal also began to embrace the message of equality. Benson remembered one occasion when they posted a job opening for a maintenance man: "Somebody went up and crossed off *man* and put *person*. Everybody in that plant was just absolutely positive that I was the one who had done that. . . . To this day I'm sure that everybody thinks I was the one who did that—they would not believe me when I told them that I did not change that name up there. And I never did find out who did it."

Women at Hinson Manufacturing in Waterloo also fought to keep their jobs when the company purchased an adjacent building and tried to hire only men to work at the new plant. The company argued that women were not qualified for these jobs, but the union fought them, arguing they had the right to work there. Hinson used every excuse not to allow women to work there, even saying that they did not have rest room facilities for women so they could not transfer to the new building. The women filed grievances that went all the way to arbitration. When the company finally capitulated and hired a woman to work in the new plant, they did not pay her the same rate as the men. According to Ilene Christianson, the company had "all kinds of excuses" not to pay women the same rate as men, saying things like "she wasn't putting out," but once they actually observed a woman on the job, they realized that women were keeping up with the rate. The women eventually went out on strike to get the company to take their concerns seriously. Ilene Christianson commented that the women fought for equal rights, "because they [the company] figured a man could do more work than the women. But that is not true, because I've seen a lot of women that can outdo a man sometimes out there."[89]

These changes came about because of the Civil Rights Act, affirmative action policies, and proactive women. They benefited men as well. At Amana it was company policy that a man's spouse would be covered by his insurance, but a woman's husband was not covered. Eunice Evans began to argue for a change in the contract to insure her husband, who could no longer work due to ill health. She recalled, "[During] one contract negotiation, we wanted insurance for our spouses. Men could have it for women, but women couldn't have it for men. And so after the contract was through and they would not even consider it, I wrote a grievance. Immediately we got it. I wrote the grievance on discrimination." Evans was quite proud of her achievement and was dismayed when the company made a proposal as if it was their idea. She commented, "When it [the contract] came out and they gave the insurance to the women for their husbands, it was a company proposal. It was not ever said it was an answer to a grievance. I had the paper to prove that it was."[90]

Men had various reactions to the changes in the workplace. Usually their initial reaction was fear that women would take their jobs. Florence Jones noted that at Hormel in Fort Dodge, the men "[got] scared thinking that the women [were] going to take their jobs."[91] The men also wanted to make sure women could do the jobs they were assigned; consequently women had to prove that they could indeed handle them. Dorven Bride thought that at Morrell, they would take the easy part of a job, the "gravy" part, and give it to the women, and then make the men do the difficult aspect. When he worked at Hormel, which opened in Ottumwa after Morrell closed in 1973, the women had to perform all aspects of the job. He commented, "And I can tell you this, that when a woman bids on a job down here, if they're incapable of handling that job, they are disqualified. They don't take the gravy part off and give it to a woman and say, well, here's a man, you do the hard part. No . . . it's equal down here. If they bid on a job, they got to do that job, all the aspects of it." Over time, however, Bride grew to appreciate women's hard work and their skill in handling some of the difficult jobs. "We got a lot of women using knives down here, and they do a real good job. Matter of fact, they probably do as good a job or better than the men on the knife. They learn how to keep a knife sharp, and they do an excellent job. . . . We got them boning hams. We got them on the kill floor using knives, and they do a good job." Even though he came from John Morrell and fought against the ABC system, Bride realized that women could work just as hard as men, and he changed his attitude. "You know, the generation has growed out of that. I think the generation shows us today that women does a lot of things that they didn't do years ago."[92]

The changes occurring in the workplace during the 1970s affected the union as well. As female membership increased, women began to serve in more leadership positions. In the seventeen central labor bodies affiliated with the IFL, there were two female presidents in 1980. Susan Rhum was president of the Des Moines County Labor Council in Burlington, and Marian Morton was president of the North Central Labor Council in Mason City.[93] Bev Clinton recalled that she "was the first woman on the executive board in this local, and it's an old local, and the first woman of course who was ever president."[94] Marlene Kruger had the privilege of being the first female to give a report at the Iowa State Machinists Council. "I remember going to the state delegation one time, and I got up to give a delegate report, and when I sat down they all clapped and yelled, and I tried to figure out what I said that set these people off, and they were all clapping. I was the first woman to ever give a delegate report at a state Machinists Council. There had never been any others. There had been women there—but they had never had another woman that had given a delegate report."[95] Even though women made advances into leadership positions, women still had to deal with men's sexist attitudes. Bev Clinton endured plenty of sexism while she served in IAM Local 831, noting that the local "was an old-timer men's little cliquey league . . . and you find that men still don't think a woman's place is in the union. That's hard to say and hard to believe in this day and age, but I still think the woman has a hard time being a leader in a local. Maybe it's just harder in this local 'cause it was mostly men." Even though she was president of the local, Clinton still had to put up with little comments regarding her "proper" place, as men would say, "in a teasing way, but they'll say, 'Oh, that's women's work. You do it, Bev.' But it runs a raw nerve sometimes. It's not just women's work—it's all our work."[96]

By experiencing these changes in the workplace and the union, many women did embrace labor feminism. Women such as Carol Carter in Burlington, Ethel Jerred in Ottumwa, Doris Peick in Cedar Rapids, and Erma Wiszmann in Davenport all pioneered leadership roles and fought against gender discrimination in the workplace and the union. Other women celebrated their victories in being able to keep a single seniority job and not see it lost to men. Ethel Jerred was proud that she and her fellow workers could work on men's jobs and prove that they were hard workers, they could do the work, and still behave like ladies. After the long, hard-fought battle in UPWA Local 1, Jerred believed, "The women had proven to the men that we came up there as ladies. When we run that clock at night, we were going to be ladies." The women of Local 1 also proved to the Morrell supervisors that, as Jerred commented, "Women weren't up there looking for trouble.

. . . We proved to the company and the union that the women could go up there and do this."[97] Jerred, despite the challenges along the way, felt proud that she could work a man's job while maintaining her femininity, respectability and dignity.

## The Limits of Feminism

Not all women embraced the language of equal rights or the feminist movement. In fact, most women shunned the feminist movement and did not consider themselves feminists. Many women had misunderstandings about the movement and blamed "women's liberation" for the decline of female jobs in the factory. Carol Carter noted that at Champion, women were dissatisfied with the eradication of separate seniority lists and sex-based job categories. She believed many of the older women were "threatened by change, in the sense that they don't understand it. I think there was a feeling that women perhaps were going to be forced onto jobs that they could not handle, and then they'd be dismissed. Some of the women even still to this day comment about, 'Well, this is what women's lib has done to us,' you know." She did try to explain that this was to protect them and promote equality in the workplace, but women were still resistant to the change.[98] Marlene Gerst was one Champion worker who was adamant that there were no feminists working at the plant. She believed that women were equal and that women should have equal pay for equal work, but said, "I don't think that women are downtrodden in the plant, because I don't think that women are. They're not being treated any different." She believed because Burlington was not a "big city," they did not have "women's lib" or a strong feminist movement. She also believed that women did not want to work on men's jobs, and "men really thought it was not very manly to work on the women's jobs." She believed strongly that women "really don't want to do the jobs that have been historically men's jobs, because they've been the heavy jobs, dirty jobs. They take skill that most women don't have. . . . It's hot and it's dirty and it's oily, and they just don't really want to go back into those jobs. And I really think, unless a woman is very, very mechanically inclined, those jobs that historically were men's jobs just aren't desirable jobs for women." She also thought that women were not mechanically inclined and it was difficult for women to work on these jobs. "I don't think—and maybe I could get crucified by some of my fellow women workers—I just don't think the women have the ability mechanically. Now, there's exceptions to every one of those rules, but I wouldn't want to go back there and work with a mic [*sic*]. Some I'm sure don't know the difference between an Allen wrench and a screwdriver. You know, we're just not mechanically equipped to do it."[99]

When job categories broke down at Sheller-Globe in Keokuk, many women switched to the men's jobs. According to Carrie Azinger, men worked on big presses, and women started working on them to make more money. Betty Noe was adamantly against a woman working on the presses, unless she could prove that she could do it. Noe could never work on a press because she was too short. She commented, "Wouldn't that be swell for me to say, short as I am, because I want that almighty dollar, I'm not going to get laid off. I'm going to take that pressman's job. Now that is ridiculous." She thought that some of the women were "paying through their nose" working on such jobs: "Most of those women have female problems and hysterectomies. Every piece of their gut is taken out of them, just like me. They're not paying through the nose when they're young, but they're paying through the nose when they get older. I have had nine major operations." Women like Noe believed that if a woman did not want to take a job she could not handle, she could choose to be laid off instead. Noe commented, "It was more or less a peaceful transition, although I wasn't very happy about some of those women taking those mold jobs, because I knew from experience that eventually it was going to hurt them."[100]

Women in meatpacking also seemed to resent the change from a separate seniority system to a single system. Mickey Lockhart noted that when she started working at Wilson Foods in Cedar Rapids, "You knew when you came in there, that was a man's job, this was a women's job. In fact, I'll tell you, I kind of like it that way." She believed that when feminist groups wanted to demolish sex-based job categories, they must have been thinking about office work, because "nobody in their right mind would think that a woman should haul beef or something like that. That's ridiculous, some of them jobs. You know, they are jobs that men can do better than women, and there are jobs that women can handle better than men." As far as trying to make a more equal workplace, she "never was for it."[101] According to Marion Klaner, the women in her department did not try to challenge the men. They never had a female on a machine job. They felt "that it [wasn't] a job that we want[ed] to do." Even though she did have a license to drive a fork truck if she wanted to, she never exercised her seniority to get those jobs. Mary Ashlock, who worked at Armour in Mason City, also opposed the eradication of separate seniority, because there were many jobs in the plant that women could not do. "There wasn't very many of them that took advantage of it. A few of them did. A few of them even tried boning [hams] here in the later years, but the majority of the older ones, they didn't. They were satisfied with the jobs that they had."[102] Harriet Erzinger was pretty insistent that she did not want to work a man's job: "[I wanted] a job that was easy enough that I could do it. I didn't want to learn how to use a knife. I didn't want to carry a hundred-pound bag or a two-hundred-pound bag, or whatever I had to do. Or push a truck loaded with meat. No way."[103] Marion Klaner even believed, "Women are the weaker sex, and they are built different than men for their systems what they can endure, when it comes to a lot of lifting," and she had observed that "the women that done more of the strenuous jobs always ended up usually with a hysterectomy or something where . . . a man don't have to go through that."[104]

It almost appeared as if some women resented the feminist movement. When Marlene Kruger was asked whether she was a feminist, she immediately responded, "No, not really. I'm not a NOW person. I'm not with the National Organization of Women. There are some issues that cross my religious background where I have never felt comfortable with the issues."[105] Harriet Erzinger stated that she was not a "women's libber": "I don't believe in women doing heavy work, jobs that men have always done, and I still think that men should be breadwinners."[106] Many women were also reluctant to endorse the ERA. As Erma Wiszmann commented when she tried to get her local to become more involved in the fight for the ERA, "We support it because I'm president, but the heart isn't in it."[107] Doris Peick also noted, "Labor has not taken too great an active role, in my estimation." Even she was nonchalant about it: "I have been liberated. I have equal rights." She did support the ERA, but not actively: "I have not had time to become a participant in NOW. . . . I support financially. I donate. I donate whatever that I can because my time has always been entrenched majorly in the political scene."[108] According to Viola Juehring, the ERA was not an important issue with the women at Clinton Garment Company. She felt that she could do anything she wanted: "I'm free. Maybe some of them have husbands that dominate them, but those are personal things." She also commented, "[I could have] any job I want, but who wants to work in a coal mine or go off and drive a big truck, go up on a telephone pole? We talk about women's work and men's work. That isn't women's work. Why should we take a job away from a man?"[109]

## Conclusion

Many women found it difficult to conceive of the need for the ERA or even for a feminist movement. These women, who had worked their entire lives in working-class jobs, did not understand the need for gender equality in the workplace. Whether it was in the meatpacking industry, where they had worked in comfortable women's jobs, or in an apparel plant like Clinton Garment Company, women could not see how they were limited. What accounts for this discrepancy? The blame could fall on the union for not embracing feminism sooner or for failing to educate women on gender equality. While it may be easy to focus on the organizational shortcomings of labor and feminist groups, I argue that the discrepancy lies in the cultural grounding of midwestern women. As I have shown throughout, in the Midwest female industrial workers saw themselves within a patriarchal family unit. These fundamental building blocks created the foundation for community and social life. Women were taught from childhood that they needed to be ladies, that men's and women's work were divided, and a woman needed to stay in her place. If she strayed outside, she risked scorn, rejection, and disgrace. The idea of being a lady was so ingrained in cultural norms and values that they simply could not fathom demanding equality. As a new generation of female workers entered the workplace throughout the 1980s, who came of age during the height of the feminist movement, they began to accept and embody the values of equality. It took a new generation of female leaders to push at the hidden structures of inequality and insist on their equality.

# Epilogue

In 1981, a new Republican president was sworn into office, and as Ronald Reagan moved into the White House, a new beginning dawned in America. Reagan's presidency is easy to identify as a marker for the changes in the social, economic, and political landscape of America. Iowa was not immune to these changes, and the state experienced a decline in industry, a new conservative state government, and a renewed emphasis on family values. In industry's continual search for cheap labor, new opportunities opened in Mexico and the Southwest, and industry moved once again. Factories that had peppered the landscape for thirty years began to close, leaving vacant and desolate hulls to rot in overgrown lots. As factories left, so too did the strong union locals. Remaining unions faced an increasingly hostile environment in the state government. And as political conservatism took root in the state, so too did a renewed focus on family values. The antifeminist movement soon labeled feminists and feminism as a direct threat to American values and American families. These sweeping changes ushered in a new historical period in Iowa history.

As industries began to close their factories, women who had worked diligently for these companies lost their jobs and began to search for other types of work. The process of deindustrialization and capital decentralization changed the landscape of Iowa and depleted many towns of their well-paying jobs. The industries that stayed often decreased wages and laid off those in higher-paying job categories. For example, IRC in Burlington closed its doors in 1983 and moved its plant to Corpus Christi, Texas. The women in Burlington found it difficult to find new jobs that paid the wages they had once earned, and they lost the valuable union protection they had fought so hard for. Letha Alliman lamented when the factory closed, "You know, Iowa workers are good workers, smart workers, and I think they have used us to get things started and then just moved it somewhere else where it's cheaper."[1]

The new economics also had a detrimental effect on the model of meatpacking practiced by Morrell, Rath, and Wilson. New models emerged that took processing plants closer to the farmers and then depressed wages and kept the unions out. Iowa Beef Packers used methods that were brutal to the workers, paid them little, and then sold meat at lower prices to consumers. Consequently, the older established packers could not remain financially solvent. One by one, the old packinghouse giants closed: John Morrell in 1973, Rath Packing in 1985, and Wilson in 1990. The employees of Rath Packing attempted an innovative strategy of employee ownership of the company, but the old model of packing could not be sustained, and the employee-owned company was eventually closed.

The political landscape in Iowa also changed when Terry Branstad became Iowa's longest-serving governor, ushering in a new political era of conservatism in the state. The state's moderate politics began to swing toward the right, and a pro-business, antiunion approach took over Iowa's capitol. There was also a strong reaction to the feminist movement. Even though Iowa was one of the first states to ratify the Equal Rights Amendment, there was a conscious effort in the 1980s to de-ratify the amendment. Phyllis Schlafly's anti-ERA movement took root in Iowa, and many of those who already opposed feminism grew more vocal. As the antifeminist voices became louder, feminists were labeled radical and dangerous, attempting to tear apart the fabric of American society by demanding equal rights. Americans became afraid of the rapid changes to the order of domesticity and the supremacy of the male breadwinner, and hysterical claims of women attempting to create a matriarchal society by oppressing men spread like a virus.

What the antifeminists failed to take into account were the permanent changes in the economic and social structures of the American family in the postwar period. After 1950, women started working and, unlike after the war, they did not stop. By 1990, 62 percent of women were in the workforce, a 30 percent increase from 1950 when only 30 percent of women were counted in the workforce.[2] Women liked working. They appreciated the freedom earning their own wages brought them, and providing for their children became a core part of their identity. The single-income household was part of the past and would remain in the past.

Women's roles within the patriarchal family shifted, and they became partners with their spouses in the new dual-income households. The socioeconomic changes of the postwar period created opportunities for women, but the core structure of the patriarchal household remained. Women did not see themselves as warriors for women's rights. Far from it; they wanted to support their families and fulfill their ethic of work within the family unit. Many of the women discussed in this study became fearful of feminism. Although they had a fundamental misunderstanding of what feminism was, they still did not want to challenge the system of patriarchy. As Marlene Kruger stated, "Most of the people who know me don't consider me [a feminist]—I'm not a NOW person. There are some issues that cross my religious background where I have never felt comfortable with the issues."[3] By placing women within the sociological unit of the family, we can make sense of their reaction to this seeming dichotomy of work and feminism. The rural, midwestern ethos of doing one's part and fulfilling one's responsibility to the family and the community was prevalent in Iowa society. As the structure of the farm family and the economic demands of the postwar period shifted, the definition of women's duties also changed. Women now saw their family responsibility in a different light, and they believed it was their duty to bring in additional income.

Seeing women within this family structure and placing it within the context of a rural, midwestern culture explains working women's aversion to feminism. Yes, women should receive equal pay for equal work, but women should not be forced to work in male jobs. Men should have the more physically demanding jobs, earn higher wages, and maintain leadership roles in the union. But not all women felt this way, and here lies the fracture. As women learned about workplace rights, they also saw themselves as equal to their male coworkers and began to consciously fight for equal rights for women, essentially engaging in feminist action.

Despite these misgivings about the feminist movement, by the end of the 1980s, more women saw themselves as equal to men. The changes that followed the war irrevocably changed the landscape of the workplace. When factories closed in Iowa and moved elsewhere, women did not stop working; they simply found other jobs, though ones that did not pay nearly as much. Women pursued work in the growing service sector and the care industry as well as the skilled trades. Women became welders, plumbers, carpenters, machinists, and electricians. While these were still significantly male-dominated fields, the changes of the postwar period opened the door for women to pursue this type of higher-paying, skilled work. Whether Iowa women recognized it or not, their movement into the workforce had changed the dynamics of patriarchy. The pursuit of work and wages can be seen as a feminist action, but how can we as scholars make sense of an individual's sense of self and identity if it contradicts their actions? As I have argued, these women did not see themselves as individuals but as a function of the family unit. Pursuing work, to them, was not an act of feminism but a fulfillment of their familial duties.

The political landscape in Iowa stayed conservative and slowly moved further to the right. What happened in the state to push Iowans toward conservatism is another study yet to be written. What I suggest, however, is that one cannot understand the changes in politics without looking at the family within the context of rural and midwestern culture. As this study shows, when rapid changes happen to a society, such as deindustrialization and the emergence of feminism, people begin to hold contradictory ideas about themselves and their identities. Pulling apart these contradictions is what is necessary to arrive at the reality of societal change. In this case, working women engaged in feminist activity while rejecting the identity of feminism. Dismissing women's self-identities when they appear contradictory hides pockets of society from the historical record and creates blind spots for the causes of future action. Only by seeking to understand their individual sense of self and perceptions of their own identity can scholars provide a fuller picture of social change. In this case, Iowa women wanted to work, but in the words of Rosemary Hayes, "I think most women do like to be treated like ladies."[4]

# Notes

## Introduction

1. Eunice Evans, Amana, interview by Janet Clements, March 6, 1995, Iowa Labor History Oral Project, Iowa Federation of Labor, AFL-CIO, State Historical Society of Iowa, Iowa City, Iowa (hereafter cited as ILHOP).
2. Alice Kessler-Harris reported that women were 24.3 percent of the workforce in 1930, which increased slightly to 25.1 percent in 1940. Alice Kessler-Harris, *Out to Work: A History of Wage-Earning Women in the United States* (New York: Oxford University Press, 2003), 258.
3. According to the 1960 Census, urban population "comprises all persons in . . . places of 2,500 inhabitants or more incorporated as cities . . . and towns" (U.S. Bureau of the Census, *Census of Population: 1960*).
4. Leland Sage, *A History of Iowa* (Ames: Iowa State University Press, 1974), 316; and Dorothy Schwieder, *Iowa: The Middle Land* (Ames: Iowa State University Press, 1996), 289.
5. According to the 1960 U.S. Census, Iowa's population was 2,786,365, with 2,757,537 of the residents categorized as white and 28,828 as nonwhite. Only 5 percent of nonwhite residents lived in rural areas (U.S. Bureau of the Census, *Census of Population: 1960*, table 14).
6. Bruce Fehn, "African American Women and the Struggle for Equality in the Meatpacking Industry, 1940–1960," *Journal of Women's History* 10 (Spring 1998): 45–69.
7. Mary Neth, *Preserving the Family Farm: Women, Community, and the Foundations of Agribusiness in the Midwest, 1900–1940* (Bloomington: Indiana University Press, 1995). See also Jenny Barker Devine, *On Behalf of the Family Farm: Iowa Farm Women's Activism since 1945* (Iowa City: University of Iowa Press, 2013).
8. Andrew R. L. Cayton and Susan Gray, *The Identity of the American Midwest: Essays on Regional History* (Bloomington: Indiana University Press, 2001), 13.
9. Dorothy Sue Cobble was the first to coin the term *labor feminists.* She described them as feminists "because they recognized that women suffer disadvantages due to their sex and because they sought to eliminate sex-based advantages," and they were labor feminists "because they articulated a particular variant of feminism that put the needs of the working-class women

at its core." Dorothy Sue Cobble, *The Other Women's Movement: Workplace Justice and Social Rights in Modern America* (Princeton, NJ: Princeton University Press, 2004), 3; see also Nancy Gabin, *Feminism in the Labor Movement: Women and the United Auto Workers, 1935–1975* (Ithaca, NY: Cornell University Press, 1990); Dennis Deslippe, *"Rights Not Roses": Unions and the Rise of Working Class Feminism, 1945–80* (Urbana: University of Illinois Press, 2000).

10. Erin Kempker demonstrates how conservative midwestern women opposed feminism during the 1960s and '70s. While the midwestern women discussed in this book did not adopt the language of staunch antifeminists, they were very much aware of the antifeminist rhetoric of the day. See Erin Kempker, *Big Sister: Feminism, Conservatism, and Conspiracy in the Heartland* (Urbana: University of Illinois Press, 2018).
11. Gabin, *Feminism in the Labor Movement*; Cobble, *The Other Women's Movement*; Deslippe, *"Rights Not Roses."* See also Nancy MacLean, *Freedom Is Not Enough: The Opening of the American Workplace* (Cambridge, MA: Harvard University Press, 2006); Bruce Fehn, "Striking Women: Gender, Race and Class in the United Packinghouse Workers of America (UPWA), 1938–1968" (PhD diss., University of Wisconsin, 1990); and Louise Lamphere, Patricia Zavella, and Felipe Gonzales, *Sunbelt Working Mothers: Reconciling Family and Factory* (Ithaca, NY: Cornell University Press, 1993).

## Chapter One

1. Dixie Bigger, Burlington, interview by Merle Davis, January 12, 1982, ILHOP.
2. The plant in Burlington would be unionized by the UAW in 1963.
3. Burlington, Iowa, Vertical Files, State Historical Society of Iowa (hereafter SHSI) Library, Iowa City, Iowa.
4. Keach Johnson provides an excellent overview of industry in Iowa at the turn of the twentieth century in "Iowa's Industrial Roots, 1890–1919," *Annals of Iowa* 44 (Winter 1978), 163–90. Dorothy Schwieder also provides an excellent overview of Iowa's political economy during the first half of the twentieth century in *Iowa: The Middle Land* (Ames: Iowa State University Press), 1996. Wilson Warren provides excellent context to the industrial background of the Midwest in his chapter "Beyond the Rust Bowl," in *The Rural Midwest since World War II*, edited by J. L. Anderson (DeKalb: Northern Illinois University Press, 2014). Last, Derek Oden illustrates the importance of the canning industry in Iowa in "From Cob to Can: The Development of Iowa's Canning Industry in the Late Nineteenth and Early Twentieth Centuries," *Annals of Iowa* 63 (Fall 2004), 390–418.
5. See also Lisa Ossian, *The Home Fronts of Iowa, 1939–1945* (Columbia:

University of Missouri, 2009), for more on war production in Iowa during World War II.

6. For more on product cycle theory and the spatial redistribution of industry, see also Warren, "Beyond the Rust Bowl"; Dennis Roth, "Thinking about Rural Manufacturing: A Brief History," *Rural America* 15 (January 2000), 12–19; and John Fraser Hart, "Small Towns and Manufacturing," *Geographical Review* 78 (July 1988), 272–87.
7. *Iowa Development Digest*, December 13, 1952, SHSI Library, Iowa City.
8. U.S. Bureau of the Census, *Census of Population*, 1940, 1950, and 1960.
9. Johnson, "Iowa's Industrial Roots," 44. See also Warren, "Beyond the Rust Bowl."
10. This rural class structure developed all across the rural Midwest and was not unique to Iowa. For more on the rural class structure and a rural collective conscious, see Jane Adams, *The Transformation of Rural Life: Southern Illinois, 1890–1990* (Chapel Hill: University of North Carolina Press, 1994), 125–31.
11. "Iowa: Where Farms and Factories Share in Progress," Iowa Development Commission, Vertical File, SHSI.
12. "Industrial Development in Iowa Is Vital to Population Growth," *Iowa Development Bulletin*, February 27, 1954; and "Our Role: Past, Present, and Future," *Iowa Development Bulletin*, December 30, 1953, SHSI.
13. "Industry: Will It Help or Hurt the Farmer?," *Iowa Development Digest*, October 1956, SHSI.
14. Keith Orejel has provided a history of the Iowa Development Commission from its creation to the end of World War II in "The Origins of the Iowa Development Commission: Agricultural Transformation and Industrial Development in Mid-Twentieth-Century Iowa," *Annals of Iowa* 76 (Winter 2017): 47–70.
15. "Our Role: Past, Present, and Future."
16. Memo from the Iowa Development Commission, February 21, 1963, Iowa Development Commission Vertical File, SHSI.
17. "Industry's Road to Opportunity Leads to Iowa," Iowa Development Commission, Vertical File, SHSI.
18. These included Des Moines, Sioux City, Davenport, Cedar Rapids, Waterloo, Dubuque, Council Bluffs, Ottumwa, Burlington, Clinton, Mason City, Iowa City, and Fort Dodge.
19. "Iowa: Where Farms and Factories Share in Progress," April 1951, Iowa Development Commission, Vertical File, SHSI.
20. "Nearly 200 Attend First Iowa Industrial Development Clinic," *Iowa Development Bulletin*, November 1954, SHSI.
21. "Industrial Development in Iowa Is Vital to Population Growth."

22. "Iowa: The Land Between Two Rivers," Iowa Development Commission, Vertical File, SHSI; "Industrial Development in Iowa Is Vital to Population Growth."
23. Roth, "Thinking about Rural Manufacturing."
24. "Plant Locations Are Determined Scientifically in Modern Industrial Decentralization Program," *Iowa Development Bulletin*, February 15, 1954, SHSI.
25. "Business Climate Important to Community Development," *Iowa Development Digest*, July 1956, SHSI.
26. "Plant Locations Are Determined Scientifically."
27. Wilson Warren argues in *Struggling with "Iowa's Pride": Labor Relations, Unionism, and Politics in the Rural Midwest since 1877* (Iowa City: University of Iowa Press, 2000) that the United Packinghouse Workers of America joined with other unions in the state to reform the Democratic Party in Iowa, making the state more lenient toward labor during the 1960s and '70s.
28. "Manufacturers View: Iowa's People Top Attraction for New Industry," *Iowa Development Digest*, February 1955, SHSI.
29. "Plant Locations Are Determined Scientifically."
30. *Industrial Development*, July 1962, Clinton, Iowa, Vertical Files, SHSI.
31. Warren, "Beyond the Rust Bowl."
32. Some of these firms included Quaker Oats, American Agriculture Company, Dubuque Tank Terminal Company, General Mills Cereal, Modern Industries, Wilton Junction Cob Company, Tipton Process Company, Cornoco Processing Plant, and Allied Mills.
33. "9 New Iowa Firms in 2nd Quarter, 17 So Far in 1953," *Iowa Development Bulletin*, July 15, 1953, SHSI.
34. J. I. Case and John Deere were the two largest farm equipment manufacturers, and Armour, Dubuque Packing Company, Iowa Packing Company, Oscar Meyer, John Morrell, and Wilson were the largest meatpackers.
35. *Industrial Development*, July 1962, Clinton, Iowa, Vertical Files, SHSI.
36. "Iowa Manufacturers Important in Nation's Industrial Life," *Iowa Development Digest*, May 1955, SHSI.
37. Warren, *Struggling with "Iowa's Pride."*
38. "Non-farm Employment for Nearly 63 Percent of All Iowans," *Iowa Development Digest*, September 1955, SHSI.
39. *Clinton Herald*, April 2, 1962, Clinton Vertical Files, SHSI.
40. "Small Firms Play Major Part in Iowa Industry," *Iowa Development Digest*, June 1956, SHSI.
41. "Plenty of Labor, Cooperation Pays Off for Clinton," *Iowa Development Bulletin*, April 16, 1963, SHSI.
42. In 1955, Polk County (Des Moines) had 347 manufacturing firms, and there were 200 in Linn County (Cedar Rapids), 163 in Black Hawk County

(Waterloo), 146 in Scott County (Davenport), and 232 in Woodbury (Sioux City). "Industry in Iowa," *Iowa Development Digest*, February 1955, SHSI.

43. "More Than Half of Iowa's Factories Located in Smaller Cities, Towns," *Iowa Development Digest*, May 1955, SHSI.
44. "Iowa Industry Settled in Iowa Community of 1,200," *Iowa Development Digest*, December 1954, SHSI.
45. "Growth of Big Industry in Iowa Shows Adequate Labor Supply," *Iowa Development Digest*, February 1954, SHSI.
46. Hart, "Small Towns and Manufacturing," 284; Roth, "Thinking about Rural Manufacturing," 17.
47. Polk, Linn, Black Hawk, Scott, Dubuque, Des Moines, Woodbury, Wapello, Lee, Jasper, Clinton, Webster, Muscatine, Cerro Gordo, Marshall, Floyd, Jackson, Jefferson, Pottawattamie, Iowa.
48. "Industry in Iowa," *Iowa Development Digest*, February 1955, SHSI.
49. Burlington, Iowa, Vertical Files, SHSI.
50. "Burlington Does HAVE It," *Burlington Hawkeye Gazette*, August 24, 1961; *Burlington Hawkeye Gazette*, August 16, 1961.
51. *Burlington Hawkeye Gazette*, January 25, 1957.
52. Clinton, Iowa, Vertical Files, SHSI.

## Chapter Two

1. Pauline Fisher, Oskaloosa, interview by Janet Clements, April 18, 1995, ILHOP.
2. See also Nan Enstad, *Ladies of Labor, Girls of Adventure: Working Women, Popular Culture, and Labor Politics at the Turn of the Twentieth Century* (New York: Columbia University Press, 1999); Susan Glenn, *Daughters of the Shtetl: Life and Labor in the Immigrant Generation* (Ithaca, NY: Cornell University Press, 1990); and Jacquelyn Dowd Hall et al., *Like a Family: The Making of a Southern Cotton Mill World* (New York: Norton, 1987).
3. Alice Kessler-Harris, *Out to Work: A History of Wage-Earning Women in the United States* (New York: Oxford University Press, 1982), 301.
4. Julia Kirk Blackwelder, *Now Hiring: The Feminization of Work in the United States, 1900–1995* (College Station: Texas A&M University Press, 1997), 148, 153; and Kessler-Harris, *Out to Work*, 302.
5. Governor Harold Hughes to the members of the Governor's Commission on the Status of Women, October 11, 1963, Box 1, Governor Ray's Commission on the Status of Women, Iowa Women's Archives (hereafter cited as IWA).
6. "Employment Practices Concerning Women," Box 1, Governor Ray's Commission on the Status of Women, IWA.
7. U.S. Bureau of the Census, Iowa, 1960, Table 62, p. 17-188.

8. Jenny Barker Devine, *On Behalf of the Family Farm: Iowa Farm Women's Activism since 1945* (Iowa City: University of Iowa Press, 2013); and Mary Neth, *Preserving the Family Farm: Women, Community and the Foundations of Agribusiness in the Midwest, 1900–1940* (Baltimore, MD: Johns Hopkins University Press, 1995).
9. Edith Arendt, Cedar Rapids, interview by Greg Zieren, October 31, 1979, ILHOP.
10. Mary Speer, Des Moines, interview by Greg Zieren, February 16, 1980, ILHOP; Artis Hatland England, Autobiographical Sketches of Rural Women, Folder: Johnson County, IWA.
11. Josephine Gerard, Amana, interview by Janet Clements, January 12, 1982, ILHOP; Eunice Evans, Amana, interview by Janet Clements, March 6, 1995, ILHOP; Fern Klopp, Cedar Rapids, interview by Greg Zieren, September 12, 1980, ILHOP.
12. The term *rural farm women* refers to those whose household operated an active farm located outside a designated urban area.
13. "The Family Farm Has a Future If . . . ," *Farm Journal Magazine*, April 1963, Beverly Everett papers, Box 6, IWA.
14. Deborah Fink, *Open Country, Iowa: Rural Women, Tradition and Change* (Albany: State University of New York Press, 1986), 190; Jane Adams, *The Transformation of Rural Life: Southern Illinois, 1890–1990* (Chapel Hill: University of North Carolina Press, 1994).
15. Luella Zmolek, interview by Doris Malkmus, September 10, 2001, Voices from the Land: Oral History Project in Iowa, Special Collections Department, Iowa State University and IWA, University of Iowa; Ilo Rhines, interview by Doris Malkmus, October 26, 2001, Voices from the Land: Oral History Project in Iowa.
16. Bev Clinton, Cedar Rapids, interview by Dan Holub, August 6, 1991, ILHOP; Susan Rhum, Burlington, interview by Merle Davis, February 14, 1983, ILHOP; Carol Carter, Burlington, interview by Merle Davis, January 12, 1982, ILHOP.
17. Joyce Burrows, Dubuque, interview by Dan Holub, May 21, 1991, ILHOP; Helen Erdmann, Waterloo, interview by Merle Davis, June 2, 1982, ILHOP.
18. Edith Arendt, interview, October 31, 1979, ILHOP; Marlene Kruger, interview by Dan Holub, June 27, 1991, ILHOP; Jeannette Haymond, Cedar Rapids, interview by Paul Kelso, November 9, 1977, ILHOP.
19. Doris Peick, Cedar Rapids, interview by Merle Davis, August 24, 1982, ILHOP.
20. Bruce Fehn, "African American Women and the Struggle for Equality in the Meatpacking Industry, 1940–1960," *Journal of Women's History* 10 (Spring 1998): 45–69; Mercedes Aguilera, interview by Janet Weaver, September 22,

2005, Mujeres Latinas Oral History Project, IWA. See also Janet Weaver, "From Barrio to '!Boicoteo!': The Emergence of Mexican American Activism in Davenport, 1917–1970," *Annals of Iowa* 68 (Summer 2009): 215–54.

21. Martha Linn, interview by Doris Malkmus, September 18, 2001, Voices from the Land: An Oral History Project in Iowa; Eunice Evans, March 6, 1995, ILHOP; Esther Witmer, interview by Doris Malkmus, April 3, 2001, Voices from the Land: Oral History Project in Iowa; Sally Putman, interview by Doris Malkmus, October 27, 2000, Voices from the Land: Oral History Project in Iowa.
22. "Women Outnumber Men in Seven Major Industries," *Iowa Industrial Bulletin*, November 28, 1952, SHSI.
23. Ronald Schatz, *The Electrical Workers: A History of Labor at General Electric and Westinghouse, 1923–60* (Urbana: University of Illinois Press, 1983), 30–33, 120; Ruth Milkman, *Gender at Work: The Dynamics of Job Segregation by Sex during World War II* (Urbana: University of Illinois Press, 1987), 15.
24. James Barrett, *Work and Community in the Jungle: Chicago's Packinghouse Workers, 1894–1922* (Urbana: University of Illinois Press, 1987), 51; Milkman, *Gender at Work*, 8; Rick Halpern, *Down on the Killing Floor: Black and White Workers in Chicago's Packinghouses, 1904–54* (Urbana: University of Illinois Press, 1997), 16; Roger Horowitz, *"Negro and White, Unite and Fight!" A Social History of Industrial Unionism in Meatpacking, 1930–90* (Urbana: University of Illinois Press, 1997), 163.
25. Violet Boharty, Ottumwa, interview by Merle Davis, September 15, 1981, ILHOP; Lucille Bremer, Waterloo, interview by Merle Davis, June 2, 1982, ILHOP; Velma Wetzel, Waterloo, interview by Greg Zieren, October 12, 1979, ILHOP.
26. Darlene Croft, Estherville, interview by Merle Davis, November 11, 1982, ILHOP; Fink, *Open Country, Iowa*, 192.
27. Schatz, *The Electrical Workers*, 30.
28. Schatz, *The Electrical Workers*, 30.
29. Leona Roberts, Amana, interview by Janet Clements, February 27, 1995, ILHOP; Folder 21, Box 13, IAM Lodge 105 Records, SHSI.
30. Kate Rousmaniere, "The Muscatine Button Workers' Strike of 1911–1912: An Iowa Community in Conflict," *Annals of Iowa* 46, no. 4 (1982): 243–62.
31. Fink, *Open Country, Iowa*, 190–93; Florence Paul, Oskaloosa, interview by Merle Davis, April 5, 1982, ILHOP.
32. Waterloo, Industry, Vertical File, SHSI; Wilma Riley, Waterloo, interview by Merle Davis, July 22, 1980, ILHOP; Ilene Christianson, Waterloo, interview by Merle Davis, June 11, 1981, ILHOP.
33. "Where Industry and Agriculture Meet," Clinton, Iowa, Vertical Files, SHSI;

Viola Juehring, Clinton, interview by Merle Davis, July 8, 1982, ILHOP; Alice Oltmanns, Clinton, interview by Merle Davis, June 28, 1982, ILHOP; Irene Vaughn, Clinton, interview by Dan Holub, June 15, 1991, ILHOP.

34. Sandra Avery, Fort Madison, interview by Merle Davis, March 1, 1983, ILHOP; Tom Cale, Fort Madison, interview by Merle Davis, March 3, 1983, ILHOP; Fort Madison Vertical Files, SHSI; Ted Sloat, *Fort Madison: A Pictorial History* (St. Louis: G. Bradley, 1988).
35. Carrie Azinger, Keokuk, interview by Merle Davis, December 11, 1981, ILHOP; Betty Noe, Keokuk, interview by Merle Davis, December 10, 1981, ILHOP; Keokuk, Vertical Files, SHSI.
36. Meeting Minutes, January 19, 1949, Folder 1, Box 22, American Federation of Grain Millers, Local 6, Records, SHSI.
37. Everett Shadle, Quad Cities, interview by Merle Davis, March 13, 1982, ILHOP.
38. Wilma Haynes, Burlington, interview by Merle Davis, January 18, 1983, ILHOP; Susan Rhum, February 14, 1983, ILHOP.
39. Wilma Haynes, January 18, 1983, ILHOP; Letha Alliman, interview by Merle Davis, February 12, 1983, ILHOP.
40. Wilma Haynes, January 18, 1983, ILHOP; Employee Lists, Folder 6, Box 6, IAM District Lodge 102 Records, SHSI.
41. Marlene Gerst, Burlington, interview by Merle Davis, January 14, 1982, ILHOP; Marlene Kruger, June 27, 1991, ILHOP.
42. Katrina Sanders, "The Burlington Self-Survey in Human Relations: Interracial Efforts for Constructive Community Change, 1949–1951," *Annals of Iowa* 60 (Summer 2001): 244–69.
43. Billye Smith Williams, Burlington, interview by Merle Davis, February 17, 1983, ILHOP.
44. Betty Noe, October 10, 1981, ILHOP; Janet Weaver, "Barrio Women: Community and Coalition in the Heartland," in *Breaking the Wave: Women, Their Organizations and Feminism, 1945–1985*, ed. Kathleen Laughlin and Jacqueline Castledine (New York: Routledge, 2011).

## Chapter Three

1. Alice Jackson, Burlington, interview by Merle Davis, December 4, 1981, ILHOP.
2. E. P. Thompson, *The Making of the English Working Class* (New York: Vintage, 1963). See also Herbert Gutman, *Work, Culture and Society in Industrializing America* (New York: Vintage, 1966).
3. The scholarship that has informed my thinking about class and class consciousness includes James Barrett, *Work and Community in the Jungle:*

*Chicago's Packinghouse Workers, 1894–1922* (Urbana: University of Illinois Press, 1987); Mary Blewett, *Men, Women, and Work: Class, Gender, and Protest in the New England Shoe Industry, 1780–1910* (Urbana: University of Illinois Press, 1988); Ardis Cameron, *Radicals of the Worst Sort: Laboring Women in Lawrence, Massachusetts, 1860–1912* (Urbana: University of Illinois Press, 1993); Jacquelyn Dowd Hall et al., *Like a Family: The Making of a Southern Cotton Mill World* (New York: Norton, 1987); Thomas Dublin, *Women at Work: The Transformation of Work and Community in Lowell, Massachusetts, 1826–1860* (New York: Columbia University Press, 1979); Nan Enstad, *Ladies of Labor, Girls of Adventure: Working Women, Popular Culture, and Labor Politics at the Turn of the Twentieth Century* (New York: Columbia University Press, 1999); Laurie Mercier, *Anaconda: Labor, Community, and Culture in Montana's Smelter City* (Urbana: University of Illinois Press, 2001); and David Montgomery, *The Fall of the House of Labor: The Workplace, the State, and American Labor Activism, 1865–1925* (New York: Cambridge University Press, 1987.)

4. Several important scholars have pioneered the connection between the labor movement and the rise of the feminist movement and argue for the concept of labor feminists. Dorothy Sue Cobble in several different works has been very influential in forming these concepts; see *The Other Women's Movement: Workplace Justice and Social Rights in Modern America* (Princeton, NJ: Princeton University Press, 2004), and her edited works, *The Sex of Class: Women Transforming American Labor* (Ithaca, NY: Cornell University Press, 2007), and *Women and Unions: Forging a Partnership* (Ithaca: Cornell University Press, 1993). Nancy Gabin in *Feminism in the Labor Movement: Women and United Auto Workers, 1935–1975* (Ithaca, NY: Cornell University Press, 1990) and Dennis Deslippe, *"Rights Not Roses": Unions and the Rise of Working Class Feminism, 1945–1980* (Urbana: University of Illinois Press, 2000), have both shown the importance of female consciousness in fighting for both workplace rights and gender equality. Alice Kessler-Harris argues for the importance of gender in understanding the basic ideas of class construction in *Gendering Labor History* (Urbana: University of Illinois Press, 2007). Xiaolan Bao, in *Holding Up More Than Half the Sky: Chinese Women Garment Workers in New York City, 1948–92* (Urbana: University of Illinois Press, 2001), has also greatly informed this study by showing how immigrant Chinese garment workers formed a class consciousness through a shared culture and community. Louise Lamphere et al., *Sunbelt Working Mothers: Reconciling Family and Factory* (Ithaca, NY: Cornell University Press, 1993), has also been very informative about women on the shop floor in the 1980s in Albuquerque, New Mexico.
5. Wilson Warren, in *Struggling with "Iowa's Pride": Labor Relations,*

*Unionism, and Politics in the Rural Midwest since 1877* (Iowa City: University of Iowa Press, 2000), shows the importance of working-class neighborhoods in Ottumwa in the late nineteenth century, and also succinctly illustrates how they are dispersed across south central Iowa.

6. Ruth Milkman, *Gender at Work: The Dynamics of Job Segregation by Sex during World War II* (Urbana: University of Illinois Press, 1987).
7. Susan Rhum, February 14, 1983, ILHOP; Edith Arendt, October 31, 1979, ILHOP; Betty Noe, October 10, 1981, ILHOP.
8. Company reply to grievance, Dorothy Garringer, February 13, 1961, Folder 7, Box 16, IAM District Lodge 105 Records, SHSI. Garringer also filed numerous grievances through the union, and anytime there was a chance at overtime, or missed overtime, she would submit a request or a grievance.
9. Pat Marshall, Cedar Rapids, interview by Merle Davis, August 24, 1982, ILHOP.
10. Ralph Helstein, Chicago, interview by Merle Davis, May 12, 1983, ILHOP.
11. Letha Alliman, February 12, 1983, ILHOP; Bev Clinton, August 6, 1991, ILHOP; Betty Noe,October 10, 1981, ILHOP; Carol Carter, Burlington, interview by Merle Davis, January 12, 1982, ILHOP.
12. Letha Alliman, February 12, 1983, ILHOP; Wilma Haynes, January 18, 1983, ILHOP; Dixie Bigger, January 13, 1982, ILHOP.
13. Grievance submitted by Erma Mantz, October 1953, Folder 1, Box 15; grievance submitted by Eunice Evans, December 7, 1954, Folder 2, Box 15; grievance submitted by Patricia McGuire and Barbara Sexton, March 3, 1970, Folder 4, Box 21; grievance submitted by Wanda Beasley, February 23, 1970, Folder 3, Box 21, all in IAM District Lodge 105 Records, SHSI.
14. Pat Marshall, August 24, 1982, ILHOP; Susan Rhum, Burlington, second interview by Merle Davis, May 17, 1990, ILHOP; Fern McCarthy, Burlington, interview by Merle Davis, December 12, 1981, ILHOP.
15. Pat Marshall, August 24, 1982, ILHOP; Fern Klopp, September 12, 1980, ILHOP.
16. Grievance, Betty Fry, March 12, 1954, Folder 2, Box 15, and grievance, Wilma Funk, October 3, 1968, Folder 4, Box 20, IAM District Lodge 102 Records; Gladys Accord, Amana, interview by Janet Clements, March 14, 1995, ILHOP.
17. Bud Sanders, Amana, interview by Janet Clements, March 15, 1995, ILHOP.
18. Birtman Employee Records, Folder 7, Box 6, Folder 4, Box 7, IAM District Lodge 102 Records, SHSI; Fern Klopp, September, 12, 1980, ILHOP.
19. Pat Marshall, August 24, 1982, ILHOP; Doris Peick, August 24, 1982, ILHOP.
20. Article II, Wage Rules, Section 1, 1955–1957 IAM Contract Agreement with Birtman Electronics, Folder 3, Box 20, and "Electronics Handbook for IAM Representatives," 1962, Folder 2, Box 20, IAM Lodge 102 Records, SHSI.

21. Gellman Manufacturing Employee Records, Folder 1, Box 12, IAM Lodge 102 Records, SHSI.
22. Minimum wage in 1955 was $1.00 an hour.
23. Carrie Azinger, December 11, 1981, ILHOP; Bev Clinton, August 6, 1991, ILHOP.
24. Wilma Haynes, February 18, 1983, ILHOP.
25. Bev Clinton, August 6, 1991, ILHOP; Betty Noe, October 10, 1981, ILHOP.
26. Third Shift Steward Journal, January 11, 1969, Folder 11, Box 1, IAM Local 2303 Records, SHSI; Billye Smith Williams, February 17, 1983, ILHOP.
27. Marlene Gerst, January 14, 1982, ILHOP.
28. Betty Noe, October 10, 1981, ILHOP; Irene Christianson, June 11, 1981, ILHOP.
29. Betty Noe, October 10, 1981, ILHOP; Wilma Haynes, February 18, 1983, ILHOP.
30. Wilma Haynes, February 18, 1983, ILHOP; Billye Smith Williams, February 17, 1983, ILHOP.
31. Leona Roberts, February 27, 1995, ILHOP.
32. Susan Rhum, February 14, 1983, ILHOP; Fern McCarthy, December 12, 1981, ILHOP.
33. Susan Rhum, February 14, 1983, ILHOP; Alice Jackson, December 4, 1981, ILHOP.
34. Bev Clinton, August 6, 1991, ILHOP; Marlene Kruger, June 27, 1991, ILHOP; Union-company meeting minutes, August 23, 1957, Folder 3, Box 6, IAM Lodge 102 Records, SHSI.
35. Management meeting minutes, March 29, 1968, Folder 1, IAM Local 1373, SHSI.
36. Union meeting minutes, December 23, 1969, February 9, 1971, Folder 12, Box 26; May 15, 1972, Folder 3, Box 27; June 22, 1967, Folder 10, Box 26; February 24, 1970, Folder 1, Box 27, IAM Lodge 105, SHSI.
37. Memo to employees, September 14, 1973, Folder 1, Box 1; To Factory Employees, from T. E. Burton, Plant Manager, October 22, 1973, Folder 3, Box 1; Shop Committee Meetings, October 3, 1973, Folder 7, Box 1, IAM Local 2303, SHSI.
38. Grievances filed January 1957, Folder 1, Box 16, IAM Lodge 105, SHSI.
39. Grievances filed October 1967, Folder 5, Box 19, IAM Lodge 105, SHSI.
40. Wilma Haynes, February 18, 1983, ILHOP.
41. Third Shift Steward Journal, February 7, February 11, February 28, April 17, May 19, 1968; January 29, August 4, and September 26, 1969, Folder 11, Box 1, IAM Local 2303 Records, SHSI.
42. Edith Ardent, Cedar Rapids, interview by Greg Zeiren, October 31, 1979, ILHOP.

43. Doris Peick, August 24, 1982, ILHOP.
44. Doris Peick, August 24, 1982, ILHOP.
45. Complaint to the NLRB, September 28, 1955, Folder 9, Box 9, IAM District Lodge 102 Records, SHSI.
46. Third Shift Steward Journal, January 13, January 24, May 2, May 19, September 16, September 17, 1969, Folder 11, Box 1, IAM Local 2303 Records, SHSI.
47. Alice Jackson, December 4, 1981, ILHOP.
48. Grievance, February 14, 1969, Folder 4, Box 1, IAM Local 2303 Records, SHSI.
49. Memo for the Record, Disciplinary Action, November 4, 1974, Folder 4, Box 1; Third Level Grievance Response, Division Manager's Reply, December 20, 1974, Folder 3, Box 1, IAM Local 2303 Records.
50. Shop Committee Meetings, November 2, 1973, Folder 7, Box 1, IAM Local 2303 Records, SHSI.
51. Marlene Kruger, June 27, 1991; Contract 1962, Lennox Industries and IAM Local 1995, Folder 11, Box 10, IAM District Lodge 118 Records, SHSI.
52. Contract 1963, Eagle Signal, Folder 13, Box 13, IAM Local 2045 Records, SHSI; Contract at Birtman Electric, Folder 3, Box 6, IAM District Lodge 102 Records, SHSI; Bev Clinton, August 6, 1991, ILHOP; Ila Jean Bryne, Fort Dodge, interview by Merle Davis, July 29, 1981, ILHOP.
53. Pat Marshall, second interview by Merle Davis, May 24, 1990, ILHOP; Pauline Fisher, April 18, 1995, ILHOP.
54. This data was gathered from a sample of twenty-five female interviewees in the Iowa Labor History Oral Project.
55. Edith Arendt, October 31, 1979, ILHOP; Susan Rhum, February 14, 1983, ILHOP.
56. Billye Smith Williams, February 17, 1983, ILHOP.
57. Billye Smith Williams, February 17, 1983, ILHOP; Ila Jean Byrne, July 29, 1981, ILHOP; Fern Klopp, September 12, 1980, ILHOP; Edith Arendt, October 31, 1979, ILHOP; Third Shift Steward Journal, September 9, 1969, Folder 11, Box 1, IAM Local 2303, SHSI.
58. Doris Peick, August 24, 1982, ILHOP; Joyce Burrows, May 21, 1991, ILHOP.
59. Third Shift Steward's Journal, August 28–September 16, 1969, Folder 11, Box 1, IAM Local Lodge 2303, Records 1966–1976, SHSI.
60. Third Shift Steward's Journal, January 21, February 10, April 17, April 28, and May 8–9, 1969, Folder 11, Box 1, IAM Local Lodge 2303, Records 1966–1976, SHSI.
61. Waterloo Industries, Labor-Management Minutes, March 29 and October 28, 1969, Folder 1, IAM Local Lodge 1373, Records 1968–1974, SHSI; Third Shift Steward's Journal, December 23, 1968, March 14, 1969, Folder 11, Box 1, IAM Local Lodge 2303, Records 1966–1976, SHSI.

62. Union meetings with management, July 2, 1971, Folder 2, Box 27, IAM Local Lodge 105, SHSI.
63. Third Shift Steward's Journal, Folder 11, Box 1, IAM Local 2303 Records, SHSI.

## Chapter Four

1. Ruth Lubert, Waterloo, interview by Merle Davis, July 21, 1981, ILHOP.
2. Jenny Barker Devine discusses farm women in Iowa and their activism in a variety of social and farm organizations. She demonstrates how farm women had a rich cultural tradition of volunteerism and activism in social organizations. Jenny Barker Devine, *On Behalf of the Family Farm: Iowa Farm Women's Activism since 1945* (Iowa City: University of Iowa Press, 2013).
3. Kevin Boyle, ed., *Organized Labor and American Politics, 1894–1994: The Labor-Liberal Alliance* (Albany: State University of New York Press, 1998).
4. For more on the history of the women's auxiliaries, see Judy Aulette and Trudy Mills, "Something Old, Something New: Auxiliary Work in the 1983–1986 Copper Strike," *Feminist Studies* 14 (Summer 1988): 251–68; Melinda Chateauvert, *Marching Together: Women of the Brotherhood of Sleeping Car Porters* (Urbana: University of Illinois Press, 1998); Elizabeth Faue, *Community of Suffering and Struggle: Women, Men, and the Labor Movement in Minneapolis, 1915–1945* (Chapel Hill: University of North Carolina Press, 1991); Dana Frank, "Gender, Consumer Organizing, and the Seattle Labor Movement, 1919–1929," in *Work Engendered: Toward a New History of American Labor*, ed. Ava Baron (Ithaca, NY: Cornell University Press, 1991), 273–95; Marjorie Penn Lasky, "'Where I Was a Person': The Ladies' Auxiliary in the 1934 Minneapolis Teamsters' Strikes," in *Women, Work and Protest: A Century of U.S. Women's Labor History*, ed. Ruth Milkman (Boston: Routledge and Kegan Paul, 1985), 181–205; Susan Levine, "Workers' Wives: Gender, Class and Consumerism in the 1920s United States," *Gender and History* 48 (Spring 1991): 45–64; Caroline Merithew, "'We Were Not Ladies': Gender, Class, and a Woman's Auxiliary's Battle for Mining Unionism," *Journal of Women's History* 18 (2006): 63–94; Annelise Orleck, "'We Are That Mythical Thing Called the Public': Militant Housewives during the Great Depression," *Feminist Studies* 19 (Spring 1993): 147–73; Paula Pfeffer, "The Women behind the Union: Halena Wilson, Rosina Tucker, and the Ladies' Auxiliary to the Brotherhood of Sleeping Car Porters," *Labor History* 36 (Fall 1995): 557–78; Emily E. L. Twarog, *Politics of the Pantry: Housewives, Food, and Consumer Protest in Twentieth-Century America* (New York: Oxford University Press, 2017).
5. Dorothy Sue Cobble, *The Other Women's Movement: Workplace Justice and Social Rights in Modern America* (Princeton, NJ: Princeton University Press, 2004), 23–25.

6. Resolutions, 9th Annual Convention of the Iowa Federation of Labor, 1964, Folder 21, Box 1, Doris Peick Papers, SHSI.
7. The two auxiliaries were Auxiliary Local 25, and IAM Local 363 Auxiliary, which was called the Riverside Auxiliary. Attendance records, Folder 1, Box 1, Fort Madison Trades and Labor Assembly Records. In Burlington there was an auxiliary to the Electrical Workers Local 735, one to the Upholsterers union, and one to IAM Local 1010, Burlington Trades and Labor Assembly Records, SHSI.
8. Folder 13, Box 84, Iowa Federation of Labor Records, SHSI.
9. History of the Women's Auxiliary to the Tri-City Federation of Labor, Folder 10, Box 1, Women's Auxiliary to the Tri-City Federation of Labor Records, SHSI; Minutes, September 28, 1954, October 16, 1954, Folder 7, Box 1, Burlington Trades and Labor Assembly Records, SHSI. The IAM Auxiliary Tall Corn Lodge 262 also started in 1938, and by the late 1950s it had around seventy active members. Informal history by Mae Zinzer, 1976, Folder 4, Box 1, Ladies Auxiliary to the International Association of Machinists and Aerospace Workers, Tall Corn Lodge 262, SHSI.
10. *Dubuque Telegraph Herald*, April 25, 1971, Folder 1, Box 1, David Hart Packinghouse Scrapbook, SHSI; "Form First Union Auxiliary," *Spencer Reporter Times*, September 25, 1972, David Hart Packinghouse Scrapbook, SHSI.
11. Box 1, Doris Peick Papers, SHSI.
12. "How to Organize AFL-CIO Auxiliaries, n.d., Folder 25, Box 5, George O'Hara Papers, SHSI.
13. Ruby Hinrichs, Quad Cities, interview by Greg Zieren, June 5, 1980, ILHOP.
14. Julie Fritz, Fort Dodge, interview by Paul Kelso, September 13, 1978, ILHOP; Esther DuPey with Earl DuPey, Fort Dodge, interview by Paul Kelso, September 12, 1978, ILHOP.
15. Anna Kelsey, "Ten Good Reasons Why Union Men's Wives Should Join an Auxiliary," circa 1950, Folder 6, Box 1, Women's Auxiliary to the Tri-City Federation of Labor Records, SHSI.
16. Cobble, *The Other Women's Movement*, 23.
17. Constitution of the American Federation of Women's Auxiliaries of Labor (AFWAL), n.d., Folder 2, Box 1, Women's Auxiliary to the Tri-City Federation of Labor, Records, SHSI.
18. Women's Auxiliary to the Tri-City Federation of Labor to Mrs. George Kennedy, October 19, 1951, Folder 7, Box 1, Women's Auxiliary to the Tri-City Federation of Labor, SHSI.
19. *Dubuque Telegraph Herald*, April 23, 1972, Folder 4, Box 1, David Hart Scrapbook, SHSI; Constitution of the Ladies Auxiliary to the UPWA Local P-38, 1965, Folder 1, AMC&BW Local 38 Records, SHSI.
20. John Evans, Secretary to the Plaster Tenders and General Construction Laborers Local 23, to George O'Hara, May 26, 1960, George O'Hara Papers, SHSI.

21. "How to Conduct the Organizational Meeting," in How to Organize AFL-CIO Auxiliaries, n.d., Folder 25, Box 5, George O'Hara Papers, SHSI.
22. Evans to O'Hara, May 26, 1960; How to Organize AFL-CIO Auxiliaries; Nellie Reeves, President of the State Auxiliary, to Marcella Beatty, October 24, 1969, Folder 20, Box 60, Iowa Federation of Labor Records, SHSI; Ladies Auxiliary to the UPWA Local P-38, Folder 1, AMC&BW Local 38 Records, SHSI.
23. How to Organize AFL-CIO Auxiliaries.
24. Ibid.
25. See also Chateauvert, *Marching Together*, for more information on how the auxiliary stressed the ideologies of middle-class domesticity.
26. "Duties of the President," in How to Organize AFL-CIO Auxiliaries.
27. Elda Luebbert to Mr. D. L. Williams, President of the Quad City Federation of Labor, August 24, 1961; D. L. Williams to Elda Luebbert, Secretary-Treasurer of the National AFL-CIO Auxiliary, August 29, 1961, Folder 25, Box 5, George O'Hara Papers, SHSI.
28. "How to Organize AFL-CIO Auxiliaries," Folder 25, Box 5, George O'Hara Papers, SHSI.
29. The auxiliary to the Brotherhood of Sleeping Car Porters also had a clearly defined ritual for meetings and initiations, which stressed the importance of ladylike behavior and respectable behavior of all members. See Chateauvert, *Marching Together*; Pfeffer, "The Women behind the Union."
30. Ritual 1960, Ladies Auxiliary to the IAM, Folder 11, Box 1, Tall Corn Lodge 262 Records, SHSI.
31. Mae Zinzer, Informal History, 1981, Folder 4, Box 1, Ladies Auxiliary to the IAM, Tall Corn Lodge 262 Records, SHSI.
32. History of the Women's Auxiliary, Folder 10, Box 1, Women's Auxiliary to the Tri-City Federation of Labor, Records, SHSI; *Dubuque Telegraph Herald*, April 25, 1971, Folder 1, Box 1, David Hart Packinghouse Scrapbook, SHSI.
33. Anna Kelsey to "Sister Secretary," July 22, 1951, Folder 6, Box 1, Women's Auxiliary to the Tri-City Federation of Labor Records, SHSI.
34. Several scholarly works have addressed the various tactics auxiliary women used in promoting the labor movement through consumer organizing; see especially Frank, "Gender, Consumer Organizing, and the Seattle Labor Movement."
35. Women's Auxiliary to the Tri-City Federation of Labor to Mrs. George Kennedy, October 19, 1951.
36. Women's Auxiliary to the Tri-City Federation of Labor to Theodore Satnat, Business Agent, January 13, 1949, Folder 10, Box 1, Women's Auxiliary to the Tri-City Federation of Labor Records, SHSI.
37. Leona Adams, Waterloo, interview by Merle Davis, July 3, 1981, ILHOP.
38. Marjorie Penn Lasky showed how women organized into auxiliaries during the Teamsters' strike in Minneapolis in the 1930s because they could fulfill

the domestic roles such as preparing food in support of the strike in "'Where I Was a Person.'" Women could show militancy themselves by organizing their own rallies during a strike. See Aulette and Mills, "Something Old, Something New"; and Faue, *Community of Suffering and Struggle.*

39. History of the Women's Auxiliary, Folder 10, Box 1, Women's Auxiliary to the Tri-City Federation of Labor Records, SHSI.
40. Julie Fritz, September 13, 1978, ILHOP.
41. Meeting Minutes, October 14, 1952, Folder 7; November 22, 1955, Folder 8; January 1, 1956, February 11, 1958, and January 26, 1960, Folder 9, Box 1, Burlington Trades and Labor Assembly Records, SHSI.
42. Meeting minutes, March 9, April 13, May 25, 1954, Folder 7, Box 1, Burlington Trades and Labor Assembly Records, SHSI.
43. Della Peters to IAM District 118, February 27, 1951, Folder 21, Box 1; Velma Bare, Recording Secretary to the Ladies Auxiliary, to IAM District 118, June 15, 1950; meeting minutes, August 3, 1950, March 1, 1951, April 5, 1951, Folder 28, Box 1, IAM District Lodge 118 Records, SHSI.
44. Exchange between Jessie Connery and Mrs. John Reagan, November 1950, Folder 6, Box 1, Women's Auxiliary to the Tri-City Federation of Labor Records, SHSI.
45. Executive board meeting minutes, February 12, 1974, Folder 8, Box 47, UFCW Local 3 Records, SHSI.
46. *Iowa State AFL-CIO Auxiliary News,* February 1, 1967, Folder 13, Box 84, Iowa Federation of Labor, SHSI.
47. Leona Adams, July 3, 1981, ILHOP.
48. Charity was a main activity of several church groups and club women in Iowa. Several club records at the Iowa Women's Archives at the University of Iowa in Iowa City illustrate the activities of Iowa club women. See the Best Ever Club, Box 1, and Fort Madison Women's Clubs, Boxes 1 and 2, for examples. The Farm Bureau Women's Clubs also conducted similar activities. See Jenny Barker Devine, "'The Secret to Successful Farm Organization': Township Farm Bureau Women's Clubs in Iowa, 1945–1970," *Annals of Iowa* 69 (Fall 2010): 418–48.
49. Leona Adams, July 3, 1981, ILHOP.
50. Women's Auxiliary to the Tri-City Federation of Labor to Mrs. George Kennedy, October 19, 1951.
51. Women's Auxiliary to the Tri-City Federation of Labor to the AFLO Manufacturing Company, July 6, 1948, Folder 4, Box 1, Women's Auxiliary to the Tri-City Federation of Labor Records, SHSI.
52. Meeting minutes, December 1955, and February 14, 1956, Folder 8, Burlington Trades and Labor Assembly Records, SHSI; Women's Auxiliary to the Tri-City Federation of Labor to Mrs. George Kennedy, October 19, 1951.

53. Meeting minutes, November 11, 1955, Folder 7; January 25, 1956, February 14, 1956, November 8, 1957, February 11, 1958, Folder 8, Box 1, Burlington Trades and Labor Assembly Records, SHSI.
54. Ditty bags were "small bags made by volunteers at Red Cross chapters given out to soldiers and sailors and they contained personal items such as combs, sewing kits, shaving cream and razors." Women would volunteer to make them and then send them to the Red Cross to hand out to the troops. This was a popular activity among women's groups, as women in the Farm Bureau also took time to make ditty bags. American Red Cross, http://www.redcross.org/museum/exhibits/ww2.asp, page no longer available; Vivian Wieny, Iowa State AFL-CIO Auxiliary News, February 1, 1967; Devine, "'The Secret to Successful Farm Organization.'"
55. Women's Auxiliary to the Tri-City Federation of Labor to Mrs. George Kennedy, October 19, 1951.
56. *Dubuque Telegraph Herald*, April 25, 1971, Folder 1, Box 1, David Hart Packinghouse Scrapbook, SHSI.
57. Women's Auxiliary to the Tri-City Federation of Labor to Mrs. George Kennedy, October 19, 1951.
58. Meeting minutes, June 13, 1954, September 1954, Folder 7, Box 1, Burlington Trades and Labor Assembly Records, SHSI.
59. History of the Women's Auxiliary, Folder 7; Women's Auxiliary to the Tri-City Federation of Labor to Mrs. George Kennedy, October 19, 1951; Mae Zinzer, Informal History, 1981, Folder 4, Box 1, Ladies Auxiliary to the IAM, Tall Corn Lodge 262 Records, SHSI.
60. Vivian Weiny, *Iowa State AFL-CIO Auxiliaries News*, February 1, 1967, Folder 13, Box 84, Iowa Federation of Labor Records, SHSI.
61. Mae Zinzer, Informal History, 1976–, Folder 4, Box 1, Ladies Auxiliary to the IAM, Tall Corn Lodge 262 Records, SHSI.
62. Attendance Records, Folder 6, Box 1, Ladies Auxiliary to the IAM, Tall Corn Lodge 262 Records, SHSI.
63. Gabin, *Feminism in the Labor Movement*; Deslippe, *"Rights Not Roses"*; and Cobble, *The Other Women's Movement*, have all discussed the role of the women's committee within the UWA, UPWA, and the UE. See also Twarog, *Politics of the Pantry*, 56–63, for the uneasy switch from auxiliary to women's committee.
64. The IAM did not create a women's committee until 1996. "General History," History of the IAM, Georgia State University Library, September 26, 2022, https://research.library.gsu.edu/c.php?g=115643&p=751388.
65. Gabin, *Feminism in the Labor Movement*, 91–93.
66. Meeting minutes, August 24, 1970, Folder 5, Box 1, UAW Local 838, Hinson Unit Records, SHSI.

67. Ralph Helstein, May 12, 1983, ILHOP; Cobble, *The Other Women's Movement*, 87; Deslippe, *"Rights Not Roses,"* 81–84.
68. Deslippe, *"Rights Not Roses,"* 83.
69. Constitution of the Women's Committee, UPWA Local 3, Folder 3, Box 79, UFCW Local P-3 Records, SHSI.
70. Executive Board meeting minutes, April 5, 1954, Folder 3, Box 47, UFCW Local P-3 Records, SHSI.
71. Meeting minutes, March 3, 1955, Folder 3, Box 47, UFCW P-3 Records, SHSI.
72. Meeting minutes, July 6, 1955; October 5, 1955; March 7, 1956; May 2, 1956, Folder 3, Folder 47, UFCW Local P-3 Records, SHSI.
73. Meeting minutes, February 6, 1957, Executive Board meeting minutes, February 18, 1957, Folder 3, Box 47, UFCW Local P-3 Records, SHSI.
74. Darlyn Porter, Chairwoman of the Women's Committee, to Members of UPWA Local 3, May 17, 1957, Folder 3, Box 79, UFCW Local P-3 Records, SHSI.
75. Meeting minutes, September 4, 1957, Folder 4, Box 47, UFCW Local P-3 Records, SHSI.
76. Meeting minutes, March 5, 1958, February 18, 1959, March 1, 1960, Folder 4, Box 47, UFCW Local P-3 Records, SHSI.
77. *Bulletin*, June 14, 1971, Folder 12, Box 4, AMC&BW Local P-1 Records, SHSI.
78. *Bulletin*, March 27, 1967, Folder 8, Box 4, AMC&BW Local P-1 Records, SHSI.
79. *Bulletin*, December 4, 1967, Folder 8, Box 4, AMC&BW Local P-1 Records, SHSI.
80. *Bulletin*, August 1969, Folder 10, Box 4, AMC&BW Local P-1 Records, SHSI.
81. Ethel Jerred, Ottumwa, interview by Merle Davis, October 5, 1981, ILHOP.
82. Betty Talkington to Lyle Taylor, President of AMC&BW Local 46, September 17, 1969, Folder 13, Box 84, Iowa Federation of Labor Records, SHSI.
83. "Soda Pop Hop," November 2, n.d., Folder 3, Box 79, UFCW Local 3 Records, SHSI.
84. Carol Carter, January 12, 1982, ILHOP.
85. Marlene Gerst, January 14, 1982, ILHOP; Carol Carter, January 12, 1982, ILHOP.
86. Ibid.
87. Marlene Gerst, January 14, 1982, ILHOP; Dixie Bigger, January 13, 1982, ILHOP.
88. Iowa Committee on Political Education, "A Word about COPE," Folder 5, Box 14, Iowa Federation of Labor Records, SHSI.
89. "COPE's Women's Activities," Folder 5, Box 14, Iowa Federation of Labor Records, SHSI.
90. 1st Annual Iowa WAD Conference, 1963, "Leadership and Programming," Folder 10, Box 84, Iowa Federation of Labor Records, SHSI.
91. Ibid.

92. 1st Annual Iowa WAD Conference, 1963, "Never Underestimate the Power of a Woman," Folder 10, Box 84, Iowa Federation of Labor Records, SHSI.
93. *Bulletin*, April 22, 1963, Folder 4, Box 4, AMC&BW, Local P-1 Records, SHSI.
94. *Bulletin*, August 12, 1963, Folder 4, Box 4, AMCBW, Local P-1 Records, SHSI.
95. 1st Annual Iowa WAD Conference, 1963, "Never Underestimate the Power of a Woman," and "History of Women's Activities Department," Folder 10, Box 84, Iowa Federation of Labor Records, SHSI.
96. These women included Pat Olson in Sioux City; Vi Martinek, Fort Dodge; Lucile Bremer, Waterloo; Alice Oltmanns, Clinton; Doris Peick, Cedar Rapids; Minnie Lindsey, Dubuque; Lucille Hendrie, Keokuk; Mrs. Alan Lee, Davenport; Mrs. Chester Smith, Muscatine; Marilyn Larons, Burlington; all in Folder 13, Box 84, Iowa Federation of Labor Records, SHSI.
97. James Couch, "Why Women in Politics?," Ottumwa, July 1965, Folder 12, Box 84, Iowa Federation of Labor Records, SHSI.
98. Don Lewis to Betty Talkington, September 1, 1966; and Don Lewis to Betty Talkington, September 6, 1966, Folder 12, Box 84, Iowa Federation of Labor Records, SHSI.
99. "Recruitment of WAD Volunteers," Folder 5, Box 14, Iowa Federation of Labor Records, SHSI.
100. Meeting minutes, November 25, 1958, Folder 8, Box 1, Burlington Trades and Labor Assembly Records, SHSI.
101. Flier, Summer 1958, Folder 6, Box 1, Burlington Trades and Labor Assembly Records, SHSI.
102. Meeting minutes, August 26, 1958, Folder 8, Box 1, Burlington Trades and Labor Assembly Records, SHSI.
103. "Recruitment of WAD Volunteers."
104. "Awards to Volunteers," Folder 5, Box 14, Iowa Federation of Labor Records, SHSI.
105. "Award Winners," Box 85, Folder 1, Iowa Federation of Labor Records, SHSI.
106. "Never Underestimate the Power of a Woman," Folder 10, Box 84, Iowa Federation of Labor Records, SHSI.
107. Ibid.
108. "Meet the Iowa WADs," Folder 13, Box 84, Iowa Federation of Labor Records, SHSI.
109. Ibid.
110. Ethel Jerred to Betty Talkington, September 23, 1968, Folder 12, Box 84, Iowa Federation of Labor Records, SHSI.

## Chapter Five

1. Carol Carter, January 12, 1982, ILHOP.
2. Dennis Deslippe, *"Rights Not Roses": Unions and the Rise of Working-Class*

*Feminism, 1945–80* (Urbana: University of Illinois Press, 2000); Nancy Gabin, *Feminism in the Labor Movement: Women and the United Auto Workers, 1935–1975* (Ithaca, NY: Cornell University Press, 1990), both eloquently argue how women in the UAW, UPWA, and the IUE embraced working-class feminism.

3. Dorothy Sue Cobble has an interesting discussion on how airline stewardesses organized around gender-specific issues in "A Spontaneous Loss of Enthusiasm: Workplace Feminism and the Transformation of Women's Service Jobs in the 1970s," *International Labor and Working Class History* 56 (Fall 1999): 23–44. See also Cobble, *The Other Women's Movement*, 207–14; and Dorothy Sue Cobble, *Dishing It Out: Waitresses and Their Unions in the 20th Century* (Urbana: University of Illinois Press, 1992). The following also provide analysis on the ways in which women organized: Ruth Meyerowitz, "Organizing the United Auto Workers: Women Workers at the Ternstedt General Motors Parts Plant," and Sharon Hartman Strom, "'We're No Kitty Foyles': Organizing Office Workers for the Congress of Industrial Organizations, 1937–50," in *Women, Work and Protest: A Century of U.S. Women's Labor History*, ed. Ruth Milkman (Boston: Routledge & Kegan Paul, 1985); Cynthia Costello, "Working Women's Consciousness: Traditional or Oppositional?," in *"To Toil the Livelong Day": America's Women at Work, 1780–1980*, ed. Carol Groneman and Mary Beth Norton (Ithaca, NY: Cornell University Press, 1987); Gabin, *Feminism in the Labor Movement*; and Louise Lamphere et al., *Sunbelt Working Mothers: Reconciling Family and Factory* (Ithaca, NY: Cornell University Press, 1993).
4. Edith Arendt, October 31, 1979, ILHOP.
5. David Hart, "Rejected 5 Cent Raise—Now Madrid Firm Is Struck," n.d., Box 1, Packinghouse Scrapbook, SHSI.
6. *UAW News*, May 1968, Folder 11, Box 2, Fort Madison Trades and Labor Assembly Records, SHSI.
7. *UAW News*, Special election issue, "UAW Organizing Committee," May 1968, Folder 11, Box 2, Fort Madison Trades and Labor Assembly Records, SHSI.
8. Tom Cale, March 3, 1983, ILHOP.
9. Employee List, Lindfelt Glove Company, 1963, Folder 17, Box 2; Employee List, Des Moines Glove Company, 1963, Folder 3, Box 2, George O'Hara Papers, SHSI.
10. Memo to employees at the Des Moines Glove and Manufacturing Company, 1963, Folder 3, Box 2, George O'Hara Papers, SHSI.
11. Memo, 1963, Folder 3, Box 2, George O'Hara Papers, SHSI.
12. Pamphlet by the AMC&BW, n.d., Folder 17, Box 2, George O'Hara papers.
13. "Are You Getting Yours?," AMC&BW, September 1963, Folder 3, Box 2, George O'Hara Papers, SHSI.

14. Des Moines Glove Company Organizing Drive, Folder 3, Box 2, George O'Hara Papers, SHSI.
15. Hart, "Rejected 5 Cent raise—Now Madrid Firm Is Struck."
16. E. G. Freund, Plant Manager, to employees of Des Moines Glove Company, September 17, 1963, Folder 3, Box 2, George O'Hara Papers, SHSI.
17. Affidavit submitted by Marcella Foley, July 1959, Folder 13, Box 5, George O'Hara Papers, SHSI.
18. Ibid.
19. Affidavit submitted by Marcella Foley, July 15, 1959, Folder 13, Box 5, George O'Hara Papers, SHSI.
20. Statement by Burdine Mulder, 1972, Folder 21, Box 1, IAM District Lodge 105 Records, SHSI.
21. Statement by Patty Eddy, August 3, 1972, Folder 21, Box 1, IAM District Lodge 105 Records, SHSI.
22. "Our Industrial Success," editorial, *Iowegian and Citizen*, June 7, 1972, Folder 22, Box 1, IAM District Lodge 105 Records, SHSI.
23. "Seven Employees at Union Meet," *Iowegian and Citizen*, June 9, 1972, Folder 22, Box 1, IAM District Lodge 105 Records, SHSI.
24. Hazel Lee-Cichosz, editorial, July 1972; Hazel Cichosz, editorial, June 5, 1972, Folder 22, Box 1, District Lodge 105 Records, SHSI.
25. Letha Alliman, February 12, 1983, ILHOP.
26. Wilma Haynes, February 18, 1983, ILHOP.
27. Deslippe, *"Rights Not Roses,"* 98–100.
28. Letha Alliman, February 12, 1983, ILHOP.
29. Wilma Haynes, February 18, 1983, ILHOP.
30. Ibid.
31. Ibid.
32. Lila McCallister, Amana, interview by Janet Clements, February 24, 1995, ILHOP; Harriet Erzinger, Ottumwa, interview by Merle Davis, September 10, 1981, ILHOP; Pauline Fisher, April 18, 1995, ILHOP; Pat Marshall, August 24, 1982, ILHOP; Marion Nadine Klaner, Cedar Rapids, interview by Merle Davis, August 26, 1981, ILHOP.
33. Union Participation and Representation Workshop, UPWA District 3, Women's Conference, 1959–1961, Folder 6, Box 70, UFCW Local 3 Records, SHSI.
34. Bev Clinton, August 6, 1991, ILHOP; Marlene Gerst, January 14, 1982, ILHOP; Carol Carter, January 14, 1982, ILHOP; Letha Alliman, February 12, 1983, ILHOP; Marion Klaner, August 26, 1982, ILHOP.
35. Union Participation and Representation Workshop, UPWA District 3 Women's Conference, 1959–1961, Folder 6, Box 70, UFCW Local 3 Records, SHSI.
36. The UPWA Local 3's activities committee had nine women serving out of a

total of thirty-three members. Meeting minutes, Folder 9, Box 1, February 17, 1954, and Folder 3, Box 47, UFCW Local 3 Records, SHSI.

37. Meeting minutes, February 2, 1955, May 5, 1955, Folder 3, Box 47, UFCW Local 3 Records, SHSI.
38. Unions at Hinson Manufacturing in Waterloo and Globe Union in Fort Dodge are good examples of female-controlled unions. Ila Jean Byrne, July 29, 1981, ILHOP; UAW Local 838, Hinson Unit, SHSI. Alice Jackson, December 4, 1981, ILHOP.
39. Ideal was organized by the Machinists, and Turner Microphone was organized by the IBEW, Folder 28, Box 1, Doris Peick Papers, SHSI; Folder 22, Box 27, IAM District Lodge 105 Records, SHSI.
40. Folder 7, Box 2, IAM District Lodge 102 Records, SHSI.
41. Marion Nadine Klaner, August 26, 1982, ILHOP.
42. Ethel Jerred, October 5, 1981, ILHOP.
43. Warren, *Struggling with Iowa's Pride*.
44. Ethel Jerred, October 5, 1981, ILHOP.
45. Jane Burleson, Fort Dodge, interview by Merle Davis, August 5, 1981, ILHOP.
46. Florence Jones, Fort Dodge, interview by Merle Davis, August 12, 1981, ILHOP.
47. Bev Clinton, August 6, 1991, ILHOP.
48. Mickey Lockhart, Cedar Rapids, interview by Greg Zieren, October 21, 1979, ILHOP.
49. Marlene Kruger, June 27, 1991, ILHOP.
50. Pat Marshall, August 24, 1982, ILHOP.
51. Women served on organizational, educational, public relations, union label, scholarship, legislative, constitution, and labor news committees. Meeting minutes, February 23, 1965, Folder 9, Box 1, Burlington Trades and Labor Assembly Records, SHSI.
52. Bev Clinton also served as the president of the Machinists Local 831 at Square D in Cedar Rapids. Bev Clinton, August 6, 1991, ILHOP.
53. Dee Ralles, "Union's Gavels in Women's Hands," *Omaha Morning World-Herald*, July 30, 1972.
54. There was a noticeable increase in the number of women serving as a local's president during the 1970s. Marlene Kruger was president of the Machinists local at Waterloo Industries; Lila McCallister was president of the Machinists at Amana; and Pat Marshall was president of IBEW Local 1362 at Collins Radio, which was one of the largest locals in the state.
55. Mary Gulick, Velma Rucker, and Ruth Hopper all reported to UPWA Local 3 after attending women's conferences sponsored by the UPWA. Meeting 3-3-59, Folder 4, Box 47, UPWA Local 3 Records, SHSI.
56. Union Participation and Representation, UPWA District 3 Women's Conference, 1959–1961, Folder 6, Box 70, UFC Local 3 Records, SHSI.
57. Recording Secretary of UPWA Local 3 to Mayor Heaghan, Cedar Rapids,

June 16, 1960, Box 70; Mayor Heaghan to Leonard Sipe, June 20, 1960, Folder 3, Box 79, UFCW Local 3 Records, SHSI.

58. Delegates to the Women's Conference, July 18, 1960, Folder 6, Box 70, UFCW Local 3 Records, SHSI.
59. Workshop A, Women's Conference in Cedar Rapids, July 15–16, 1960, Folder 6, Box 70, UFCW, Local 3 Records, SHSI.
60. Report of Workshop C, Women's Conference in Cedar Rapids, July 15–16, 1960, Folder 6, Box 70, UFCW, Local 3.
61. "Sheaffer-UAW Group Appears Wider," Folder 1, UAW Local 1551 Records, SHSI; "Picket Injunction Petition, Testimony Continues," *Democrat*, December 11, 1974, Folder 1, UAW Local 1551 Records, SHSI.
62. Ila Jean Byrne, July 29, 1981, ILHOP.
63. Paul Larsen to James Wengert, Secretary-Treasurer of the Iowa Federation of Labor, April 17, 1974, Box 23, Iowa Federation of Labor, SHSI.
64. "Sheaffer-UAW Group Appears Wider"; "Picket Injunction Petition, Testimony Continues."
65. Jeannette Haymond, November 9, 1977, ILHOP.
66. Kathy Alter, "Support for Strike Shown," Folder 1, UAW Local 1551 Records, SHSI.
67. Executive Board Minutes, April 2, 1975, Folder 7, Box 47, UFCW Local 3 Records, SHSI.
68. Ila Jean Byrne, July 29, 1981, ILHOP.
69. "Open Letter to the Public," *Democrat*, March 13, 1975, Folder 1, UAW Local 1551 Records, SHSI.
70. March 13, 1975, Folder 2, UAW Local 1551 Records, SHSI.
71. Floyd McIntosh, Financial Secretary of IAM District 105, to Floyd Smith, IAM International President, May 14, 1971, Folder 21, Box 9, IAM District Lodge 105 Records, SHSI.
72. Leah McCracken, letter, May 5, 1971, Folder 21, Box 9, IAM District Lodge 105 Records, SHSI.
73. Marie Bennett to President Smith of the IAM, May 7, 1971, Box 9, Folder 21, IAM Lodge 105 Records, SHSI.
74. Gilbert Brunner, General Vice President of the IAM, to Jarret Molen, Special Representative, May 25, 1971, Folder 21, Box 9, IAM District Lodge 105 Records, SHSI.
75. Letha Alliman, February 12, 1983, ILHOP; Wilma Haynes, February 18, 1983, ILHOP.
76. "Need Pay Hike Now," May 14, 1974, *Hawkeye*; Mrs. Nyal Thomas, letter to the editor, Dallas City, Illinois, Folder 8, Box 1, IAM Local 2303 Records, SHSI.
77. Letha Alliman, February 12, 1983, ILHOP; Wilma Haynes, February 18, 1983, ILHOP.

78. Darrel Schleif, "Open Letter," *Hawkeye*, May 12, 1974, Folder 8, Box 1, IAM Local Lodge 2303 Records, SHSI.
79. Letha Alliman, February 12, 1983, ILHOP; Wilma Haynes, February 18, 1983, ILHOP.
80. "Labor Group Meets Police," *Hawkeye*, May 17, 1974.
81. Letha Alliman, February 12, 1983, ILHOP; Wilma Haynes, February 18, 1983, ILHOP.
82. Marlene Gerst, January 14, 1982, ILHOP; and Dixie Bigger, January 13, 1982, ILHOP.
83. Ilene Christianson, August 11, 1981, ILHOP.

## Chapter Six

1. Betty Talkington, Cedar Rapids, interview by Merle Davis, May 5, 1983, ILHOP.
2. Dorothy Sue Cobble, *The Other Women's Movement: Workplace Justice and Social Rights in Modern America* (Princeton, NJ: Princeton University Press, 2004); Dennis Deslippe, *"Rights Not Roses": Unions and the Rise of Working-Class Feminism, 1945–80* (Urbana: University of Illinois Press, 2000); Nancy Gabin, *Feminism in the Labor Movement: Women and the United Auto Workers, 1935–1975* (Ithaca, NY: Cornell University Press, 1990); Nancy MacLean, *Freedom Is Not Enough: The Opening of the American Workplace* (Cambridge, MA: Harvard University Press, 2006). For more on the feminist movement, see Sara Evans, *Tidal Wave: How Women Changed America at Century's End* (New York: Free Press, 2003); and Ruth Rosen, *The World Split Open: How the Modern Women's Movement Changed America* (New York: Penguin, 2000). For more on feminism in Iowa, see Louise Noun, *More Strong-Minded Women: Iowa Feminists Tell Their Stories* (Ames: Iowa State University Press, 1992).
3. "Summary of Accomplishments and Plans of the Governor's Commission on the Status of Women," November 9, 1965, Folder 2, Box 85, Iowa Federation of Labor Records, SHSI.
4. Sue Peterson, "State Commission Looks into Status of Iowa Women," *Sioux City Journal*, June 28, 1970, Folder: Brown, Ralph Administrative, 1969–1975, Box 1, Governor Ray's Commission on the Status of Women Records, Iowa Women's Archives (IWA), University of Iowa.
5. Report from Committee on Legislation Affecting Civil and Political Rights, April 17, 1970, Box 1, Governor Ray's Commission on the Status of Women, IWA.
6. William Kuncel, "Female Job Rights Stir Praise in Quad Cities," *Times-Democrat*, June 11, 1970, Governor Ray's Commission on the Status of Women, IWA.

7. "Guidelines for Women on the Job," *Hawkeye*, June 9, 1970, Folder History Newspaper Clippings, 1970–1973, Box 1, Governor Ray's Commission on the Status of Women, IWA.
8. Committee Recommendations, June 30, 1972, Folder: An Informal Retrospective on Iowa Governor Robert Ray's Commission on the Status of Women, 1969–1972, Box 1, Governor Ray's Commission on the Status of Women, IWA.
9. Interview with Alice McKee, October 30, 2002, Folder: An Informal Retrospective on Iowa Governor Robert Ray's Commission on the Status of Women, 1969–1972, Box 1, Governor Ray's Commission on the Status of Women, IWA.
10. Governor Ray's Commission on the Status of Women to Governor Ray, December 30, 1971, Box 1, Governor Ray's Commission on the Status of Women, IWA.
11. Employment Project, Iowa Commission on the Status of Women, June 2, 1979, Folder 6, Box 8, Paul Larsen Papers, SHSI.
12. Memo from Louise Lex, Employment Project Director, November 28, 1979, Folder 6, Box 8, Paul Larsen Papers, SHSI.
13. State of Iowa Commission on the Status of Women, 2nd Annual Report, February 1, 1974, Folder ICSW, Reports, 1973–75, Box 2, Governor Ray's Commission on the Status of Women, IWA.
14. State of Iowa Commission on the Status of Women, 3rd Annual Report, February 1, 1975, Folder ICSW, Reports, 1973–75, Box 2, Governor Ray's Commission on the Status of Women, IWA.
15. Committee Recommendations, June 30, 1972, Folder: An Informal Retrospective on Iowa Governor Robert Ray's Commission on the Status of Women, 1969–1972, Box 1, Governor Ray's Commission on the Status of Women, IWA.
16. General Background Information, May 1970, Folder: History Reports, 1970–1972, Box 1, Governor Ray's Commission on the Status of Women, IWA.
17. Governor's Commission on the Status of Women, letter, 1969, Box 10, Beverly Everett Papers, IWA; Governor's Commission on the Status of Women, Meeting Minutes, June 5, 1971, Folder: Governor's Commission on the Status of Women, Box 10, Beverly Everett Papers, IWA.
18. Memo from Louise Lex, Employment Project Director, to Waterloo Advisory Council, January 16, 1980, Folder 6, Box 8, Paul Larsen Papers, SHSI.
19. Memo from YWCA, February 15, 1965, Folder 2, Box 85, Iowa Federation of Labor Records, SHSI.
20. American Association of University Women, 1973–1986, Box 7, Beverly Everett Papers, IWA.
21. "Background Information on Iowa Civil Rights Committee," memo, October 10, 1972, Box 54, League of Women Voters of Iowa, IWA.

22. Statement: League of Women Voters to Civil Rights Commission and Minority Groups Study Committee, November 7, 1973, Folder: Civil Rights, 1969–1973, Box 54, League of Women Voters of Iowa, IWA.
23. Sex Discrimination Memo, September 1972, Folder: Civil Rights, 1969–1973, Box 54, League of Women Voters, IWA.
24. Ibid.
25. Number of participants: Burlington 7, Cedar Falls 47, Cedar Rapids 54, Clinton 13, Davenport 62, Des Moines 402, Dubuque 22, Fort Dodge 14, Fort Madison 4, Iowa City 131, Keokuk 2, Mason City 14, Mount Pleasant 4, Muscatine 18, Oskaloosa 7, and Waterloo 54. Iowa Women's Meeting Brochure, Box 5, Lonabelle Kaplan Spencer Papers, IWA.
26. Executive Board meeting minutes, June 7, 1977, Folder 2, Box 48, UFCW Local 3 Records, SHSI.
27. Rural Iowans Meeting for Women, Scrapbook 1, Box 1, Virginia Becker Papers, IWA; Folder 10, Box 24, Iowa Federation of Labor, SHSI.
28. Report, Iowa Women's Meeting, September 1977, Folder: State Women's Conference, Iowa, 1977, Box 12, Beverly Everett Papers, IWA.
29. Dave Hart, "Seniority Policy Review," *Packinghouse Worker*, August 1966, Folder 1, Box 1, David Hart Packinghouse Scrapbook, SHSI.
30. Deslippe, *"Rights Not Roses,"* 85.
31. Betty Talkington, speech, ca. 1960, Folder 8, Box 85, Iowa Federation of Labor Records, SHSI.
32. Automation Committee, Folder 10, Box 84, Iowa Federation of Labor Records, SHSI; Report of Workshop C, Women's Conference in Cedar Rapids, July 15–16, 1960, Folder 6, Box 70, UFCW, Local 3 Records, SHSI.
33. Betty Talkington, "Where Are Women Needed in Labor's Field," speech, ca. 1960, Folder 8, Box 85, Iowa Federation of Labor Records, SHSI.
34. Ethel Jerred, October 5, 1981, ILHOP.
35. Wilson Warren, *Struggling with "Iowa's Pride": Labor Relations, Unionism, and Politics in the Rural Midwest since 1877* (Iowa City: University of Iowa Press, 2000), 67.
36. Harriet Erzinger, September 10, 1981, ILHOP; Jesse Merrill, Ottumwa, interview by Merle Davis, September 16, 1981, ILHOP.
37. Virgil Bankson, Ottumwa, interview by Merle Davis, March 11, 1983, ILHOP.
38. Ethel Jerred, October 5, 1981, ILHOP.
39. Bankson's journals contain a lot of references to the layoffs of several female employees: September 7, 1963, September 24, 1963, Folder 9, Box 3, AMC&BW Local 1 Records, SHSI.
40. *Bulletin*, January 29, 1962, July 23, 1962, Folder 3, Box 4, AMC&BW Local 1 Records, SHSI.
41. *Bulletin*, March 13, 1961, Folder 2, Box 4, AMC&BW Local 1 Records, SHSI.

42. Ethel Jerred, October 5, 1981, ILHOP.
43. Bankson's journal, November 4, 1963, December 9, 1963, Box 3, Folder 9, AMC&BW Local 1 Records, SHSI; Ethel Jerred, October 5, 1981, ILHOP.
44. *Bulletin*, Box 4, Folder 6, AMC&BW Local 1 Records, SHSI.
45. Box 5, Folder 6, AMC&BW Local 1 Records, SHSI.
46. Ethel Jerred, October 5, 1981, ILHOP.
47. Ethel Jerred, October 5, 1981, ILHOP; Jesse Merrill, September 16, 1981, ILHOP; Virgil Bankson, March 11, 1982, ILHOP; Dorven "Arky" Bride, interview by Merle Davis, January 19, 1983, ILHOP; *Bulletin*, March 14, 1966, Box 4, Folder 7, AMC&BW Local 1 Records, SHSI.
48. Ethel Jerred, October 5, 1981, ILHOP.
49. Virgil Bankson, March 11, 1983, ILHOP.
50. *Bulletin*, March 28, 1966, Box 4, Folder 7, AMC&BW Local 1 Records, SHSI.
51. Virgil Bankson, March 11, 1983, ILHOP; Ethel Jerred, October 5, 1981, ILHOP.
52. Dennis Deslippe, "'We Had an Awful Time with Our Women': Iowa's United Packinghouse Workers of America, 1945–1975," *Journal of Women's History* 5, no. 1 (1993): 10–26; Bruce Fehn, "'Chickens Come Home to Roost': Industrial Reorganization, Seniority, and Gender Conflict in the United Packinghouse Workers of America, 1956–1966," *Labor History* 34, no. 2–3 (1993): 324–41.
53. Harriet Erzinger, September 10, 1981, ILHOP; Ethel Jerred, October 5, 1981, ILHOP; Ruth Morrow, Ottumwa, interview by Merle Davis, September 8, 1981, ILHOP.
54. Dorven Bride, January 19, 1983, ILHOP.
55. Deslippe, "'We Had an Awful Time with Our Women'"; Fehn, "'Chickens Come Home to Roost.'"
56. Meeting notes, Sausage Pack Department, April 14, 1959, Folder 18, Box 19, and Special Meeting, May 26, 1955, and Meeting, May 7, 1958, Folder 4, Box 47, UFCW Local 3 Records, SHSI.
57. Elizabeth Smith, Ottumwa, interview by Merle Davis, September 5, 1981, ILHOP.
58. Meeting minutes, Night Workers, June 13, 1974, Folder 3, Box 79, UPWA Local 3 Records, SHSI.
59. Marion Nadine Klaner, August 26, 1982, ILHOP.
60. Esther Kadlec, Chairman of the Women's Committee, AMC&BW Local 3, to EEOC Office, June 20, 1974, Folder 2, Box 1, UFCW Local 3 Records, SHSI.
61. Esther Kadlec, Women's Committee, to Dave Hansel, September 6, 1974, Folder 3, Box 79, UPWA Local 3 Records, SHSI.
62. Meetings, July, August, November 1974, Folder 1, Box 48; Minutes, Night Workers, June 13, 1974, Folder 3, Box 79, UFCW Local 3 Records, SHSI.

63. Special Board Meeting, September 29, 1955, and May 26, 1955, Folder 3, Box 47, UFCW Local 3, SHSI.
64. Noun, *More Strong-Minded Women*, 210–12.
65. The other women included Marie Kannegieter, Lucille Bremer, Shirley Squire, and Shirley Wilson.
66. Erma Wiszmann, President of CWA Local 7117, to Hugh Clark, President of the Iowa Federation of Labor, April 29, 1976, Folder 5, Box 80, Iowa Federation of Labor Records, SHSI.
67. Hugh Clark to Erma Wiszmann, April 29, 1976, Folder 5, Box 80, Iowa Federation of Labor Records, SHSI.
68. Erma Wiszmann to Hugh Clark, May 1, 1976, Folder 5, Box 80, Iowa Federation of Labor Records, SHSI.
69. Treva Doggett, Founding Conference, Coalition of Labor Union Women, March 23–24, 1974, Folder 33, Box 15, South Central Iowa Federation of Labor Records, SHSI.
70. Meeting, March 1974, Folder 8, Box 47; Executive Board Meeting, June 8, 1977, Folder 2, Box 48, UFCW Local 3 Records, SHSI.
71. Erma Wiszmann, Quad Cities, interview by Merle Davis, February 16, 1982, ILHOP.
72. Conference for Union Women, Flier, July 1972, Folder 33, Box 15, South Central Iowa Federation of Labor Records, SHSI.
73. Second Annual Conference, Folder 33, Box 15, South Central Iowa Federation of Labor Records, SHSI.
74. Meeting minutes, July 11, 1972, Folder 7; Executive Board Meeting, May 16, 1973, Folder 8, Box 47; Executive Board Meeting, April 16, 1975, Folder 1, Box 48, UFCW Local 3 Records, SHSI.
75. Some of the guest speakers: Addie Wyatt, Harry Smith (labor attorney, Sioux City), Sally Hacker (NOW), and Betty Talkington. Conference on Unions and Discrimination at the University of Iowa and the Center for Labor and Management, March 1975, Folder 10, Box 2, Doris Peick Papers, SHSI.
76. In April 1977, UFCW Local 3 sent two people to the Trade Union Women's Seminar in Iowa City, with the local paying for lost time and one half per diem for each day. Meeting, April 6, 1977, Folder 2, Box 48, UFCW Local 3 Records, SHSI.
77. Seminar for Trade Union Women, April 1976, University of Iowa, Center for Labor and Management in Cooperation with the IFL, Folder 16, Box 116, Iowa Federation of Labor Records, SHSI.
78. Meeting Minutes, June 15, 1978, Folder 3, Box 28; Donald Southwood, Representative of the U.S. Department of Labor, to T. N. Bass, Secretary, Clinton Corn, June 26, 1978, Folder 21, Box 4, AFGM Local 6 Records, SHSI.
79. Donald Southwood to T. N. Bass, June 26, 1978.

80. *Bulletin*, December 21, 1976, and August 10, 1977, Folder 4, Box 8, AFGM Local 6 Records, SHSI.
81. Michael Krajnovich, Clinton, interview by Merle Davis, June 22, 1982, ILHOP.
82. Ibid.
83. Folder 3, Box 32; Folder 5, Box 32; Folder 3, Box 15, AFGM Local 6 Records, SHSI.
84. Folder 6, Box 32, AFGM, Local 6 Records, SHSI; Michael Krajnovich Clinton, June 22, 1982, ILHOP.
85. William Brown, Burlington, interview by Merle Davis, February 10, 1981, ILHOP.
86. Tom Larkin, Amana, interview by Janet Clements, March 20, 1995, ILHOP.
87. Darlene Croft, Estherville, interview by Merle Davis, November 11, 1982, ILHOP.
88. Cheryl Benson, Oskaloosa, interview by Janet Clements, April 18, 1995, ILHOP.
89. Ilene Christianson, June 11, 1981, ILHOP; meeting minutes, November 15, 1969, Folder 5, Box 1, UAW Local 838 Records, SHSI.
90. Eunice Evans, March 6, 1995, ILHOP; memo, May 6, 1970, Box 27, IAM District Lodge 105 Records, SHSI.
91. Florence Jones, August 12, 1981, ILHOP.
92. Dorven Bride, January 19, 1983, ILHOP.
93. Central Body Presidents, 1980, Box 3, UFCW Local 3 Records, SHSI.
94. Bev Clinton, August 6, 1991, ILHOP.
95. Marlene Kruger, June 27, 1991, ILHOP.
96. Bev Clinton, August 6, 1991, ILHOP.
97. Ethel Jerred, October 5, 1981, ILHOP.
98. Carol Carter, January 12, 1982, ILHOP.
99. Marlene Gerst, January 14, 1983, ILHOP.
100. Betty Noe, December 10, 1981, ILHOP; Carrie Azinger, December 11, 1981, ILHOP.
101. Mickey Lockhart, October 21, 1979, ILHOP.
102. George Ashlock and Mary Ashlock, Mason City, interview by Merle Davis, November 17, 1981, ILHOP.
103. Harriet Erzinger, September 10, 1981, ILHOP.
104. Marion Nadine Klaner, August 26, 1982, ILHOP.
105. Marlene Kruger, June 27, 1991, ILHOP.
106. Harriet Erzinger, September 10, 1981, ILHOP.
107. Erma Wiszmann, February 16, 1982, ILHOP.
108. Doris Peick, August 24, 1982, ILHOP.
109. Viola Juehring, July 8, 1982, ILHOP.

## Epilogue

1. Letha Alliman, February 12, 1983, ILHOP.
2. U.S. Bureau of the Census, *Census of Population*, 1950 and 1980.
3. Marlene Kruger, June 27, 1991, ILHOP.
4. Rosemary Hayes, Waterloo, interview by Dan Holub, June 27, 1991, ILHOP.

# Bibliography


## Archival and Manuscript Collections

*Iowa Women's Archives, University of Iowa Libraries, Iowa City*

Aguilera, Maria Mercedes, papers
Autobiographical Sketches of Rural Women
Becker, Virginia, papers
Best Ever Club (Percival, Iowa) Records
Block, Marjorie Bertalot, papers
Blundall, Joan, papers
Boyd, June Lundy, papers
Burleson, Jane, papers
Christen, Inez, papers
Cleona Township Women's Club (Scott County, Iowa) records
Crawford, Anita, papers
Dix, Dorothy Pearl Unmack, papers
Everett, Beverly, papers
Ferns, Grace, papers
Fort Madison Women's Club, records
Governor Ray's Commission on the Status of Women (Iowa) records
Her Own Story: Ten Benton County Women Collection
Herr, Catharine King, papers
Iowa ERA Coalition, records
League of Women Voters of Iowa, records
McNeill, Amelia, papers
National Organization for Women, Iowa records
O'Brien, Denise, papers
Schramm, Dorothy, papers
Spencer, Lonabelle Kaplan, papers
Stoner, Jean Minish, papers
Voices from the Land: Oral History Project in Iowa

*State Historical Society of Iowa Library, Iowa City*

Amalgamated Meat Cutters and Butcher Workmen of North America, Local P-1, Ottumwa, Z 23
Amalgamated Meat Cutters and Butcher Workmen of North America, Local P-38, Mason City, ZZ 19

Amalgamated Meat Cutters and Butcher Workmen of North America, Local P-1135, Fort Dodge, Z 42
American Federation of Grain Millers, Local 6, Clinton, Z 49
American Federation of Grain Millers, Local 48, Keokuk, Z 39
Burlington Trades and Labor Assembly, Burlington, Z 15
Delevan Strike of 1978–1979, Des Moines, ZZ 55
Dubuque Federation of Labor Records, Dubuque, Z 46
Fort Madison Trades and Labor Assembly, Fort Madison, Z 7
Hart, David, Packinghouse Scrapbook, Z 16
International Association of Machinists, Lodge 102, Quad Cities, Z 6
International Association of Machinists, Lodge 105, Fairfield, Z 30
International Association of Machinists, Lodge 1238, Dubuque, ZZ 36
International Association of Machinists, Lodge 1373, Waterloo, ZZ 6
International Association of Machinists, Lodge 2303, Burlington, Z 20
International Ladies Garment Workers Union, Clinton, ZZ 55
Iowa Federation of Labor, Z 61
Ladies Auxiliary to the International Association of Machinists Lodge 262, Des Moines, Z 29
Larsen, Paul, Waterloo, Z 60
North Iowa Area Development Labor Council, Mason City, Z 26
Peick, Doris, Cedar Rapids, Z 27
South Central Iowa Federation of Labor, Des Moines, Z 28
Tri-City Federation of Labor, Quad Cities, Z 12
United Auto Workers, Local 838, Waterloo, Z 24
United Auto Workers, Local 1551, Fort Madison, ZZ 57
United Food and Commercial Workers, Local 431, Ottumwa, Z 58
United Food and Commercial Workers, Local P-3, Cedar Rapids, Z 50
United Food and Commercial Workers, Local P-31, Fort Dodge, Z 41
United Food and Commercial Workers, Local P-46, Waterloo, Z 33
United Packinghouse Workers of America, Local 1128, Fort Dodge, Z 43
United Rubber Workers, Local 444, Keokuk, ZZ 11
Women's Auxiliary to the Tri-City Federation of Labor, Quad Cities, Z 13

*Iowa Labor History Oral Project,*
*State Historical Society of Iowa, Iowa City*

Accord, Gladys, Amana
Adams, Leona, Waterloo
Alliman, Letha, Burlington
Arendt, Edith, Cedar Rapids
Avery, Sandra, Fort Madison
Azinger, Carrie, Keokuk
Bankson, Virgil, Ottumwa
Benson, Cheryl, Oskaloosa
Bigger, Dixie, Burlington
Bohaty, Violet, Ottumwa
Bremer, Lucille, Waterloo
Bride, Dorven, Ottumwa

Burleson, Jane, Fort Dodge
Burrows, Joyce, Dubuque
Byrne, Ila Jean, Fort Dodge
Carter, Carol, Burlington
Christianson, Ilene, Waterloo
Clinton, Bev, Cedar Rapids
Croft, Darlene, Estherville
Evans, Eunice, Amana
Fisher, Pauline, Oskaloosa
Gerard, Josephine, Amana
Gerst, Marlene, Burlington
Hamlyn, Luella, Waterloo
Hannah, Cheryl, Waterloo
Hayes, Rosemary, Waterloo
Haymond, Jeannette, Cedar Rapids
Haynes, Wilma, Burlington
Helstein, Ralph, Chicago
Jackson, Alice, Burlington
Jerred, Ethel, Ottumwa
Juehring, Viola, Clinton
Klaner, Marion Nadine, Cedar Rapids
Klopp, Fern, Cedar Rapids
Kruger, Marlene, Waterloo
Leedom, Michael, Burlington
Lockhart, Mickey, Cedar Rapids
Lubert, Ruth, Waterloo
Marshall, Pat, Cedar Rapids
McCallister, Lila, Amana
McCarthy, Fern, Burlington
Merrill, Jesse, Ottumwa
Morrow, Ruth, Ottumwa
Noe, Betty, Keokuk
Oltmanns, Alice, Clinton
Otterman, Velma, Waterloo
Peick, Doris, Cedar Rapids
Rhum, Susan, Burlington
Speer, Mary, Des Moines
Talkington, Betty, Des Moines
Vaughn, Irene, Clinton
Weems, Anna Mae, Waterloo
West, Lana, Keokuk
Williams, Billye Smith, Burlington
Wiszmann, Erma, Quad Cities
York, Ruth, Quad Cities

## Wisconsin Historical Society Archives, Madison, Wisconsin

*United Packinghouse Workers of America Oral History Project*

Bremer, Lucille, Waterloo, Rath
Fetter, Tony, Cedar Rapids, Wilson
Fields, Magnolia, Cedar Rapids, Wilson
Hammond, Jeannette, Cedar Rapids, Wilson
Jones, Viola, Waterloo, Rath
Lamb, Goldie, Waterloo, Rath
Melsha, Stella, Cedar Rapids, Wilson
Mueller, Charles, Waterloo, Rath
Otterman, Velma, Waterloo, Rath
Taylor, Lyle, Waterloo, Rath
Townsend, Louise, Cedar Rapids, Wilson
Treadwell, Ada, Waterloo, Rath
Weems, Anna Mae, Waterloo, Rath
Zarudsky, Helen, Cedar Rapids, Wilson

*Manuscript Collections*

United Packinghouse, Food and Allied Workers Records, Parts 1 and 2
Amalgamated Meat Cutters and Butcher Workmen of North America, Parts 1–4

## Secondary Sources

Adams, Jane. *The Transformation of Rural Life: Southern Illinois, 1890–1990*. Chapel Hill: University of North Carolina Press, 1994.

Anderson, J. L., ed. *The Rural Midwest since World War II*. DeKalb: Northern Illinois University Press, 2014.

Aulette, Judy, and Trudy Mills. "Something Old, Something New: Auxiliary Work in the 1983–1986 Copper Strike." *Feminist Studies* 14 (Summer 1988): 251–68.

Bao, Xiaolan. *Holding Up More Than Half the Sky: Chinese Women Garment Workers in New York City, 1948–92*. Urbana: University of Illinois Press, 2001.

Baron, Ava, ed. *Work Engendered: Toward a New History of American Labor*. Ithaca, NY: Cornell University Press, 1991.

Barrett, James. *Work and Community in the Jungle: Chicago's Packinghouse Workers, 1894–1922*. Urbana: University of Illinois Press, 1987.

Blackwelder, Julia Kirk. *Now Hiring: The Feminization of Work in the United States, 1900–1995*. College Station: Texas A&M University Press, 1997.

Blewett, Mary. *Men, Women, and Work: Class, Gender, and Protest in the New England Shoe Industry, 1780–1910*. Urbana: University of Illinois Press, 1988.

Boyle, Kevin, ed. *Organized Labor and American Politics, 1894–1994: The Labor-Liberal Alliance*. Albany: State University of New York Press, 1998.

Brody, David. *Workers in Industrial America: Essays on the Twentieth-Century Struggle*. New York: Oxford University Press, 1993.

Cameron, Ardis. *Radicals of the Worst Sort: Laboring Women in Lawrence, Massachusetts, 1860–1912*. Urbana: University of Illinois Press, 1993.

Cayton, Andrew R. L., and Susan Gray. *The Identity of the American Midwest: Essays on Regional History*. Bloomington: Indiana University Press, 2001.

Chateauvert, Melinda. *Marching Together: Women of the Brotherhood of Sleeping Car Porters*. Urbana: University of Illinois Press, 1998.

Cobble, Dorothy Sue. *Dishing It Out: Waitresses and Their Unions in the 20th Century*. Urbana: University of Illinois Press, 1992.

Cobble, Dorothy Sue. *The Other Women's Movement: Workplace Justice and Social Rights in Modern America*. Princeton, NJ: Princeton University Press, 2004.

Cobble, Dorothy Sue, ed. *The Sex of Class: Women Transforming American Labor*. Ithaca, NY: Cornell University Press, 2007.

Cobble, Dorothy Sue. "A Spontaneous Loss of Enthusiasm: Workplace Feminism and the Transformation of Women's Service Jobs in the 1970s." *International Labor and Working Class History* 56 (Fall 1999): 23–44.

Cobble, Dorothy Sue, ed. *Women and Unions: Forging a Partnership*. Ithaca, NY: Cornell University Press, 1993.

Cohen, Lizabeth. *Making a New Deal: Industrial Workers in Chicago, 1919–1939*. Cambridge: Cambridge University Press, 1990.

Costello, Cynthia. "Working Women's Consciousness: Traditional or Oppositional?" In *"To Toil the Livelong Day": America's Women at Work, 1780–1980*, edited by Carol Groneman and Mary Beth Norton. Ithaca, NY: Cornell University Press, 1987.

Cowie, Jefferson. *Capital Moves: RCA's Seventy-Year Quest for Cheap Labor.* New York: New Press, 1999.

Cowie, Jefferson. *Stayin' Alive: The 1970s and the Last Days of the Working Class.* New York: New Press, 2010.

Deslippe, Dennis. *"Rights Not Roses": Unions and the Rise of Working Class Feminism, 1945–80.* Urbana: University of Illinois Press, 2000.

Deslippe, Dennis. "'We Had an Awful Time with Our Women': Iowa's United Packinghouse Workers of America, 1945–75." *Journal of Women's History* 5, no. 1 (1993): 12–28.

Devine, Jenny Barker. *On Behalf of the Family Farm: Iowa Farm Women's Activism since 1945.* Iowa City: University of Iowa Press, 2013.

Devine, Jenny Barker. "'The Secret to Successful Farm Organization': Township Farm Bureau Women's Clubs in Iowa, 1945–1970." *Annals of Iowa* 69 (Fall 2010): 418–48.

Dowd Hall, Jacquelyn, James Leloudis, Robert Korstad, Mary Murphy, Lu Ann Jones, and Christopher Daly. *Like a Family: The Making of a Southern Cotton Mill World.* New York: Norton, 1987.

Dublin, Thomas. *Women at Work: The Transformation of Work and Community in Lowell, Massachusetts, 1826–1860.* New York: Columbia University Press, 1979.

Dubofsky, Melvin. *The State and Labor in Modern America.* Chapel Hill: University of North Carolina Press, 1994.

Echols, Alice. *Daring to Be Bad: Radical Feminism in America, 1967–1975.* Minneapolis: University of Minnesota Press, 1989.

Eldersveld Murphy, Lucy, and Wendy Hammand Venet. *Midwestern Women: Work, Community, and Leadership at the Crossroads.* Bloomington: Indiana University Press, 1997.

Enstad, Nan. *Ladies of Labor, Girls of Adventure: Working Women, Popular Culture, and Labor Politics at the Turn of the Twentieth Century.* New York: Columbia University Press, 1999.

Evans, Sara. *Tidal Wave: How Women Changed America at Century's End.* New York: Free Press, 2003.

Faue, Elizabeth. *Community of Suffering and Struggle: Women, Men, and the Labor Movement in Minneapolis, 1915–1945.* Chapel Hill: University of North Carolina Press, 1991.

Fehn, Bruce. "African American Women and the Struggle for Equality in the Meatpacking Industry, 1940–1960." *Journal of Women's History* 10 (Spring 1998): 45–69.

Fehn, Bruce. "'Chickens Come Home to Roost': Industrial Reorganization, Seniority, and Gender Conflict in the United Packinghouse Workers of America, 1956–1966." *Labor History* 34, no. 2–3 (1993): 324–41.

Fehn, Bruce. "Striking Women: Gender, Race and Class in the United Packinghouse Workers of America (UPWA), 1938–1968." PhD diss., University of Wisconsin, 1990.

Feurer, Rosemary. *Radical Unionism in the Midwest, 1900–1950*. Urbana: University of Illinois Press, 2006.

Fine, Lisa. *REO Joe: Work, Kin, and Community in Autotown, U.S.A.* Philadelphia: Temple University Press, 2004.

Fink, Deborah. *Cutting into the Meatpacking Line: Workers and Change in the Rural Midwest*. Chapel Hill: University of Illinois Press, 1998.

Fink, Deborah. *Open Country, Iowa: Rural Women, Tradition and Change*. Albany: State University of New York Press, 1986.

Frank, Dana. "Gender, Consumer Organizing, and the Seattle Labor Movement, 1919–1929." In *Work Engendered: Toward a New History of American Labor*, edited by Ava Baron, 273–95. Ithaca, NY: Cornell University Press, 1991.

Friedberger, Mark. *Farm Families and Change in Twentieth-Century America*. Lexington: University of Kentucky Press, 1988.

Gabin, Nancy. *Feminism in the Labor Movement: Women and the United Auto Workers, 1935–1975*. Ithaca, NY: Cornell University Press, 1990.

Glenn, Susan. *Daughters of the Shtetl: Life and Labor in the Immigrant Generation*. Ithaca, NY: Cornell University Press, 1990.

Groneman, Carol, and Mary Beth Norton, eds. *"To Toil the Livelong Day": America's Women at Work, 1780–1980*. Ithaca, NY: Cornell University Press, 1984.

Gutman, Herbert. *Work, Culture and Society in Industrializing America*. New York: Vintage, 1966.

Halpern, Rick. *Down on the Killing Floor: Black and White Workers in Chicago's Packinghouses, 1904–1954*. Urbana: University of Illinois Press, 1997.

Hart, John Fraser. "Small Towns and Manufacturing." *Geographical Review* 78 (July 1988): 272–87.

Hartman Strom, Sharon. *Beyond the Typewriter: Gender, Class, and the Origins of Modern American Office Work, 1900–1930*. Urbana: University of Illinois Press, 1992.

Horowitz, Roger. *"Negro and White, Unite and Fight!" A Social History of Industrial Unionism in Meatpacking, 1930–90*. Urbana: University of Illinois Press, 1997.

Jellison, Katherine. *Entitled to Power: Farm Women and Technology, 1913–1963*. Chapel Hill: University of North Carolina Press, 1993.

Johnson, Keach. "Iowa's Industrial Roots, 1890–1919." *Annals of Iowa* 44 (Winter 1978): 163–90.

Jones, Jacqueline. *Labor of Love, Labor of Sorrow: Black Women, Work and the Family from Slavery to the Present.* New York: Vintage, 1985.

Kempker, Erin. *Big Sister: Feminism, Conservatism, and Conspiracy in the Heartland.* Urbana: University of Illinois Press, 2018.

Kessler-Harris, Alice. *Gendering Labor History.* Urbana: University of Illinois Press, 2007.

Kessler-Harris, Alice. *In Pursuit of Equity: Women, Men, and the Quest for Economic Citizenship in 20th Century America.* New York: Oxford University Press, 2001.

Kessler-Harris, Alice. *Out to Work: A History of Wage-Earning Women in the United States.* New York: Oxford University Press, 2003.

Lamphere, Louise, Patricia Zavella, and Felipe Gonzales, with Peter Evans. *Sunbelt Working Mothers: Reconciling Family and Factory.* Ithaca, NY: Cornell University Press, 1993.

Lasky, Marjorie Penn. "'Where I Was a Person': The Ladies' Auxiliary in the 1934 Minneapolis Teamsters' Strikes." In *Women, Work and Protest: A Century of U.S. Women's Labor History,* edited by Ruth Milkman, 181–205. Boston: Routledge and Kegan Paul, 1985.

Levine, Susan. "Workers' Wives: Gender, Class and Consumerism in the 1920s United States." *Gender and History* 48 (Spring 1991).

Lichtenstein, Nelson. *State of the Union: A Century of American Labor.* Princeton, NJ: Princeton University Press, 2002.

MacLean, Nancy. *Freedom Is Not Enough: The Opening of the American Workplace.* Cambridge, MA: Harvard University Press, 2006.

Martin, Lou. *Smokestacks in the Hills: Rural-Industrial Workers in West Virginia.* Urbana: University of Illinois Press, 2015.

Mercier, Laurie. *Anaconda: Labor, Community, and Culture in Montana's Smelter City.* Urbana: University of Illinois Press, 2001.

Merithew, Caroline. "'We Were Not Ladies': Gender, Class, and a Woman's Auxiliary's Battle for Mining Unionism." *Journal of Women's History* 18 (2006): 63–94.

Meyerowitz, Joanne, ed. *Not June Cleaver: Women and Gender in Postwar America, 1945–1960.* Philadelphia: Temple University Press, 1994.

Meyerowitz, Ruth. "Organizing the United Auto Workers: Women Workers at the Ternstedt General Motors Parts Plant." In *Women, Work and Protest: A Century of U.S. Women's Labor History,* edited by Ruth Milkman. Boston: Routledge and Kegan Paul, 1985.

Milkman, Ruth. *Farewell to the Factory: Auto Workers in the Late Twentieth Century.* Berkeley: University of California Press, 1997.

Milkman, Ruth. *Gender at Work: The Dynamics of Job Segregation by Sex during World War II.* Urbana: University of Illinois Press, 1987.

Milkman, Ruth, ed. *Women, Work and Protest: A Century of US Women's Labor History*. Boston: Routledge and Kegan Paul, 1985.

Montgomery, David. *The Fall of the House of Labor: The Workplace, the State, and American Labor Activism, 1865–1925*. New York: Cambridge University Press, 1987.

Neth, Mary. *Preserving the Family Farm: Women, Community, and the Foundations of Agribusiness in the Midwest, 1900–1940*. Baltimore, MD: Johns Hopkins University Press, 1995.

Noun, Louise. *More Strong-Minded Women: Iowa Feminists Tell Their Stories*. Ames: Iowa State University Press, 1992.

Noun, Louise. *Strong-Minded Women: The Emergence of the Woman-Suffrage Movement in Iowa*. Ames: Iowa State University Press, 1969.

Oden, Derek. "From Cob to Can: The Development of Iowa's Canning Industry in the Late Nineteenth and Early Twentieth Centuries." *Annals of Iowa* 63 (Fall 2004): 390–418.

Orejel, Keith. "The Origins of the Iowa Development Commission: Agricultural Transformation and Industrial Development in Mid-Twentieth-Century Iowa." *Annals of Iowa* 76 (Winter 2017): 47–70.

Orleck, Annelise. "'We Are That Mythical Thing Called the Public': Militant Housewives during the Great Depression." *Feminist Studies* 19 (Spring 1993): 147–73.

Ossian, Lisa. *The Home Fronts of Iowa, 1939–1945*. Columbia: University of Missouri, 2009.

Pfeffer, Paula. "The Women behind the Union: Halena Wilson, Rosina Tucker, and the Ladies' Auxiliary to the Brotherhood of Sleeping Car Porters." *Labor History* 36 (Fall 1995): 557–78.

Riley, Glenda. *Frontierswomen: The Iowa Experience*. Ames: Iowa State University Press, 1981.

Rosen, Ruth. *The World Split Open: How the Modern Women's Movement Changed America*. New York: Penguin, 2000.

Roth, Dennis. "Thinking about Rural Manufacturing: A Brief History." *Rural America* 15 (January 2000): 12–19.

Rousmaniere, Kate. "The Muscatine Button Workers' Strike of 1911–1912: An Iowa Community in Conflict." *Annals of Iowa* 46, no. 4 (1982): 243–62.

Sage, Leland. *A History of Iowa*. Ames: Iowa State University Press, 1974.

Sanders, Katrina. "The Burlington Self-Survey in Human Relations: Interracial Efforts for Constructive Community Change, 1949–1951." *Annals of Iowa* 60 (Summer 2001): 244–69.

Schatz, Ronald. *The Electrical Workers: A History of Labor at General Electric and Westinghouse, 1923–60*. Urbana: University of Illinois Press, 1983.

Schwieder, Dorothy. *Iowa: The Middle Land*. Ames: Iowa State University Press, 1996.

Sloat, Ted. *Fort Madison: A Pictorial History.* St. Louis: G. Bradley, 1988.

Stecklein, Heather. "Workers' Control and Militancy in an Iowa Labor Movement: The Use of Wildcat Strikes at the Des Moines Firestone Tire and Rubber Company, 1950–1959." *Annals of Iowa* 63 (2005): 246–65.

Strom, Sharon Hartman. "'We're No Kitty Foyles': Organizing Office Workers for the Congress of Industrial Organizations, 1937–50." In *Women, Work and Protest: A Century of U.S. Women's Labor History*, edited by Ruth Milkman. Boston: Routledge and Kegan Paul, 1985.

Stromquist, Shelton. *Solidarity and Survival: An Oral History of Iowa Labor in the Twentieth Century.* Iowa City: University of Iowa Press, 1993.

Stromquist, Shelton, and Marvin Bergman, eds. *Unionizing the Jungles: Labor and Community in the Twentieth Century Meatpacking Industry.* Iowa City: University of Iowa Press, 1997.

Teaford, Jon. *Cities of the Heartland: The Rise and Fall of the Industrial Midwest.* Bloomington: Indiana University Press, 1993.

Thompson, E. P. *The Making of the English Working Class.* New York: Vintage, 1963.

Turk, Katherine. *Equality on Trial: Gender and Rights in the Modern American Workplace.* Philadelphia: University of Pennsylvania Press, 2016.

Twarog, Emily E. L. *Politics of the Pantry: Housewives, Food, and Consumer Protest in Twentieth-Century America.* New York: Oxford University Press, 2017.

U.S. Bureau of the Census. *Census of Population: 1960*, vol. I, part 17, Iowa. Washington, DC: Government Printing Office.

Walker, Melissa. *All We Knew Was to Farm: Rural Women in the Upcountry South, 1919–1941.* Baltimore, MD: Johns Hopkins University Press, 2000.

Walzer, Norman. *The American Midwest: Managing Change in Rural Transition.* London: M. E. Sharpe, 2003.

Warren, Wilson. "Beyond the Rust Bowl." In *The Rural Midwest since World War II*, edited by J. L. Anderson. DeKalb: Northern Illinois University Press, 2014.

Warren, Wilson. *Struggling with "Iowa's Pride": Labor Relations, Unionism, and Politics in the Rural Midwest since 1877.* Iowa City: University of Iowa Press, 2000.

Warren, Wilson. *Tied to the Great Packing Machine: The Midwest and Meatpacking.* Iowa City: University of Iowa Press, 2007.

Weaver, Janet. "Barrio Women: Community and Coalition in the Heartland." In *Breaking the Wave: Women, Their Organizations and Feminism, 1945–1985*, edited by Kathleen Laughlin and Jacqueline Castledine. New York: Routledge, 2011.

Weaver, Janet. "From Barrio to '!Boicoteo!': The Emergence of Mexican American Activism in Davenport, 1917–1970." *Annals of Iowa* 68 (Summer 2009): 215–54.

Whites, Lee Ann, Mary Neth, and Gary Kremer, eds. *Women in Missouri*

*History: In Search of Power and Influence*. Columbia: University of Missouri Press, 2004.

Wilkerson, Jessica. *To Live Here, You Have to Fight: How Women Led Appalachian Movements for Social Justice*. Urbana: University of Illinois Press, 2018.

Windham, Lane. *Knocking on Labor's Door: Union Organizing in the 1970s and the Roots of a New Economic Divide*. Chapel Hill: University of North Carolina Press, 2017.

Wood, Sharon. *The Freedom of the Streets: Work, Citizenship, and Sexuality in a Gilded Age City*. Chapel Hill: University of North Carolina Press, 2005.

# Index

IOWA AND THE MIDWEST EXPERIENCE

*Angel De Cora, Karen Thronson, and the Art of Place: How Two Midwestern Women Used Art to Negotiate Migration and Dispossession*
by Elizabeth Sutton

*The Archaeological Guide to Iowa*
by William E. Whittaker, Lynn M. Alex, and Mary C. De La Garza

*Atlas of Iowa*
edited by Robert C. Shepard, Patrick Bitterman, J. Clark Archer, and Fred M. Shelley

*Carnival in the Countryside: The History of the Iowa State Fair*
by Chris Rasmussen

*Dakota in Exile: The Untold Stories of Captives in the Aftermath of the U.S.-Dakota War*
by Linda M. Clemmons

*The Drake Relays: America's Athletic Classic*
by David Peterson

*Dubuque's Forgotten Cemetery: Excavating a Nineteenth-Century Burial Ground in a Twenty-First-Century City*
by Robin M. Lillie and Jennifer E. Mack

*Duffy's Iowa Caucus Cartoons: Watch 'Em Run*
by Brian Duffy

*Equal Before the Law: How Iowa Led Americans to Marriage Equality*
by Tom Witosky and Marc Hansen

*From Warm Center to Ragged Edge: The Erosion of Midwestern Literary and Historical Regionalism, 1920–1965*
by Jon K. Lauck

*Harvest of Hazards: Family Farming, Accidents, and Expertise in the Corn Belt, 1940–1975*
by Derek S. Oden

*Imaging Animal Industry: American Meatpacking in Photography and Visual Culture*
by Emily Kathryn Morgan

*Iowa Past to Present: The People and the Prairie, Revised Third Edition*
by Dorothy Schwieder, Thomas Morain, and Lynn Nielsen

*The Iowa State Fair*
by Kurt Ullrich

*The Jefferson Highway: Blazing the Way from Winnipeg to New Orleans*
by Lyell D. Henry Jr.

*The Lost Region: Toward a Revival of Midwestern History*
by Jon K. Lauck

*Main Street Public Library: Community Places and Reading Spaces in the Rural Heartland, 1876–1956*
by Wayne A. Wiegand

*Necessary Courage: Iowa's Underground Railroad in the Struggle against Slavery*
by Lowell J. Soike

*On Behalf of the Family Farm: Iowa Farm Women's Activism since 1945*
by Jenny Barker Devine

*The Plea: A True Story of Young Wesley Elkins and His Struggle for Redemption*
by Patricia L. Bryan and Thomas Wolf

*The Sacred Cause of Union: Iowa in the Civil War*
by Thomas R. Baker

*The Small-Town Midwest: Resilience and Hope in the Twenty-First Century*
by Julianne Couch

*A Store Almost in Sight: The Economic Transformation of Missouri from the Louisiana Purchase to the Civil War*
by Jeff Bremer

*Transcendental Meditation in America: How a New Age Movement Remade a Small Town in Iowa*
by Joseph Weber

*What Happens Next?: Matters of Life and Death*
by Douglas Bauer

*Woman Suffrage and Citizenship in the Midwest, 1870–1920*
by Sara Egge